CW00685199

THE
51st (HIGHLAND) DIVISION
IN THE
GREAT WAR
–
ENGINE OF DESTRUCTION

1/8th Argylls in winter goatskins, 1915-1916

THE
51ST (HIGHLAND) DIVISION
IN THE
GREAT WAR

–

ENGINE OF DESTRUCTION

COLIN CAMPBELL

Pen & Sword
MILITARY
AN IMPRINT OF PEN & SWORD BOOKS LTD.
YORKSHIRE – PHILADELPHIA

First published in Great Britain in 2013 by Argyll Publishing

Reprinted in this format in 2018 by
Pen & Sword Military
An imprint of
Pen & Sword Books Ltd
Yorkshire – Philadelphia

ISBN 978 1 52674 703 7

A CIP catalogue record for this book is
available from the British Library.

Printed and bound in the UK by TJ International Ltd, Padstow, Cornwall

Pen & Sword Books Limited incorporates the imprints of Atlas, Archaeology, Aviation, Discovery, Family History, Fiction, History, Maritime, Military, Military Classics, Politics, Select, Transport, True Crime, Air World, Frontline Publishing, Leo Cooper, Remember When, Seaforth Publishing, The Praetorian Press, Wharncliffe Local History, Wharncliffe Transport, Wharncliffe True Crime and White Owl.

For a complete list of Pen & Sword titles please contact

PEN & SWORD BOOKS LIMITED
47 Church Street, Barnsley, South Yorkshire, S70 2AS, England
E-mail: enquiries@pen-and-sword.co.uk
Website: www.pen-and-sword.co.uk
Or
PEN AND SWORD BOOKS
1950 Lawrence Rd, Havertown, PA 19083, USA
E-mail: Uspen-and-sword@casematepublishers.com
Website: www.penandswordbooks.com

Dedicated to
the Scottish Soldier,
Yesterday, Today and Tomorrow

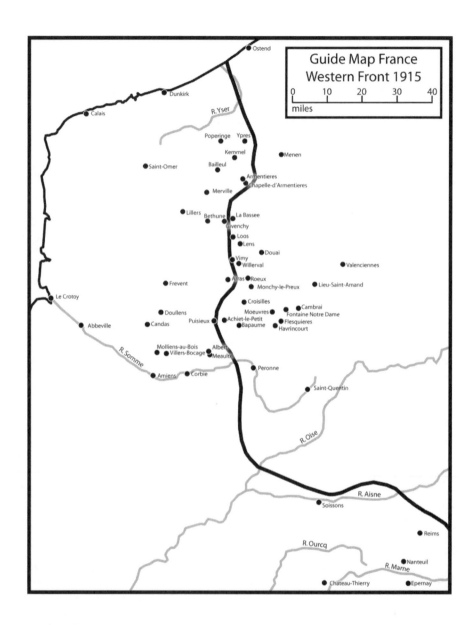

Guide Map France
Western Front 1915

miles
0   10   20   30   40

Ostend

Dunkirk

Calais

R. Yser

Poperinge   Ypres

Kemmel

Menen

Saint-Omer   Bailleul

Armentieres
Chapelle-d'Armentieres

Merville

Lillers   La Bassee
Bethune
Givenchy
Loos
Lens
Douai
Vimy
Willerval
Valenciennes

Frevent   Arras   Roeux
Monchy-le-Preux   Lieu-Saint-Amand

Croisilles

Doullens   Moeuvres   Cambrai
Puisieux   Fontaine Notre Dame
Abbeville   Candas   Achiet-le-Petit   Flesquieres
Bapaume   Havrincourt

Molliens-au-Bois   Albert
Villers-Bocage   Meaulte

R. Somme

Amiens   Corbie   Peronne

Le Crotoy   Saint-Quentin

R. Oise

R. Aisne

Soissons

Reims

R. Ourcq

Nanteuil
R. Marne
Chateau-Thierry   Epernay

CONTENTS

INTRODUCTION

Engine of Destruction: The 51st (Highland) Division in the Great War was the last book published by Argyll Publishing of Glendaruel before its owner, Derek Rodger, retired. It is an unexpected privilege and a delight to have the opportunity to write an introduction to this Pen and Sword reprint, with its amended title, *The 51st (Highland) Division in the Great War: Engine of Destruction.*

When jointly researching *Can't Shoot a Man with a Cold. Lt. E.A.Mackintosh M.C. 1893-1917. Poet of the Highland Division* with Rosalind Green, the lack of a modern overview of the 51st (Highland) Division from 1914-1918 was conspicuous. The only narrative widely available, *The History of the Fifty First (Highland) Division 1914-1918*, by Major Frederick William Bewsher, was published in 1921. Some of the restraints on him are touched upon in the prologue to this book, but his greatest obstacle was that he was writing whilst serving with the Headquarters of the 3rd (Lahore) Division of the Indian Army in Bir Salem, Palestine. Production costs forced him to reduce the number of maps and details. He reflected that, *it is doubtful if full justice can be done to the part played by the British Army in the Great War until a generation not intimately involved in it has arisen and has come to regard the burdens sustained for over four years by the British soldier in the true perspective.* He understood that he was too close to the events and personalities of the division and that time and emotional detachment should produce a more balanced overview of its history. In 2004 the time seemed ripe for a second history of the division and this book was the first twenty-first century 51st (Highland) Division history, but not, as it has already turned out, the last.

One of the delights of studying history is the fact that a review of events tends not to produce well defined conclusions. 'Much', as Joseph Addison wrote, 'can (usually) be said on both sides.' The author has to exercise objectivity, an almost impossible feat. Conclusions are based on a study of the facts, but these facts frequently reflect the bias of those who recorded them, particularly in battalion war diaries, where writers were trying to penetrate the fogs of war, minimizing their battalion's failings and, metaphorically, defending their flanks.

I am of direct Highland and Western Isles ancestry, was in the Glasgow University Officers Training Corps, became, by invitation, a member of the Lowland Territorial, Auxiliary and Reserve Forces Association at the time of the Strategic Defence Review in 1998 and believe that the reserve element of the forces should be expanded: these factors may militate against objectivity, but I have done my best – the reader will have to judge! One of the book's aims is to 'touch upon others' views of its reputation'. Over the years a number of criticisms, often unsubstantiated, have been made by veterans, the Official History or by modern authors. As no one had ever answered these criticisms and as some of them appeared to be mere opinion, the book was in part intended to challenge them.

In The Hell they called High Wood - The Somme 1916, by Terry Norman, the author asserted that the 51st's vain attacks on High Wood gave it the experience that made it an elite formation 'in its own estimation at least'. Almost every division failed at High Wood, as did the divisions on the 51st's flanks during its attacks. That the author saw fit to include the comment in parentheses suggested that the he did not share the opinion of historians who numbered it among the best.

Brynn Hammond in *Cambrai 1917, The Myth of the First Great Tank Battle* described the 51st as 'Scottish', his inverted commas implying that there were so many 'outsiders' as to negate that definition. In this book that is challenged on the basis of the birthplaces of the dead in *Soldiers Died* in several sample battalions, from varying recruitment areas. In Craig French's *Friends are good on the day of battle: the 51st (Highland) Division during the First World War*, the author's more detailed analysis, on a month by month recruitment basis, divided recruit categories into: 1. Those born or enlisted in the battalion's recruiting region; 2. Those from elsewhere in Scotland; 3. Those from other places. He also factored in places of enlistment. The 1/7th Black Watch, from Fife, features in analyses of their composition in both this book and Craig French's: the first puts the Scottish element at 93%, the latter at 90.4%, well within the acceptable margins of error. Using the same, differing methods with other battalions, in both books, proved conclusively that the Highland Division was genuinely Scottish. If Brynn Hammond had enclosed 'Highland' in inverted commas, he would have been correct. One wonders why the point was made in the first place. Craig French confirms that until early 1918 Scottish soldiers were posted to Scottish battalions and that attempts to post Scottish reinforcements to non-Scottish battalions met with so much vigorous dissent that the authorities reverted to the former policy. This maintained the high proportion of Scots in the Highland Division until the end of the war.

This book suggests that the Scottish educational system was a factor in the success of the 51st. Craig French's opening page confirms this: *Long after the war was over a distinguished Irish General expressed the hope that if ever he had troops under him again they might be Scots. A Scotsman present expressed surprise at his preference for foreigners, to which the General replied that he held that hope because of the high standard of Scottish education, which ensured that the youngest lance-corporal would intelligently carry on his Commander's intentions even after all his officers were killed.* This perception cannot be taken as proof of the universal ability of all Scottish junior NCOs or privates to exercise unexpected initiative confidently in the absence of officers, because evidence exists to the contrary; but it does reflect a view that assuming an unaccustomed leadership role was a more visible characteristic amongst Scottish soldiers than amongst others.

Whereas this book draws brief conclusions on all the Highland Division's engagements, Craig French chose four and subjected them to meticulous investigation under the headings of narrative, analysis, artillery, combined arms, training, command and control, organisation and administration, strength and casualties and, lastly, esprit de corps. He selected Festubert, Beaumont-Hamel, Cambrai and the 1918 March Offensive. He traced the division's experience on the 'learning curve', when it was newly in France and raw, through to its peak as an elite division in 1917 and its hardships in 1918. It would have been useful to have seen his conclusions before this book was completed.

One of the most contentious aspects of the Highland Division's history is the reference to the autumn 1917 German short list of the three most feared British divisions, which placed the Highland Division at the top of the list, above the 29th Division and the Guards Division. Bewsher's history, Neil Munro in Fred A Farrell's *The 51st Division, War Sketches* and practically every history of battalions that served in the Highland Division repeat this story. The fact that no one has a copy of the list, or may never have had a copy, or may never even have seen it, is grist to the mill of the 51st (Highland) Division's critics and its competitors. It is likely that it caused scuffles between the Guards and the 51st as the former relieved the latter in the Battle of Cambrai.

Attempting to grade the performance of divisions is problematic as every division was composed of individuals, with differing experiences, whose reactions to the sustained alarms of war cannot be expected to be uniform, however well trained they have been. The characteristics of their battalion, brigade and divisional commanders clearly impinged on the performance of divisions, as did over prolonged exposure to battle. Divisions also experienced performance peaks and troughs. From the safety of late twentieth century peace time, the SHLM project rated the 46th (North Midland) Division as 65th out of 66 and Simon Peaple in his *Mud, Blood and Determination.*

The History of the 46th (North Midland) Division in the Great War put it in the lowest quartile, although stating that it finally matured when it broke the Hindenburg Line in late September 1918 by crossing the St. Quentin Canal. Interestingly, a German rating of January 1918 judged it to be a good average division, which raises the question 'who is best qualified to judge?' – historians separated by events by many years, or the division's adversaries? There is a danger in league tables, but they are here to stay, will always be controversial and are worth exploring. The British Army's learning process is touched upon in this book. *Learning to Fight* by Aimée Fox (2018), provides highly detailed analysis of the process.

This book was designed to be read both by those drawn to it by an ancestor's service in the 51st, or by those with a desire to learn more about the division, as well as appealing to a military historian's interest in the issues revealed by the division's experiences. It includes reminiscences that were safely held by families and that had never entered the public domain. It has been an especial responsibility and honour to let those modest but experienced voices be heard. 'Engine of Destruction' derives from an unnamed commentator who told M.M. Haldane, author of the *History of the 4th Seaforth Highlanders*, that *the two most terrible engines of destruction ever made by man were the 51st and 15th Divisions, both Scottish....* This is not a description that might be politically correct nowadays, but attitudes were different a hundred years ago.

If the book stimulates interest, illuminates a family's history or increases the stock of human knowledge and experience, it will have been worthwhile. However, its main purpose was to pay tribute to a generation that met hitherto unimagined horrors with fortitude, adaptability, resilience and humour and, despite the terrible price that they paid in lives, broken bodies and minds, carried on until the job was done. It was not through any lack of effort on their part that their task had to be fully completed in 1945. Just as the Great War is a memorial to the failures of emperors and politicians, so too is the failure of the peace settlement and the war of 1939—1945.

Colin Campbell, July 2018

Prologue

In 1921 Major F.W. Bewsher D.S.O., M.C. published *The History of the Fifty First (Highland) Division 1914-1918*. Frequent reference is made to his book, and to war diaries, written as soon after events as possible, and factual, to the best of the diarists' knowledge. Most immediate post-1919 divisional and battalion histories were reluctant to criticise their own soldiers, or others, out of deference to comrades, dead or alive, and to avoid blame. They tend to be limited to their own isolated part in a battle. This book will try to place the 51st in context, diminish isolated perspectives, review its performance, and touch upon others' view of its reputation.

The American Civil War of 1861-1865 rehearsed many aspects of the war on the Western Front. Many battles involved attacks on entrenched positions, with heavy casualties and the USA's General Grant drew from a large population and accepted that a ratio of up to 3:1 on the part of the attackers facing entrenched defenders was needed to succeed. The siege of Petersburg included deep entrenchments and gun positions, and mining the enemy with explosives piled in underground chambers. The USA's small regular army provided leadership to both sides. State volunteer militias expanded for the war. Individuals raised new regiments, in which rank was often attained through friendship and influence, and in which discipline was lax. All of which presaged the problems incurred in the rapid expansion of the British Army in 1914. The Boer War of 1889-1901/2 drove home the supremacy of concealed riflemen against exposed infantry, and after the Boer War marksmanship was actively encouraged in the British Army.

Mass armies participated in the Russo-Japanese War of 1904-1905.

Summarising its lessons Lieutenant Colonel Yoda, Imperial Japanese Army, concluded that trench warfare made battles more stubborn, that heavier artillery was necessary, and that outflanking movements were needed. Yoda thought that better logistics and casualty evacuation were needed to conserve the attackers' numbers and maintain morale. Night was needed for re-establishing control, resupply, planning for the next day, and maintaining contact with the enemy. He thought that full divisional attacks at night were unlikely, and that night attacks would be at regimental strength. The weapons of choice were the bayonet, bullets and grenades. His predictions were surprisingly accurate. [1]

While optimists might have hoped that a war of movement would characterise any future European war, trench warfare did not come as a surprise, as army manuals covered the construction of defensive positions. Lack of reserves, supplies, military intelligence, experience, artillery support, reliable communications, time for reconnaissance and planning, were all known factors in battlefield failure before 1914. So too were over-optimism, and failure to realise when further attacks were futile. It took too long for the lessons of previous wars to be re-applied. What was unprecedented was a continuous trench system from Belgium to Switzerland that made outflanking by land impossible.

For numbering and nomenclature of battalions and divisions see Appendix I.

An asterisk * against a man's name refers the reader to Appendix II listing wartime deaths.

All battles are described from right to left.

NOTE

1. Kuikosha Kiji (Officers' Club Journal) No. 352, 1906 translated by Capt. E.F. Calthrop RFA* *The Journal of the Royal United Services Institute*, Vol LI

1/6th Seaforths leaving Bedford,1915

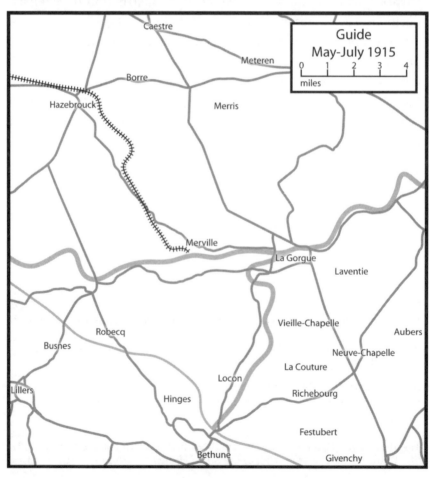

CHAPTER 1

INNOCENCE
Bedford

'It's a' richt, we're here noo.' [1]

Scotland has a long military tradition. Families in the Scottish Borders disputed the frontier lands with England, and raided their enemies on both sides of the boundary. Highland clansman took up arms at their chief's behest to defend his interests. Skill at arms and poverty took Scots as mercenaries to Europe: from the fifteenth century until 1831 they served in the French king's *Garde d'Ecosse*, and in the Thirty Years War (1618-1648) they served in the Polish, Danish, Dutch and Swedish armies. A plaque in the English Church, Amsterdam, commemorates MacKay's Regiment, which served the Dutch States General from 1572 to 1782. Patrick Gordon (1635–1699) of Aberdeenshire joined the Swedish Army in 1655, then the Polish Army and lastly the Russian Army, eventually becoming its general in chief.

In 1633 the Royal Scots, the oldest infantry regiment in the British Army, was established. After the 1715 Jacobite Rising, the Black Watch was raised in 1739 to police the Highlands. Within ten years of the defeat of the second Jacobite Rising at Culloden in 1746, Highland regiments were recruited by the British Army, where they wore regimental tartan and confirmed their reputation as close quarter warriors. With the lifting of the post-Culloden civilian ban on tartan in 1782, Sir Walter Scott's tales of Scottish history, and King George IV's kilt wearing on his Edinburgh visit in 1822, there was a tartan revival. Queen Victoria's attachment to Balmoral, and the tartanisation of her entourage made tartan the internationally recognised costume of the Scot. After the army reforms of 1881 all the Scottish infantry wore tartan. Tartan reinforced the Scots' fierce sense of identity.'

The Treaty of Union of 1707 safeguarded the distinctive law and religion of Scotland, and until the 1830s there were four Scottish universities to England's two, which made higher education more accessible in Scotland than in England. Post 1707 Scotland suffered from cultural imperialism, much of it led by a rapidly Anglicised Scottish aristocracy.

Written Scots was saved from oblivion by Robert Burns, and a few authors used it before and during the First World War; even an establishment figure like John Buchan wrote poems in Scots. The much disparaged kailyard school of literature portrayed Scottish life sentimentally, but had a wide readership. Gaelic was discouraged in classrooms and playgrounds, but it survived.

Between 1889 and 1914 a Scottish Home Rule Bill was debated fifteen times, and one reached a second reading in 1913. The Scottish National Portrait Gallery, opened in 1889, was a tangible affirmation of Scottish identity. In 1902 a petition circulated in Scotland against the assumption of the numeral VII by King Edward, who was neither the seventh Edward to be king of Scotland, nor had there been a previous King Edward of the United Kingdom. Harry Lauder, world renowned before 1914, portrayed a mean and comic Scot, offensive to some, but touching the hearts and humour of many with his sentimental songs: he reflected the Scots' inclination for self mockery.

The people of Scotland knew that they were Scots, or more precisely, that they were not English! On matters of history the Scots had and have long memories: a former C.O. of 1/8th Argylls remembered that when he and his adjutant, Alex MacDonald from Glencoe, were under severe bombardment in a trench MacDonald turned to him and said,

'Sir, in case we do not get out of this alive, I would just like to thank you.'

'For what?'

'Well, Sir, when you took command of this Battalion there were seventeen Campbells in the Mess: now there are only three-God be praised.' [2]

A throwback to the notorious Massacre of Glencoe in 1692!

. . .

The territorial regiments of the 51st Highland Division derived from the Volunteers, formed in 1796 to oppose French invasion, and largely disbanded at the end of the Napoleonic Wars in 1815. The resurgence of French military ambition, demonstrated by Napoleon III of France, alarmed the British, and in 1859 the Volunteers were re-established.

In February 1860 'The Old Guard of Glasgow' was formed from survivors of units dating back to the Glasgow Light Horse of 1796. These ancients neither drilled, nor had uniforms, but became the 78th Lanark, which merged with the 3rd Lanark Rifle Volunteers. Volunteers were to be 'a useful auxiliary to the regular army and militia' [3] and harass the enemy's flanks and lines of communication. The Voluntary Artillery Corps manned coastal batteries. Initially there was enormous enthusiasm, and a member of the Queen's Edinburgh Rifle Brigade recollected that 'many went regularly to two or even three drills a day'.[4] Appearances were most important. 'Every shade of grey, green and brown was adopted and the uniforms were often richly decorated with braid or lace, especially in the corps equipped at their own expense.'[5]

Subsequently cavalry, mobile artillery, signals, supply and bearer units (medical units) were established, and in 1890 the companies were formed into seven regional brigades.

Between 1859 and 1900 the Volunteers were formalised with criteria for officer training, standards of shooting, attendance at drills, upper age limits, and physical fitness. Being a volunteer was like membership of a social club, with drill nights, camps, sports, smokers, and the occasional trip to Bisley for the expert marksman. A memorial in a Kilbarchan, Renfrewshire, cemetery lists nineteen volunteers who had died between 1869 and 1889 under the motto 'Rest from War', but war was a figment of the imagination for most of them.

That changed during the Boer War, with a call on January 2nd, 1900, for each regular regiment's Volunteers to raise a company of 116 officers and men, recruited on regular army terms, for one year or the duration of the war. Eleven special service companies were formed. Cycle troops, engineers, medical personnel and a Fife and Forfar Light Horse company also volunteered.

In 1902 nine brigades were established: Argyll and Sutherland Highlanders, Black Watch, Gordon Highlanders, Highland Light Infantry, Ist Lothian, 2nd Lothian, Scottish Borders, Scottish Rifles, and the Seaforth and Cameron Highlanders. A tenth brigade was created by splitting the Argyll and Sutherland Brigade. The proportion of volunteers in the male population in 1901 is significant – in England it was 1 in 68, in Scotland 1 in 36. [6]

In 1908 Secretary of State for War Haldane replaced the Volunteers with the Territorial Force (T.F.), intended for home defence. There were fourteen infantry divisions in the United Kingdom: the Lowland and Highland Divisions represented 14.2% of the T.F., from Scotland's U.K. population share of 11.27%. (1911 census: UK 42,138,000, Scotland 4,751,000) [7] Therein lies the genesis of Scotland's higher wartime casualty rate.

At mobilisation in August 1914 the 1/1st Highland Division had three brigades.

Argyll and Sutherland Brigade:1/6th (Renfrewshire), 1/7th (from Stirlingshire and Clackmannan), 1/8th (Argyllshire) and 1/9th (Dumbartonshire) Battalions of the Argyll and Sutherland Highlanders.

- Seaforth and Cameron Brigade: 1/4th (Ross Highland), 1/5th (Sutherland and Caithness), 1/6th (Morayshire) Battalions of the Seaforth Highlanders, and 1/4th Battalion of the Cameron Highlanders (from Invernesshire and the Hebrides)

- Gordons Infantry Brigade: 1/4th (from Aberdeen city), 1/5th (Buchan and Formartin), 1/6th (Banff and Donside), 1/7th (Deeside Highland) Battalions of the Gordon Highlanders.

- The 4th (City of Dundee), 5th (Angus and Fife), 6th (Perthshire) and 7th (Fife) Battalions of the Black Watch Brigade were allocated to coastal defence.

The 1/1st Highland Division also had its own artillery, medical, veterinary, engineer and supply units.

The territorials responded well to mobilisation. In a 1/6th Gordons' company only one man failed to report for duty, and he was at sea. In another company all reported including a former territorial who took the place of a man who was seriously ill. [8] 1/8th Argylls brought their companies up to strength with recruits, one of whom was the pier porter at Ardrishaig, Loch Fyne, who leapt aboard the steamer leaving with the departing Lochgilphead company. [9] There were no territorial limits to recruitment: 1/5th Seaforths recruited in the Belfast docks; 1/8th Argylls and the 2/4th Seaforths had Mancunians and in 2/4th Seaforths, 'when it came to the turn of the company containing the Manchester boys to be next the band the Commanding Officer used to hear a song to this effect:

'We are the Seaforth 'ighlanders,
Our 'ome is were the 'eather grows,
We dance the fling on 'eels and toes,
An' we're 'ighly respected werever we goes.' [10]

The division mustered around Perth, then entrained to its War Station at Bedford. Its G.O.C., Major-General Colin Mackenzie was replaced on 23rd August by Brigadier-General Bannatine-Allason, (1855-1940). Walter Nicholson, a regular officer on the Highland Division's staff, found him uninspiring and complained that he enjoyed over-long meals, silently watching passing troops from his window, and that he was a bad conversationalist. Nicholson thought him short of knowledge and over-reliant on force of personality. [11]

Bannatine-Allason contributed the first chapter of Bewsher's *The History of the 51st (Highland) Division* and, having noted the numerical strengths of the battalions, but not the quality of the men, he recorded that the horses and transport were 'inferior in quality, though many of the animals actually went overseas and did good work.' [12] He observed that the artillery was badly harnessed and that very few of the men knew about horse management. The army had been gifted 100 polo ponies from Madras, and, when others rejected them, Bannatine-Allason wrote (of himself), 'the G.O.C., with considerable

Major General
Bannatine-Allason

experience of such animals gladly accepted the offer . . . with the result that the company commanders and staffs of the Highland Division went to France better mounted than any other.' [13] Finally he noted: 'the determination of all to 'play the game' . . . no praise can be too great for the regimental officers and men.' [14]

For most of the men, whose previous furthest trip may have been a camp in Scotland, England was a novelty. A company of 1/8th Argylls, led by its Company Sergeant Major went out 'in good order and got deliberately drunk to a man to mark the occasion of their first expedition across the Border.' [15] The time at Bedford exposed conspicuous inadequacies. The men were billeted in houses. The lucky were cared for by their hosts, the others were left to their own devices in rented houses. Private James Rennie, 1/6th Gordons remembered that 'six of us slept in a little room. . . three slept on the bed and three slept on the mattress on the floor.' [16] Billets become dirty and lousy and in the winter some men burned the woodwork in their billets to stay warm. Sergeant John Bruce Cairnie, 1/5th Seaforths, on 13th March 1915 was in Foster Hill Rd, Bedford 'estimating the damage done by the men in some of the empty houses. A good deal of damage, much of it apparently wilful, but I believe nothing to what has been the case in some of the Morayshire billets. Banisters, wainscoting, etc burnt up and marble mantelpieces in smithereens, but I didn't see any as bad as that.' [17] Both coal and supervision were lacking. Once this was discovered a day a week was devoted to housekeeping.

The junior officers, busy mastering their new roles, had little time, experience or even inclination, to monitor the men's living conditions. The differences between territorials and regulars were great: Nicolson's willing clerical staff knew nothing of army procedures and had to be taught what to do, otherwise they did nothing. The territorial doctors waited on patients to report sick, whereas regular army doctors emphasised preventive measures. [18]

Orders were often questioned. Sergeant John Cairnie 1/5th Seaforths:

'there was nearly a mutiny this morning when the men were told to parade with their equipment which still wringing wet

20

on. The Adjie wouldn't give in but when half the battalion paraded without it he had to send them back for an hour to get great coats. Route-march round by Rinhold and Cleat Hill raining most of the way. I enjoyed it very much. Afternoon pay and rations. Lecture from Sergt-Major. He thought this about wet equipment 'a damn good joke'. He insisted on punctuality on parade, which is certainly necessary. Our men aren't smart enough yet at turning out. [19]

'Laurie and I got a swearing from the Adjie today because he saw some of the men scratching their faces when they were at attention. He's getting very snotty about details, so I suppose we'll have to stiffen up too.' [20]

It was difficult for men who may have shared the same school classrooms as their officers to adopt the regular army's habit of instant obedience. [21] Prospects for instilling such habits were dashed by the removal of regulars who provided the professional input to territorial battalions: NCOs went first, then the adjutants, all posted to New Army battalions, or to regular battalions in France. This was not unique to the Highland Division. The division's artillery, the rifles and much of the equipment was out of date: transport had been commandeered from civilian sources and replacement wagons came slowly. [22]

In November and December of 1914 an epidemic struck: out of 18,200 men 529 caught measles, of whom 57 died: 7 others died from scarlet fever and one from diphtheria.[23] Men from the Highlands were more susceptible to illness than those who had acquired immunities in overcrowded industrial towns. Amongst those from north and west of the southern boundaries of Banff, Inverness and Argyll, 477 caught measles, of whom 59 died, whereas only 52 cases occurred from south of that line, with 6 deaths. Private James Rennie, 1/6th Gordons, caught measles and scarlet fever and was in Goldington Road School, a temporary hospital:

'I was at the big doorway of the hallway and everything went out and in past me. Nine of them were packed out in one day . . . there were 35 of them died in one week . . . with measles and scarlet fever. . . They wrote home and told Mother I was a 'goner'. And if she wanted to see her boy she had better show up pretty quick. . . And then I got home on sick leave. . . I was humped backed and skinny as a rail. I was at home for a couple of months. . .' [24]

Sergeant John Cairnie, 1/5th Seaforths noted:

'20 Jan 15 Route march to Turvey, somehow I felt less fit than usual. . . 20 men on the sick-list this morning, mostly with chest-colds. No cases of measles in our Company today, but one death in 'G'.
'21 Jan 15 Company drill under Joe Robertson with Ritson in the background and a military funeral over the wall. Quite cheerful sounds on the pipes. One death in 'A' today, and I believe 2 in 'H' yesterday.' [25]

In the midst of the epidemic units were taken to reinforce the depleted B.E.F. None had the six months training needed for territorial battalions willing to serve overseas. First to go were 1/1st Highland Field Ambulance R.A.M.C. and 1/2nd Highland Field Company R.E., both from Aberdeen and the Highland Mobile Veterinary Section. Bannatine-Allason thought that their second line replacements made rapid progress in their training. [26] On 10th March 1915 IV (Mountain) Brigade Royal Garrison Artillery (R.G.A.) was removed and on 3rd May the heavy guns of the R.G.A. were transferred.

1/4th Seaforths, 1/6th Gordons and 1/7th Argylls went in November and December 1914 to be followed in February 1915 by 1/4th Camerons, 1/4th Gordons, and 1/9th Argylls. They were all replaced by their second line battalions, e.g 2/4th Seaforths, but they were undertrained and sent back to Scotland. When John Rennie recovered from his illnesses he was with the 2/6th Gordons at Scone where a malingerer was asked by an officer why he was not on parade:

'Oh, John Bull told me to get off parade and stay off until I got cleaned. . . so I just stayed off parade. And Captain Robertson he says: 'Who?' Smithy says; 'John Bull, that wee fat mannie wi' the tartan breeks and the black leggings.' Well did Captain Robertson laugh. We were all tittering too. So Captain

Robertson says ,'You better get cleaned up and after dinner you come out on parade. . . And see that you turn out on parade every day from now on, and no more of this going sick all the time.' [27]

The 1/6th and 1/8th Argylls, from the Argyll and Sutherland Brigade, brought the Seaforths and Camerons brigade up to strength in April 1915. The Gordon Brigade's departed battalions were replaced by 1/6th (Perthshire) and 1/7th (Fife) Battalions of the Black Watch, which had been on coastal defence duties.

1/6th Black Watch had left the Tay defences on 15th April, arriving in Bedford on the 16th, after which 'a fortnight of feverish energy followed . . . during which the Battalion was completely reclothed and re-equipped, and all the unfit men were weeded out and replaced from the second line. A complete transport section, which up to this time had consisted of a few commandeered civilian vehicles, was also organised.' [28] There were 204 replacements from 2/5th Black Watch.[29] Bannatine-Allason thought that the 'Black Watch battalions were splendid in physique and appearance on parade. . . and soon proved their value.' [30] For over a month the original battalions were aware that their division was incomplete, under-trained, and worried that the Highland Division might not get to the Front, a coveted destination for those who had not yet been there. The division was still short of a brigade.

As the artillery prepared to go overseas Lieutenant James Dandie, R.G.A. noted that 'binoculars and revolvers have arrived. I believe we have to pay for them at once.' (22nd April) and on the 28th: 'what a day: work-ing till full pressure without a halt to 8 p.m. mostly with the telephone wagon. It was to clean and load up with wire – we wound four miles onto the big drums and two miles for the little 'uns.' [31]

The brigade vacancy was filled by the West Lancashire Division's North Lancashire Infantry Brigade: 1/4th Royal Lancaster Regiment (Ulverston), 1/4th Loyal North Lancashire Regiment (Preston), 1/8th (Irish) The King's (Liverpool Regiment), and 2/5th Lancashire Fusiliers. The Lancashire men's arrival on 18th April must have been a culture shock to all involved.

1/4th Royal Lancasters had been guarding the Great Western Railway from Paddington Station to Twyford. Their history noted 'the strain upon discipline involved in stringing out a Battalion of young and inexperienced soldiers upon a 30 mile length of railway, in close proximity to London and other places of interest and pleasure.' [32] Some men were killed on the railway track, attributed to them being country people, unused to express trains. [33] Between November 1914 and April 1915 the battalion had been moved five times. Some of its skilled tradesmen had been returned to their jobs at Vickers of Barrow-in-Furness and it was under-strength and under-trained when it went to France. [34]

There were other changes: Bannatine-Allason replaced several brigadiers, battalion commanders, the Commander Royal Engineers, the Assistant Director of Medical Services, the Assistant Director of Veterinary Services, and the Assistant Quartermaster General, and the 1/6th Argylls Commanding Officer became Base Commandant in France.[37]

The division was completely equipped when it left Bedford, although the artillery still had 15 pounder field guns. Ballantine-Allason was uneasy about its skill levels, caused by the lack of regular officers, alterations to the division's order of battle, and the weather. He thought that musketry training had been inadequate, citing difficulties with establishing ranges, and obtaining ammunition. [38]

The division began its move to France on 29th April 1915. 1/7th Gordons marched to Ampthill military siding at Bedford where a huge crowd had gathered to see them off. Captain Robert Ross wrote that the men whistled and sang as if it was a gala day and his descriptions of the battalion's cross Channel journey and first days in France reveal the excitement felt by all. [39]

The division sailed from either Folkestone for Boulogne or Southampton for Le Havre. When 1/6th Argylls detrained at Merville an innocent private, described as probably being from Paisley, approached an officer who was supervising the arrival, saluted, and asked 'Please sir, wha's winnin'?' The officer smiled but made no reply. Nonplussed the soldier responded, 'It's a' richt, we're here noo.' [40]

By 5th May the Highland Division was concentrated around Lillers,

Busnes and Robecq, west of Béthune. On 7th May General Haig visited Bannatine-Allason at Busnes and rode with him through the billets of the 1st and 3rd brigades. He described Brigadier General Walter Ross of the 1st Brigade as 'a good hard determined officer.'[41]

On 4th May 1/7th Gordons had set out for the Highland Division's next concentration area, and the night march was characterised by units losing their way, by stragglers being chivvied to keep up, by traffic jams, by the detachment of the rearguard from the battalion, a lack of maps, and of junior officers only having a vague idea of their planned destinations – all signs of amateurism at every level.[42] The Highland Division was reserve for the Indian Corps in its vain attack on Aubers Ridge on 9th May and was not needed.

Brigadier General
Walter Ross

On 11th May, 1/1 Highland Division was renamed and renumbered as the 51st (Highland) Division Territorial Force (T.F.) composed of 152nd (Seaforth and Argyll), 153rd (Gordon and Black Watch) and 154th (Lancashire) brigades. On 14th May it transferred to G.H.Q. reserve and marched to Caestre, Borre, Merris and Meteren, south west of Ypres. Haig saw it marching through Merville and 'all were in great spirits and singing 'there's a wee wify (sic) waiting', a wee but and ben'. . . one of Harry Lauder's songs. Curiously the latter's son is a lieutenant in the battalion that passed.'[43] John Lauder was in 1/8th Argylls.

The 51st was not needed for the Second Battle of Ypres and on 18th May it marched south to La Gorgue and Vieille Chapelle, north of Béthune. The Battle of Festubert had begun and some of the German line had been pushed back, at heavy cost.

Haig noted on 19th May:

Gen. Bannatine-Allason commanding 2/Highland Division (sic) (now called the 51st Div) came to see me soon after 9 a.m. He seemed a little anxious about putting his men straight into the trenches! I told him that we want them to take the offensive, and press the enemy hard, as he is already showing signs of demoralisation. Before the present operations we had made arrangements for training this Division, but the Division was placed in reserve under GHQ and no training has been done. [This placed responsibility for the lack of training on Sir John French, Commander of the British Expeditionary Force, whose job Haig wanted and obtained after the failure at Loos in September 1915.] I have arranged for the 4th Corps to give them instruction in bombing and to provide detachments to help in training in other matters.' [44]

153rd Brigade recorded on 19th May that one officer and four NCOs from each battalion were sent to la Couture for bomb (grenade) throwing training, which was being organised by the C.R.E. of 2nd (Regular) Division.

On 20th May Haig took no account of the fact that the 51st had been constantly on the move since its arrival in France. Ballantine-Allason's anxiety about his division's unpreparedness for trench warfare was totally justified.

20 May 1915 Haig:

'I also saw Major General Bannatyne Allason. . . On his remarking that his men were not yet fully trained, I replied that infantry peace training was little use in teaching a company how to capture a house occupied by half a dozen machine guns! What he wanted was grit and determination combined with the abilities of a stalker. He had a number of good shots in his division. He should urge his men to operate at wide intervals, and use cover: and try and bring converging fire on the locality to be attacked. He should also use our machine guns as much as possible.'

Thus Haig's disparaged Bannatine-Allason and exposed his own lack of knowledge of the realities of trench warfare. Haig finished:

'Allason said that he could not sleep for the noise of the guns during the night, and proposed to sleep at Locon. I agreed with this but said that he would hear the noise there too! He will have to get accustomed to the fighting!' [45]

Some officers were unable to handle the transition from peace to war.[46] Bannatine-Allason's headquarters were closer to the front than Haig's.

Officers of 1/6th Black Watch were introduced to the trenches that they would occupy, then 'towards midnight (20th) the 6th arrived in front of Indian Village near Festubert, where it took over the line from a battalion of the Coldstream Guards (2nd Division), who were not a little surprised to find a battalion of raw Territorials taking over a complicated line just captured from the enemy. The Guards, however, showed great patience in helping their successors to take over the new trenches, then a mere scrape in the ground about eighteen inches deep.'[47]

When 1/6th Black Watch came out on the 22nd, C.S.M. Guthrie wrote to his wife:

> 'We got safely back from the firing line last night after an exciting time, we had only one casualty and that was one of our ration carrying parties. We were lying just along side the Canadians. They are a brave lot, but very foolish about exposing themselves to needless danger, with the result that they are having many wounded and killed. There were several cases each day that with care shd. not have happened, & they had to get a loan of our bearers on several occasions.
>
> 'We are all very proud of our Coy. being one of the first of the Territorials to be sent into the first line of firing trenches, without any previous experience of trench work. Our men were all very cool and got into the trenches so quietly and with so little fuss that the Canadians next to us did not know a change had taken place. Their officers sent a complimentary note to Hd. Quarters regarding the manner we carried it out. There was an attack on our left but so well were the Coys in the firing line of the 6th in hand that not a single shot was fired. . . The Germans gave us a hot time with shell fire from their famous 'black marias' these are the high explosive shell guns . . . not one of their shells actually burst in our trench altho' we all got bespattered with mud, and fragments of the shells were quite plentiful all along our trench, which by the way had only been made the day before we got into it & was neither bullet nor view proof, and if we attempted to

straighten our backs, the snipers bullets immediately began to ping about our ears, but they failed to bag one of us. . . ' [48]

On the 20th-21st 153rd Brigade relieved a Canadian brigade in the Richebourg sector. 1/5th Gordons were relieved on the 23rd by 1/7th Gordons. The only communication trench was too narrow for two men to pass, and the outgoing 1/5th Gordons lay behind the parados until 1/7th Gordons had filed into the front line. Ross confessed that they did not know where or how far away the enemy was and that they were constantly looking over the parapet to see if the Germans were attacking. [49] This is not as surprising as it seems, as the 1/7th Gordons discovered that the fire steps in the trench faced the back! It was the old German front line trench which and had not been repaired or reversed i.e. firesteps cut and barbed wire erected, facing the enemy. 1/7th Gordons remedied the defects next day.

On Saturday 22nd May Haig met the GOC 1st Canadian Division:

'I saw Maj General Bannatyne-Allason at Alderson's HQ (Lt-Gen E.A.H. Alderson 1st Canadian Division). His men had never been in the trenches before, and had been unable to dig the new line which was ordered last night. They say they were attacked by the enemy. In fact the enemy never left his trenches but only fired. Alderson said that he thought that the 51st (Highland) Division was a danger, new troops etc.' [50]

1/6th Black Watch and others found the transition to battlefield conditions shocking:

'All those who were present will remember the first two days in the trenches. Men and officers suffered severely from thirst and had the unpleasant task of burying many enemy dead; in addition it was necessary to convert the shallow ditch which had been taken over into a well-built fire trench, working all the time under continuous fire from enemy snipers and machine-guns.' [51]

About 700 dead, mainly British, were buried by the men of 152nd Brigade, and large quantities of ammunition, rifles and rations were salvaged. [52] This experience would have dissipated some of the innocent optimism that had buoyed them throughout their training, and gave them a frightening insight of their own possible demise. Captain Ross of 1/7th Gordons judged that their sudden introduction to trench warfare had put them under great strain. [53]

A Franco-British offensive was planned for June, and Haig chose to attack near Givenchy, to follow up the limited successes of Festubert. The 51st was to take part and Haig visited its GOC:

> 'I said (to Bannatine-Allason) that the operation in hand was a simple one and that all that was wanted was some plucky fellows who can shoot, and who will open out when attacking so as to avoid losses which must occur, if they are in bunches. At 1 pm. the Highland Division is placed under the orders of the Indian Corps, who will provide detachments to help in the trenches, machine-guns, and sappers. Also some regular officers will go into the trenches with the regiments of the Highland Division for a few days.' [54]

Pluck, marksmanship, and not bunching were not a sophisticated recipe for a frontal attack. Not bunching depended on the enemy barbed wire being destroyed by shelling, and the determination of attackers to get at the enemy made high casualties inevitable. In the quiet before the battle C.S.M. Guthrie of 1/6th Black Watch complained:

> 'We are still supposed to be resting here. The rest means up at 6.30 travel one mile for bathing parade, or 3-4 miles running exercise – a scanty breakfast of bread and marmalade, then off in the broiling sun for a 5-6 mile march, then back for dinner – tatties and stew. . . but so tired and thirsty are we – as a rule – that we have no heart far less appetite to eat it. . . the heat is very oppressive – you may realise how hot it is when I tell you that the Zambuck or the Vaseline in boxes in my jacket pocket melt into liquid and run thro' my clothing like oil. I have managed to stick it out so far but yesterday I really thought I was laid out, as after coming in from the route march I could do naught but lie and wriggle in pain on the grass for an hour. Then the majority of the men were no better, a good number of them

had stripped and lying about with nothing on but their identity discs. . . ' [55]

1/6th Seaforths' headgear improved in early June when 'the blue Balmoral, covered with a khaki cover, was issued to us, instead of the unsightly and inconvenient kind of postman's cap to go over the Glengarry, with which we left England.' [56] This was later replaced by an all-khaki Tam O' Shanter.

On 12th June the final order was issued for the attack on the 15th, but Haig's concern about Bannatine-Allason manifested itself on the 10th:

> 'B-A knew very little about the kind of arrangements which must be made in order to achieve success. He seemed also long faced and melancholy! I therefore went to Hinges and saw Gen. H Rawlinson (IV Corps Commander). I told him to send a practical Staff Officer to help Allason and to
>
> 1. See himself the Brigadiers and two Company Commanders who are ordered to carry out the attack and go through the details of the action.
>
> 2. To arrange that the Brigadier and the troops detailed for the action are now out of the trenches, and are being exercised so as to be fit when the time comes. At present they are in the trenches!' [57]

On the 13th Rawlinson sent his Chief of Staff, Dallas, to the 51st [58], tardy and minimal help for an inexperienced division. Rawlinson calculated that the attack would be expensive in lives unless the wire could be cut, and he was pessimistic about that. [59]

The15th June attack began at 6 p.m. From right to left, the 1st Canadian Battalion (Western Ontario), 2nd Green Howards, 2nd Wiltshire and 1st Grenadier Guards of 7th (Regular) Division all failed.

1/4th Loyal North Lancashires and 1/6th Scottish Rifles, which had replaced 2/5th Lancashire Regiment in the 154th (Lancashire Brigade) advanced. A watching 1/5th Seaforths' sergeant wrote: 'at last the hour had come for the 6th Scottish Rifles. . . machine-guns swept over the

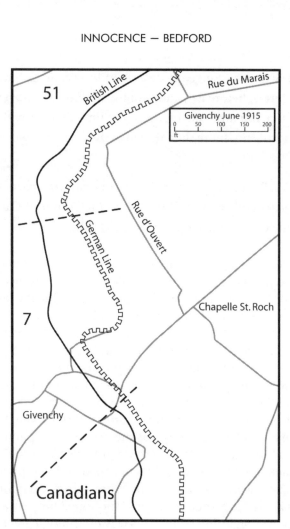

parapets and tore them to pieces . . . Their ranks thinned considerably before they were many yards from their own trenches. But 'on they went and entered the German front line, where they were lost to view.'[60] Afterwards Nicholson met a regular officer who confirmed that the men went over the parapet 'magnificently' but that they did not know what to do at the other side.'[61]

1/5th Seaforths attacked at 6.45 pm:

'One can visualize the scene, a grassy plain on a beautiful summer afternoon, no artillery barrage, no proper cutting of the enemy's wire, no firing on his batteries after the infantry started, the infantry advancing absolutely unprotected except by the rifle and machine-gun fire of their comrades, and machine-guns were few and far between in those days.' [62]

A 1/5th Seaforths' sergeant described the scene as 'just one solid sheet of bullets. . . before a distance of thirty yards was traversed all the officers of our company were hit . . . By the time we were within reach of the German wire, not more than fifteen of the company were still on the move.'[63]

Private TK Ritchie, 1/8th Argylls, was in a carrying party supporting 1/5th Seaforths and wrote to Mr Donald McCallum of Campbeltown about the fate of his son, Sergeant Alex McCallum*:

'Alex did not carry a box of bombs but had his bayonet fixed (we did not fix our bayonets, but had our rifles slung over one shoulder and box slung on the other) – he being the leader. The thunder of artillery died away and in the sudden silence 7pm June 15th the order came, No.10 Platoon fix bayonets, and at charge we all hollered and waved our bonnets and cheered as over the parapet went the first line. The second followed at ten yds intervals, and we fell in our place right behind the second line on the left flank. The bullets by this time from the enemy's machine guns and rifles were falling like heavy hail. I think Alex was the first over the parapet, and I heard him shout keep to the left flank boys, I dashed ahead and then noticed everyone had dropped and I dropped also (all this done quicker than I can write). I dropped right at Alex's heels. He turned round and motioned forward and began to wriggle and squirm his way on through green wheat. I'd a hard job following. I remember it isn't easy wriggling ahead on the ground with a box 2' x 1' x 1' on one shoulder and a rifle on the other. All the time there was an infernal hiss and ping of bullets, a whirl of pieces of shrapnel. One could see. . . fellows falling all around and I don't know how far we had gone – it seemed like a mile to me. But about a second before I was hurt we both stopped and looked and could see the German sandbags about forty yards away – just after that – I was bending down – when I felt a ton of hot nitre on my shoulder and I sank like a stone. I just recollect Alex looking round and sort of hesitating – the rest for me was a nightmare. I never saw Alex again. . .

I remember dully watching a terrible wounded chap of the Seaforths next to me and for the life of me I could not raise myself up. I think I then got suddenly frantic for I contrived to get loose from the box of bombs, my equipment and coat. But I couldn't by any means stop the blood flowing at my back. I began to feel a bit easier when I had my tunic off however and crawled back mostly on one arm. How I got back over the parapet I don't rightly know but I remember a chap hauling my shirt off and yelling to someone for iodine. Through the night I lay in a bit of trench and kept crying for water and struggling for breath – But I did not quite realise what was what until I woke up and found myself going down the canal in a hospital barge and gazing out at the passing canal bank.

I am unaware if Alex was killed or wounded but a chum writes and tells me he is missing since that charge.' [64]

1/6th Seaforths gave covering fire to 1/5th Seaforths from a crowded trench in a salient, and were showered with shrapnel, and hit by Minenwerfer mortar bombs: after three hours they had 140 casualties, roughly one per yard of their trench. [65]

Determined men had reached the German's third line, 400 yards inside enemy territory. With inadequate artillery support, a shortage of grenades, and stubborn German counter attacks the survivors were driven back to their own trenches, the last returning at 4 am. on the 16th. They were from 1/6th Scottish Rifles, and some 1/6th Seaforths who had been sent to help them. The total domination of No Man's Land by enemy machine-gun fire made reinforcement and resupply impossible. The British had insufficient grenades as their grenade store had been hit by German shells on the 15th [66] The surviving 1/5th Seaforths, hiding in No Man's Land, crawled back to their trenches.

Organisational flaws recorded in the war diary of 1/4th King's Own Royal Lancaster Regiment typify the problems facing troops moving forward in support of the attack. On 14th June , at 8 pm it 'was held up for an hour by another Unit and transport going to trenches along Route C', then on its arrival at the old British trench at 11.30 pm it managed to squeeze in although contrary to arrangements it was already occupied by the 1/6th Scottish Rifles'.

On the 15th a 'company had come into the trenches by the wrong route and this caused some confusion'. Then the 'telephone line to Brigade broke down at 6.5 pm (6.05 pm) and messages were passed by relay post.' (runners). When the battalion was ordered to advance in support of the attack 'A Coy should have arrived in fire trench by this time (8.25 pm) but owing to a bridge being broken in No.1 Communication trench their progress appears to have been delayed and they did not reach their allotted position – nor move forward to support L.North Lancs.'

At 9.30 pm an officer reported a lack of ammunition and at 10 pm 'events proved that Amm. Supply was ample.' Then at 10 pm the machine guns sent forward to reinforce the attack could not go forward because the British were retiring from the German line, while 'D Coy of this Battalion threw back right flank to try to get in touch with Grenadier Guards – this was not effected until some 2 hours later.' In this interim period the 'German counter attack was delivered. . . Retirement of the Battalion was made necessary by the falling back of assaulting Battalions & the fact that no troops were on our right.' (ie Grenadier Guards) [67]

Haig ordered further attacks, at 4.45 p.m. on the16th. The 3rd Canadian Battalion (Toronto Regiment), 2nd Royal Scots Fusiliers and 2nd Bedfordshires of 7th (Regular) Division failed, as did 1/8th (Irish) The King's (Liverpool Regiment) of the 51st. Lieutenant A.M. Clement of 152nd Brigade Grenadier Company wrote that it 'was a hot part of the line if ever there was one, especially on the 16th June when we made our big attack and got mowed down by machine-gun fire and also got messed up between the German artillery and that of our own guns.'[68] A third attack was authorised at 5 p.m. on 17th June, to take place at 3 a.m. on the 18th.

Captain Ross, 1/7th Gordons, then with 153rd Brigade's Grenadier Company, found out about the third attack on the 17th from an incredulous Guards' officer who told Ross that he would be attacking that night without artillery support over ground traversed by wide ditches and uncut barbed wire. The Guards were to support the attack, which had been postponed until 5 a.m. on the 18th. Ross' men had no rations, so they scavenged food from the dead and improvised plans of attack. It was called off, but the enemy shelled their trenches. [69]

On the 17th, 1/6th Seaforths, exhausted from a week in the line, dirty and bearded, were relieved by 1/6th Argylls 'inquiring, as they entered the line, in the real Paisley tongue, 'Have you got any good dug-outs here? We're a great mob for sleeping!' ' [70]

The Official History records the battle casualties from 15 – 21 June as 7th Division 1,344, 51st Division 1,665, Canadian Division 802. [71] Of the Canadians Rawlinson wrote, 'I don't think they meant business' [72] because they had only lost only 802 men. This takes no account of the fact that the 7th Division made five battalion strength attacks on the 15th and 16th, the 51st made four, plus two companies, and the Canadians only two. If a body count was a legitimate yardstick of effort the 51st had meant business – despite the fact that Rawlinson had previously confided in his diary on 13th June that the 51st's officers 'are not good, too few gentlemen among them.' [73]

Numbers of casualties prove nothing – fewer enemy machine-guns, the lie of the land, better use of cover, better leadership, easier lines of retreat, and luck could diminish casualties – inexperience and over-optimism could increase them.

Rawlinson congratulated Bannatine-Allason:

> 'The Corps Commander wishes you to convey his appreciation to the troops of the 51st Division for their gallant conduct of yesterday, and today, particularly to the assaulting battalions – viz., the 6th Scottish Rifles, the 4th Loyal North Lancashire Regiment, and the 8th King's Liverpool Regiment.'[74]

As he had not thought that the attack would succeed and that it was against his better judgement, the message has a hollow ring.

The 51st's inexperience had been exposed by lack of rations and water supplies, late reliefs, complicated reliefs, stores going forward too slowly, and units getting lost. Bewsher reflected that 'no opportunity was vouchsafed to officers and men of being 'put wise' before the full responsibility of holding a captured position was thrust upon them. The significance of this statement is that troops on the first occasion they enter the battle zone are liable to be 'gobrowed' (intimidated) by their new circumstances.' [75]

Compare the 51st's experience with that of 1/6th Gordons which had left in November 1914: they were with 7th (Regular) Division from 13th November 1914 and did not go into the trenches until 6th December. 'While the battalion still carried out its usual drill and attack practice, it also received instruction in relief of trenches, the posting of sentries, and other details of trench warfare.' [76] During one operation the battalion was in close support, although not actively involved, but 'it gave the men their first lesson in the confused uproar and turmoil of battle.' [77]

Maxse's 18th (Eastern) Division arrived in France in July 1915 and was instructed by 5th (Regular) Division and the 51st. They took over the line on 22nd August. [78] Maxse wrote that 18th Division's first fortnight in the trenches had given it 'just enough artillery firing, sniping, bomb throwing and consequent uncertainty to give the troops confidence without too many casualties... 150 to date.' [79] Maxse was grateful to the 51st and 5th divisions for their tutelage, although earlier in the year he had thought that the 51st was 'ill-organised and unsoldier-like'.'[80] Bewsher recognised the inexperience of the 51st.

> 'The Highland Division during its first tour of duty in the line was thus employed in the particularly trying operation of consolidating a newly won position. Few operations call for more resource and more tactical skill on the part of junior officers and NCOs, or for more detailed planning and arrangement on the part of commanders and staff. Order has immediately to be evolved from chaos... the amount of work required to make a position defensible and habitable appears overwhelming.' [81]

Nicholson thought that the 51st was not given any trench warfare instruction because it was hoped that it might bring fresh ideas for trench warfare that had been missed by experienced divisions. This is too forgiving of those who did not train it. He thought that induction had been avoided because the men of the 51st might not be able to co-exist with the men of the Indian Corps, to which the 51st was attached. [82]

Linton Andrews, who then served in 1/4th Black Watch, Bareilly Brigade, Meerut Division, noted that his battalion had been told officially not to fraternise with the Indians, because the Scots could not understand them, and because they were 'strange people'. This absurdity was exposed when Andrews' battalion halted on a march, and nearby Indians, realising that the Scots were hungry, shared their food with them. Unofficially Linton's battalion had been told that the only way to gain an Indian's respect was to treat him roughly, but they treated them as friends saying to them, 'Teek, Johnny, Allyman no bon' ('Well done, Indian soldiers. The Germans are no good.') And they would reciprocate with 'Black Watch teek. Black Watch dam good.' [83] The Indian Divisions had British battalions in their brigades, and if incompatibility with Indians was thought to be a problem, the 51st's battalions could have been attached to the British battalions. Maybe Nicholson was excusing fellow regular officers for their neglect.

Despite its rawness the 51st had proved that it could mount a spirited, if amateurish, attack. That it had not been trained to consolidate and supply itself properly, and that it was not attuned to the realities of trench warfare, lay at the door of its Corps and Army Commanders, for deploying it too soon.

NOTES
1. Anonymous private, 1/6th Argyll, Merville station, 1915. Argyll and Sutherland Highlanders Museum, Stirling.
2. George Malcolm *Argyllshire Highlanders 1860-1960* (Halberd Press 1960) Page 34
3. Major-General J.M.Grierson, *Records of the Scottish Volunteer Force 1859-1908* (Blackwood and Sons 1909) p.8.
4. Grierson p.12.
5. Grierson pp.26-27
6. Grierson p.368 Appendix I
7. House of Commons *A Century of Change. Trends in UK Statistics.* Research Paper 99/111
8. Captain D.Mackenzie M.A., M.C. *The Sixth Gordons in France and Flanders,* (Rosemount Press 1922) p.2.
9. Malcolm p.17.
10. M.M. Haldane *History of the 4th Seaforth Highlanders* (Witherby 1927) p.320.
11. W.N. Nicholson *Behind the Lines, an account of administrative staff work in the*

British Army 1914-1918 Jonathan Cape 1939/reprint Strong Oak Press and Donovan p.26

12. Major F.W. Bewsher *The History of the Fifty First (Highland) Division 1914-1918* (Blackwood 1921)p.1.

13. Bewsher p.6.

14. Bewsher p.7

15. Malcolm p.17

16. Private James Rennie 1/6th Gordons, transcript of tape made in Canada in the 1980s by his daughter Marge Rudy.

17. Cairnie diaries ww1/memoir/cairnie1915

18. Nicholson pp.50-51.

19. Cairnie diary 22.1.1915.

20. Cairnie diary 15.2.1915.

21. Bewsher p.5 and p.29.

22. See the *The 4th Cameron Highlanders at Bedford* with their civilian horse drawn carts and casual march discipline at the Scottish Film Archive *httl://ssa.nls.uk* - select Left column options Browse by decades 1910s, then 'full length videos'. The first of these is 4th Camerons.

23. Bewsher pp.22-23.

24. Rennie recollection.

25. Cairnie 20.1.1915 and 21.1.1915

26. Bewsher p.7.

27. Rennie recollection.

28. Major-General A.G.Wauchope *A History of the Black Watch (Royal Highlanders) in the Great War, Volume 2: Territorial Forces* (Medici Society) p.128.

29. 153rd Bde War Diary 21.4.15 TNA W0 95/2869.

30. Bewsher p.8

31. Dandie *Diaries* National Library of Scotland

32. Lt.Col.Wadham and Captain Crossley *The Fourth Battalion The King's Own (Royal Lancaster Regiment) and the Great War. p.* 11 (privately Pub. 1920, now available Naval and Miltary Press).

33. Wadham and Crossley p.10.

34. Wadham and Crossley p.15.

35. Nicholson p.59.

36. Martin Middlebrook *Your Country Needs You* (Leo Cooper 2000) p.110.

37. Bewsher p.8

38. Bewsher pp. 1-2.

39. Captain Robert B.Ross. *The Fifty-First in France,* (Hodder and Stoughton 1918) p.20

40. 1/6th A&SH Museum, Stirling

41. Field Marshal Sir Douglas Haig *Diary* 7.5.1915. National Library of Scotland

42. Ross Page 34

43. Haig diary 14.5.1915

44. Haig diary 19.5.1915

45. Haig diary 20.5.1915

46. Gary Sheffield and Dan Todham (editors) *Command and Control on the Western Front, The British Army's Experience 1914-1918* (Spellmount 2004) p.15

47. Wauchope Page 129

48. CSM Alick Guthrie 1/6th Black Watch, letters to his wife. Black Watch Regimental Association
49. Ross p.69
50. Haig diary 22.5.1915
51. Wauchope p.13.0
52. 152nd Brigade War Diary 29.5.15 WO 95/2861
53. Ross pp.67 – 71.
54. Haig diary 22.5.1915
55. Guthrie letters
56. Peel and MacDonald *Sixth Seaforth Highlanders: Campaign Reminiscences* 1923 p.8.
57. Haig diary 10.6.15.
58. Rawlinson diary 13.6.15 ex *Command on the Western Front Robin Prior and Trevor Wilson Command on the Western Front The Military Career of Sir Henry Rawlinson 1914-1918* (Pen and Sword) 2004 p.97.
59. Rawlinson diary 14.6.15. op cit page 97
60. Bewsher p.19.
61. Nicholson p.228.
62. Captain David Sutherland, *War Diary of the Fifth Seaforth Highlanders* p.20.
63. Bewsher p.20.
64. Pte Tom K Ritchie No.2101 1/8th A&SH Letter from Wrest Park Hospital, Ampthill, Bedfordshire 25.7.15 (A&SH Museum)
65. Peel and MacDonald *Sixth Seaforth Highlanders: Campaign Reminiscences* (Elgin) 1923 p.10.
66. Edmonds *Official History of the War Military Operations France and Belgium* (MacMillan) 1928 1915 v.2 p. 95.
67. War Diary 1/4th King's Own Royal Lancaster Regiment 14-16.5.1915.
68. Lt.Clements 1/6th A&SH letter of 19.7.15 to Whitecraigs Golf Club, A &SH Museum.
69. Ross pp. 91-94. Hand grenades were still thought of as a specialised function and each brigade had a grenadier company which could be deployed where it was most needed. These were disbanded as grenades became universally available.
70. Peel and MacDonald p.11
71. Edmonds OH 1915 v.2 p.97 footnote.
72. Rawlinson diary 17.6.1915. op cit page 98
73. Rawlinson diary 13.6.1915op cit page 97
74. Bewsher p.23.
75. Bewsher pp.14-15
76. Mackenzie p.9.
77. Mackenzie p.2.1
78. John Baynes *Far From A Donkey* Brassey's 1995 p.129.
79. Ivor Maxse letter of 5.9.1915
80. IWM: Maxse Papers 69/53/12, Box No 54. John Bourne Centre for First World War Studies
81. Bewsher p.12.
82. Nicholson p.64.
83. William Linton Andrews, *Haunting Years, The Commentaries of a War Territorial*, Hutchison. pp.64-65

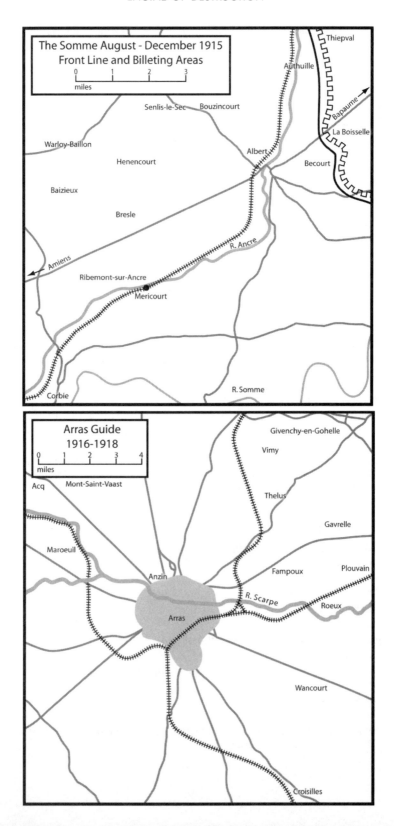

The Somme August - December 1915
Front Line and Billeting Areas

0   1   2   3
miles

Thiepval
Authuille
Bapaume
La Boiselle
Senlis-le-Sec   Bouzincourt
Warloy-Baillon
Albert
Henencourt
Becourt
Baizieux
Bresle
R. Ancre
Amiens
Ribemont-sur-Ancre
Mericourt
Corbie
R. Somme

Arras Guide
1916-1918

0   1   2   3   4
miles

Givenchy-en-Gohelle
Vimy
Acq   Mont-Saint-Vaast
Thelus
Gavrelle
Maroeuil
Fampoux   Plouvain
Anzin
R. Scarpe
Roeux
Arras
Wancourt
Croisilles

CHAPTER 2

EXPERIENCE
Somme and the Labyrinth

'Oh, four and twenty bombers,
Went out at La Boisselle,
An' only ane came back again,
Remarkin it was hell.' [1]

By 27th June 1915 the 51st Highland Division had returned to the Indian Corps in the Laventie sector, where the line was a single breastwork, built above ground, because the water table was two feet below the surface. There were isolated posts 200 to 400 yards behind it, and a line of posts over 1000 yards behind these. The enemy overlooked the area, and all the posts could be easily bombarded. The 51st began to link the posts to form a continuous support line, and to construct communication trenches, which were regularly destroyed by the enemy's artillery, making trench repairs part of daily routine.

The sector was remembered for Red Lamp corner. The front line was not a continuous breastwork, and in one place the left end of a front line trench was linked to the front line trench ahead of it by a communication trench. The men in the forward part of the line were threatened at night by rifle fire from the men behind them and to their right, so a red lamp was lit nightly to mark the end of the forward part of the line. [2]

C.S.M. Alick Guthrie of 1/6th Black Watch described the atmosphere at Laventie:

'After a night of work and silence, at daybreak the men began shouting all sorts of things to the enemy over the way, inviting them to a morning's shooting, asking for a piece of 'little Willie's' birthday cake, 'allemande no bon' etc whilst they on their part sent replies back in pure English, one being distinctly heard to say 'its alright Scotties, take off your boots and go to bed.' Then we later in the day got Piper Ferguson to tune his pipes & give us a number of selections, so you can see while we are engaged on serious business the men are in good heart. We had a visit from the Padre yesterday & he spent all the afternoon among the men, he has got more pluck than – no names – but some you would expect to see.' [3]

Curiosity and lack of discipline led to men peering over the parapet and being sniped. Deaths from asphyxiation happened when men flouted the rules and lit coke fires in enclosed dug outs. [4] Bewsher noted that enemy soldiers were often completely ignored by the troops, and that the responsibility for that lay with local commanders.[5] 'Live and let live' was common. When 1/5th Seaforths moved into the line at Laventie the enemy shouted that they were Saxons and that the Anglo-Saxons should not shoot them, and when the Saxons were being relieved they warned that the Prussians were taking over and that the Seaforths should give them hell. [6] Where the front lines were within yards of one another it made sense not to grenade the enemy, who would retaliate at once. Or for the artillery always to cause casualties, otherwise counter bombardments might eliminate the initiator of the exchange. A systematic sample of British divisions on the Western Front established that, from time to time, most regular, territorial and new army divisions 'let sleeping dogs lie' in the interests of a quiet life.[7]

The participants in the 1914 Christmas Truce were largely regular soldiers, supposedly the epitome of professionalism and aggression. Ian Hay, 10th Argylls, 9th (Scottish) Division, described night time wiring parties from both sides, each on their own side of No Man's Land, illuminated by flares, leaving each other alone to get on with their work. [8] Officers practised survival techniques. Brigadier Crozier of 40th Division wanted samples of German barbed wire from patrols to prove that they had been to it [9] and discovered that some officers kept a coil of German wire in a dug-out, lengths of which were delivered to him as proof of a task successfully accomplished. [10]

Whilst lack of aggression may have manifested itself in the 51st, it was widespread. From their less hazardous headquarters, divisional, corps and army commanders countered the human instinct for self preservation by ordering raids, to dominate No Man's Land, reconnoitre the enemy's barbed wire and positions, kill Germans, or capture prisoners for interrogation.

Bewsher refers to 'wind' as a failing of the division.[11] Inexperienced or nervous sentries, usually at night, imagined enemy activity and fired into No Man's Land, provoking a flurry of rifle, machine-gun and even artillery fire from both sides, which would fade away as it was realised that there were no raids taking place. This was universal.

Imposing military discipline on individuals who came from the same small village or town was essential. Yet these local connections provided a basic cohesion and mutual understanding difficult to achieve in newer battalions. Pipe Major Willie Lawrie* of the 1/8th (Argyllshire) Argylls was ordered by the Adjutant to turn out the pipers for an event in the officer's mess, on an evening for which he had other plans. He toasted the colonel after he had played a pibroch and said 'Your very good health, Kilberry. You're a gentleman – As for the rest, I have my own opinion.' [12] Not the kind of comment to have passed unremarked upon in a regular battalion.

At this time officers who had found conditions too severe were transferred. In 1/8th Argylls:

> ' . . . One of the casualties of age was their Colonel, John
> Campbell of Kilberry. . . his health could not stand up to it,
> and he was invalided home in September, 1915. . . policy had
> by now changed to one of appointing professional soldiers to
> command and lead the citizen armies in this long 'war of
> attrition'. . . Major Douglas Baird 12th Bengal Cavalry. . . came
> over to assume command. . . bringing with him his two Indian
> orderlies and his horses. . . his ideas on personal discipline in
> the trenches, (i.e. cleaning of brasses, shaving, care of arms
> and correct behaviour of all ranks) were not, at first, too well
> received. . . he found it difficult to obtain that instant and
> unquestioning obedience to command to which long service
> in the Indian Army had accustomed him; and, being a Ross-
> shire man himself, he consulted his Brigadier, that well-
> known and well-loved gentleman, Wattie Ross. The latter

listened sympathetically and then said, 'Do you not remember the notice on the Kirk door which used to read 'There will be a meeting in the Parish Hall tomorrow at 8 o'clock. All members are requested to attend'? Well, that's the line to take.' ' [13]

Other older C.O.s disappeared from the 51st and were replaced: MacTaggart of 5th Lancers was enthusiastic, fastidious about his new 1/5th Gordons' uniform, insisted on turning out his pipers for visitors, and emanated blood and thunder. [14] Lt. Colonel Sir Robert D Moncrieff of 1/6th Black Watch was invalided home in December 1915 and the CO of 1/4th Royal Lancasters, Lt.Colonel Walter Wadham v.D., was invalided home in June 1915, to command the 3/4th Royal Lancasters, which subsequently sent 250 officers and 4,500 men overseas, most of them to 1/4th Royal Lancasters. Good officers identified N.C.O.s and men who needed a change. C.S.M. Alex Guthrie, 1/6th Black Watch, was one of these:

'I had a talk with Captain Alexander this am about 3 o'c he called me aside and told me that he had put in my name for an appointment down at the base. . . he said I was looking rather run down & thin & would be none the worse of a month down there, as it would be a rest from the kind of work I've been doing. I thanked him for his kind thoughtfulness & I hope I'll be lucky enough to get the job.' [15] His luck held and a few weeks later he wrote to Captain Alexander:

'I have been appointed Training Sergt Major, and my duties begin at 7.30 am & finish at 9.30 pm. I am responsible for all parades, and Training, daily and weekly returns of all men passing thro' the classes. The number on parade each day varies from 2,500 to 3,500 N.C.O.s & men, and these are divided into equal parties and taught Musketry, Bombing, Skirmishing, Drill, Physical Exercises, Bayonet Fighting, Entrenching etc. . . the discipline of the division is much improved, heavy punishments being awarded for every offence. We have only a few men of the 1/6th here (none of B Coy) but they are a credit to their regts. . . ' [16]

He was fully occupied, but he had been temporarily freed from the tensions of the trenches.

At the end of July 1915 the 51st went south to the Somme, where Britain was extending its share of the Western Front, to join X Corps, 3rd Army. At a station in Amiens a French battalion greeted 1/8th Argylls with the British and French national anthems and 'not to be outdone in international courtesy. . . the battalion choir which, led by Lieutenant Taylor and assisted by those in the ranks, gave a spirited rendering of 'Scots Wha Hae'. The French, recognising its significance in our land came to the salute, and remained there throughout the song.' [17] When 1/7th Gordons detrained at Méricourt-Ribemont Captain Ross contrasted the fogs and damp mists of Flanders with the fresh clean air of the Somme Valley, and felt that he had entered a happier environment. [18] Marching towards Corbie Private John Greer*, 1/6th Argylls wrote that 'a concert started up and did not finish till we arrived, it could not have been any cheerier supposing we had got word that the war was finished.'[19]

The 51st was the first British division to arrive in the area and Lieutenant Tillyard, billeting officer of 1/4th Royal Lancasters was pleased with his reception, but was 'somewhat overshadowed by the superior attractions of the uniform of our Highland brethren of the Division, especially the kilt, which was a source of unending wonder to the local population.'[20] At the sight of his kilt 1/7th Gordons' billeting officer's reception by the French civilians had been 'violently enthusiastic.' [21] When the 51st marched through Corbie Private John Greer*, 1/6th Argylls, wrote that 'there was a great sensation because we were the first British troops to land (arrive) there. Bands played going through the town and all you could see was women with nothing on but a shirt and standing at the doors looking out of the windows. It was a splendid piece of country and reminded one of the Braes.' (Gleniffer Braes, south of Paisley) [22] C.S.M Guthrie, 1/6 Black Watch, thought 'the people here are quite different from the Flanders folk, the latter were stiff and disobliging in fact one would think they were all in German employment so ingracious were they. Here, however, they are quite nice and very French, and quite taken up with the 'Kilties' they are quite liberal in giving the men souvenirs in the shape of fruits etc.' [23]

On 26th July 152nd Brigade recorded that the 'Brigadier and Brigade

Major (were) shown round the trenches held by the 116th French Regiment Infantry of the Line between 7 a.m. and 17.30 p.m. finding the line very well organised for defence, the 116th Regiment having been in exactly the same place for seven months.' [24] Relations with the French troops were cordial. Colonel Rorie of the 1/2nd Highland Field Ambulance took over from the 16/16 French Field Ambulance at Warloy-Baillon and 'their O.C. was a true son of the Midi, a big, burly black-bearded, merry-hearted man, with a fine bass voice which he used to sing to great effect after our conjoint dinner in the hospital that evening.' . . . The French insisted on learning 'It's a Long Way to Tipperaray' and 'when their unit left the next morning, after exchanging a tricolour for a Union Jack, every mother's son of them was shouting it; and they marched tunefully enough down the village street, with the British flag flying at their head, and all of us giving them a hearty send off'. . . ' [25]

When the Bretons of the *19eme Regiment d'Infanterie* were relieved by 1/6th Black Watch 'the Highlanders were addressed in the broadest Scotch, and it was later discovered that in pre-war days he (the speaker) had been employed in selling onions on the streets of Perth!' [26]

As the Bretons left, some of the pipes and drums accompanied them for part of the way. Their appreciation of this musical farewell was reflected, said Bewsher, by the way in which they refreshed the Highland bands, probably with 'Le Pinard' the rough red wine issued to French soldiers. [27] The association between the Bretons and the 51st was commemorated in a pipe tune written by Pipe Major William Lawrie*, 1/8th Argylls, entitled 'The 8th Argyll and Sutherland Highlanders Farewell to the *116eme Regiment De Ligne.*' Lieutenant E.A. Mackintosh*, 1/5th Seaforths, wrote 'The Undying Race' celebrating the Breton and Scots common Celtic heritage and ancient struggles with the Saxons:

> Here in the narrow broken way
> Where silently we go
> Steadfast above their valiant clay
> Forgotten crosses show.
> Our whispers call to many a ghost
> Across the flare-light pale,
> And from their graves the Breton host
> Stand up beside the Gael. [28]

The trenches on the Somme were not breastworks: east of Bouzincourt 1/6th Seaforths found that 'the trenches were all dug out of the chalk to a depth of about 5 feet... and... were sumptuous in the extreme'. [29] 1/5th Seaforths, at Authuille, on the River Ancre, were pleased with the dug-outs, 12 feet down and cut in the chalk. Although the trenches were materially superior to those at Laventie, the sector was undermined by the Germans. Five hundred French tunnellers had dug mines and counter mines and on 22nd August they handed over to the three hundred men of 179th Tunnelling Company, R.E. A hundred and eighty miners from the 51st were detached to reinforce the sappers.[30]

The underground war impinged on the infantry, who removed the spoil from the front line, had the anxieties of garrisoning trenches under which there were mines, and the duty of recovering from the effects of a mine. When a mine exploded the Germans would rush to occupy the crater, to be met by the British in close quarter battle for what was the most advantageous rim of the crater – that closest to the enemy. If either side secured one rim, or both, the crater would subsequently be joined to the owners' front line trench by a sap. In the subterranean war countermining was endemic and mortaring and sniping took a toll. Lieutenant Cairnie, 1/5th Seaforths:

Lt. Cairnie

'On duty from 1 to 4 and got in about 10 hours sleep, in spite of Blackie's snoring. No work done on the trench this morning. About 11 o'clock the Germans blew up one of our mines and a number of men of the R.E. were gassed. One officer and three men or so were done for. Some Argyles who assisted at the top of the shaft were the worse of the gas too.

We took over the left sector of the line at 4 o'clock, changing over with 'D' Coy. A lot of trench mortars came over just at that time but did no damage. No. 1 platoon lost a Melvich boy at tea-time – shot through the parapet and Argyle working party had two killed and 5 wounded at night by a trench mortar.

> And after all we are just holding on and doing no good. Our sentries in the front line are sitting in little holes in the parapet, neither observing nor firing and the Germans are firing our own mines. Everybody talks in whispers and walks on tiptoe.'[31]

From August until December 1915 the 51st served in the sector from Bécourt to Thiepval and settled into the routine of trench warfare, with several days each in the front line, support, and reserve and then rest in the rear. 'Rest' was a misnomer, because in addition to kit replacement, cleaning and training, fatigue parties had to walk several miles to a dump, then carry ammunition or trench stores to their destination, or dig a trench, march back to their billets at dawn, then begin their next day's duties. From 1st to 11th September 1915, with the exception of 9th September, 152nd Brigade provided 1,000 men daily for fatigue parties.[32]

The 51st introduced the New Army's 18th (Eastern), 22nd and 36th (Ulster) Divisions to trench warfare and Lt. Cairnie of 1/5th Seaforths heard that 'there has been some friction between K's (Kitchener's Army) and Terriers, but not here.' [33] Elsewhere a naive Englishman 'in his virgin greenness and self-conceit raised the ire of some members of a rather tough lot of Paisley Highlanders (1/6th Argylls) by referring to them as 'Blooming Territorials,' so they promptly hoisted him over the top of the parapet and kept him out there for two hours among the barbed wire until he was in a rather shivering condition. Then they said, 'Now, if you like, you can come back among the blooming Territorials!' Which he thankfully did.' [34]

1/5th Seaforths introduced 1/7th Bedfords T.F. to trench life, who 'were spread over all the line, a section to a platoon. We put one of our men to two of theirs for instructional purposes, but I think the instruction mostly took the form of tall tales.' [35] 1/6th Gordons teased novices:

> 'Each saphead in front of our line was held by a 'double sentry' – two men on duty for a spell of two hours – one seasoned veteran and a new hand from the English division.

The officer on duty, going round the line, came upon two such men preparing to go to the saphead to relieve the sentries there and heard the following whispered conversation:

New Hand: 'How far off are the Germans, Jock?'

Old Hand: 'Files, they're a hunner yairds; files they're fifty; bit man (with impressiveness) files they're sa near that at nicht they'll rach ower their han' an' tak aff yer bunnet.' [36]

Private Greer of 1/6th Argylls described the hazards of training raw troops:

'August 6th A few of the 10 Essex Kitchener was sent in beside for experience in the trenches before taking them over. 8th August. They just about put all the 6th to their grave by cross firing on their own trench.' [37]

Raids were carried out, some on a whim, and others for military purposes. On 1/5th Gordons' front on 31st August 1915 patrols went out under Major McDonald and 2/Lt. Roberts, the latter on one occasion bringing in a flag posted on a mine crater by the Germans, within 15 feet of the front line. [38] Experienced men advised against such bravado. On 30th June Lieutenant Hugh Munro, 1/8th Argylls, wrote home:

'Yesterday morning our trench had a visit from our G.O.C. (Highland Division), (Bannatine-Allason) and he found me in the midst of my platoon, washing. Being in an extraordinarily genial mood he stopped and talked for a little; asked my name; declined to believe I had been out for two months, because of my 'pink and white complexion'; and finished up by earnest paternal warnings not to be rash in showing myself above the parapet! 'You young boys are the worst,' he said, 'and we don't want to send you home without an eye, or minus half your head!' [39]

Twelve weeks later the the Reverend H. Reid, 1/8th Argylls' chaplain, recorded:

'This has been a very sad day for the 8th. Word was brought in by the Cyclist that young Lieut. Hugh Munro – son of Neil Munro, the author, was killed last night about 11.15 p.m. in front of our trenches. He and a young Seaforth Lieut. had gone out to capture a German Flag, accompanied by two men, Lance-Corp. Graham and Corporal Sneddon. Munro ordered the two to lie down and cover with rifles what appeared to be German snipers, while he crept forward followed by the Seaforth Officer. He reached the flag untouched but could not tear it from the staff. Just then there was a rifle shot and he tore up the staff. A bomb had been attached to the stick and it exploded, killing Munro on the spot. The Germans then turned on the Machine Guns and the others had to retire. Volunteers were called for and the above mentioned and others went out and brought in the dead body. When the Germans saw them lift the body they opened fire on them again, but they managed to reach our own Lines. Just when they got up to the wire entanglements, Lance-Corp. Graham was shot by a bullet, but I do not think his wound is serious. . . I rode over to the trenches and brought the body back to M. . . in one of the Ambulance Cars

. . . Wrote Munro's father, giving him the sad news.' [40]

There was a steady drain on manpower. Sniping, shelling, grenading, trench mortaring, mines and raids took a steady toll. Amongst those was Private Collins*, 1/8th Argylls, who wrote home:

Dear Mum and Dad,

We are going into the trenches tonight for 1 day only and I think there will be a bayonet attack, so that is the reason I am writing this note that is the game at which we lose so many men and so we cannot all expect to come out of it. But it is a glorious death to die fighting for your King and Country. The sting of death is (I think) hardly noticeable as one is mad during the attack. Forgive me for all the wrongs I have commited toward you.

It is my sincere wish that I survive for your sake. I hope this will eventually reach you, should the worse occur. I will close.

Your loving son, Jim

Let dear Cedric join the navy and not the Arg. If fit.

Especially you, Dear Mum, I could not have had better parents, of that I am sure. [41]

The Germans were well provided with mortars, which pitched their bombs in a parabola into the trenches and, as they wobbled through the air their destination could be roughly calculated, enabling men to escape the likely points of impact, by moving round a traverse to a safer bay, but when three or four were in the air simultaneously the chances of escaping were diminished. Cairnie of 1/5th Seaforths was in charge of a fatigue party sandbagging a trench:

'There's a tremendous lot of work to be done before the trench will be suitable for winter. Carried on in the afternoon, but had to chuck it when trench mortars started coming over. They were dropping all along our line in No. 4. Fortunately it is possible to see them coming. They came from the left, but weren't of the large type. They were just like Bethune bombs, and turned over and over making a whistling noise which rapidly mounted in strength till it was like an express train coming up. Sometimes the bombs lay for a few seconds but usually they burst immediately they reached the ground.' [42]

C.S.M. Guthrie of 1/6th Black Watch reported that 'we are getting a lot of the big high explosive 'oil cans', one can see them coming, they are the size of the cistern in the bathroom and the same shape, they burst as they land and the NOISE is awful. We have had no casualties so far as they have not got our exact range.' [43]

Men could still laugh in adversity, and on 29th October Cairnie, 1/5th Seaforths, heard that 1/8th Argylls 'got it very hot this morning with oilcans, mortars and whizz-bangs. Heard later that the Argyles didn't lose a single man although the Germans put over more than 150 mortar bombs – 50 of them oil cans, and a lot of whizz-bangs as well. The Argyles gave them 'Are we downhearted? No!' after the fusillade had stopped' [44]

At night C.S.M. Alick Guthrie, 1/6th Black Watch, was illuminated when 'the enemy threw up two flares which landed just a few yards from where I was standing and at the same time they fired two of these Mortars

51

which burst quite near to us, the idea was that the light of the flares would so blind us that we would be unable to follow the flight of the Mortar's sparkling fuse and so be unable to tell where it would alight . . .'[45]

The British acquired their own mortars. One fired a 60lb bomb which looked like the solid handled Highland Games' throwing hammer–a long metal rod went down the mortar tube. Known to others as a 'toffee apple' the Highlanders nicknamed it a 'Donald Dinnie' after a famous Scottish strong man. Later the Stokes' Mortar became the standard light mortar, and fired a 4.5 kg bomb up to 1,200 yards. There was also a 9.45 inch heavy mortar which fired a colossal bomb known as a 'flying pig'. Light trench mortars were under brigade control, with 152nd, 153rd and 154th Trench Mortar Batteries; medium mortars and heavy mortars were under divisional control; X51, Y51, Z51 Medium Trench Mortar Batteries RFA (formed 28 April 1916) and V.51 Heavy Trench Mortar Battery, RFA.

The quality of replacements was not always good. 1/5th Gordons observed that 'a draft of 73 other ranks was received. . . A great number are of poor physical physique, few are innoculated, and two men should certainly never have been sent out, as they were in the first place discharged from the 1/5th at Bedford, as unfit for Foreign Service.' [46] Unusually, their war diary regularly listed the names of all the dead and wounded at the end of each month's report. Normally officers were named and other ranks combined in a total. It is a measure of the worth of their C.O., that he saw all his men as individuals.

The French dug-outs, with three or four feet of head cover, were not bomb proof, and on 21 October 1915 it was decided to dig deeper shelters in the trenches. 10 to 12 feet of head cover was sufficient to protect the men against direct hits from mortars and field guns and this specialised work was carried out by the 51st's pioneers, 1/8th Royal Scots, who had joined the 51st on 25th August 1915. [47] Bewsher footnoted that 30 feet of head cover was later needed to resist German 5.9 inch and 8 inch shells.

Each battalion had a machine-gun officer and a bombing officer. On 16th January 1916 the machine-guns were withdrawn from the battalions and formed into brigade machine-gun companies, each of

16 machine-guns; the 152nd, 153rd and 154th Brigade Machine Gun Companies, and in 1918 these became 51st Battalion Machine Gun Corps. The new arts of war were taught in a grenade school, which ran weekly courses for batches of 13 officers and 260 other ranks, who then returned to their battalions and passed on their new skills. An infantry school was established at Villers Bocage and Haig 'saw Lt.Col. Baird commanding 8th Argyle and Sutherland Highlanders. He has done very well in command of the Battalion and is now to be made Commandant of the 51st Divisional School for training officers' [48] It ran two week courses on command and tactics for 20 officers and 40 N.C.O.s. A demonstration area was constructed to show how trenches varied with the terrain. Such divisional schools were universal and met the needs of a largely amateur army. In addition to the basics they taught new methods derived from experience.

When the men were off duty they frequented estaminets where wine, beer, coffee and tobacco were available, and the luxury of an omelette. Entertainment was homespun, with concerts, competitions, and special occasions in the officers' mess. Lt.Colonel Rorie of 2/1st Highland Field Ambulance, at Warloy in 1915, described the French Non-Commissioned Officers Club that his Field Ambulance inherited:

Lt.Colonel Rorie

'which had a good stage and some rough and ready scenery had been left to us; and here we held regular concerts, largely attended by the troops of the district and by French civilians. The hall was invariably packed and the numbers present could be calculated through the near opaque fug by counting the cigarette ends glowing in the dark. A barrel of beer was presided over by the owner of the adjacent estaminet. Progammes were created by a committee, and the fall back was 'a singing competition with ten franc, 7 franc and 3 franc prizes with a panel of judges whose word was final.' [49]

1/5th Seaforths inaugurated a sergeants' mess in a farm at Hénencourt. Performer Sergeant MacKay* was asleep on a stretcher in the medical orderly's room when he was required and was brought on it to the new mess where he was given a drink and persuaded 'to cheer the company with his inimitable songs,' which were those of Harry Lauder.'[50]

C.S.M. Alick Guthrie, 1/6th Black Watch, collected the names of twenty four artists for a company concert, and 'the Concert the other night was a great success. All the Officers were there we had a blazing fire going all the time, and the programme was an excellent one, the Officers & men were all delighted with the talent of No.2 Company. The Highland reel dancing and pipe music were new to the French folk here, and was much admired by them, the Kilties are curiosities to them still.'[51]

Concert parties were started, and later, cinemas were established: the 51st's Divisional Pierrot Troupe 'The Balmorals' was commanded by Captain Eric Stanley, who organised a five hundred seat theatre in a barn in Senlis-le-Sec. Good female impersonators were rare and Stanley was making do with a very masculine impersonator who had a deep voice and large hands and feet when Private Connel, Highland Light Infantry, 32nd Division, arrived at the stage door to be auditioned. He was ideal and Stanley tried to exchange him with 32nd Division for two specialised machine gun mountings. Despite the fact that 32nd Division was not planning anything as frivolous as a concert party it refused to release him, and when negotiations broke down, he was removed to the 51st's divisional artillery, with the connivance of the Army Commander. [52]

The pioneers of 1/8th Royal Scots had all day Wednesday as a holiday, with football matches and 'a theatre of varieties having been opened for the Division at Senlis (le Sec), the companies were marched over in succession on Wednesday evenings to see the performance.' In addition 'the rate of leave to all ranks of the Battalion continued to be most satisfactory, 2 Officers and 32 other ranks leaving each week.' [53] Seven days leave was allowed, from the time soldiers left Boulogne, but this was insufficient for many Scottish soldiers, which was addressed and 'leave for those going to Scotland had been extended to nine days' to take account of travelling time, for example, to the far north of Scotland.'[54]

Off duty time was not always marked by comradely congeniality:

'No one recalled the origins of the feud between the 6th and 8th Battalions of the Argyll and Sutherland Highlanders but, after several estaminets had been wrecked in the course of wild rumpuses for which the Army was obliged to foot the bill, it had been generally recognised that, when the Division was out at rest, those in charge of the billeting arrangements of the three Brigades would be well advised to make sure that the 6th and the 8th Argylls were separated by a considerable distance. The 8th Argylls, who came from Argyllshire itself, were largely Gaelic speaking, and sneered at the idea that the 6th, who hailed from Paisley in Renfrewshire, should pass as Highlanders at all. Furthermore the 8th Argylls considered the 6th to be undeservedly spoilt. Bell's, a local tobacco company, sent out a weekly present of twenty cigarettes per man, and they were vastly superior to the ration of issue cigarettes which came the way of the 8th Argylls. Local football clubs also sent cigarettes and supplied sports kit and equipment. The 6th Argylls never lacked whisky and the Paisley thread manufacturers, J. and P. Coates, who regarded the Battalion as their own, plied the men with comforts. The last straw was when the same firm, in the kindness of its heart, presented every officer with a breast-plate and every man with a heart shaped mirror of polished steel to place in his breast-pocket as an insurance against German bullets. The fact that the 8th Argylls taunted the 6th in Gaelic simply added fuel to the fire. None of the Paisley boys spoke a word of anything but English, but they found no difficulty in understanding the insulting tone of the Highlanders' remarks.' [55]

This seems like a tale that grew in its telling.

On 24th September 1915 Bannatine-Allason left the 51st. Bewsher attributed this to 'indifferent health' and that 'the strain of the past four months, in which he had commanded the Division during its first experiences of war, had been severe, and the General therefore felt that he could not either with justice to himself or to his Division continue.'[56] He was in the same category as the commanding officers whom he had sent home, set in his ways, and physically unfitted for modern war, as Haig had noted. Bannatine-Allason commanded the 61st (2nd South Midland) Division then the 64th (2nd Highland) Division in the UK. His replacement came on 25th September 1915, and on the 28th Cairnie recorded that the new G.O.C. inspected 1/5th Seaforths, some of whom had been troublesome in estaminets the previous evening. It was:

Major-General George Harper

'Cold and raw. Inspection by new Divisional General (Harper) at 2:30 p.m., Allason having gone home in bad health. Very cold standing on parade. Short route march followed, round by Bresle and Baizieux. Got in to tea about six, and had a good spread.' [57]

Major-General George Montague Harper was commissioned in 1884, served at the School of Military Engineering, then went to India in 1890. From 1892 to 1898 he was adjutant of the 2nd West Yorkshire Royal Engineer Volunteers, which gave him experience of the mind set of part time soldiers. After service in South Africa he was appointed to the War Office's Mobilisation Division in 1902. He was a Member of the Army Railway Council, then Deputy Assistant Quarter Master General (Mobilisation), and stayed there until he took the Staff Officers' Course at Camberley: when he passed it he became the first Royal Engineer officer to be appointed to its staff. In 1911 he became a General Staff Officer, Director of Military Operations, on the Staff of the Chief of the Imperial General Staff. By then he was a Colonel. In August 1914 he was in the Head-quarters of the B.E.F., and became a temporary Brigadier-General in November 1914. In February 1915 he took command of 17th Infantry Brigade, 6th Division, until he was promoted temporary Major-General, in command of the 51st.

Nicholson contrasted Ballantine-Allason with Harper: Harper was mentally agile, adaptable, unrufflable, knew all the major military players, and, unlike Bannatine-Allason, who deferred to them, treated them familiarly. Harper's orders were clear, and when the 51st took over a badly maintained stretch of the front line Harper exhorted them to dig countless dugouts. He was tall, distinguished, wore his grey hair long, and had a sense of humour. He knew how to foster his division's esprit de corps, and fully exploited the pipe bands for special occasions, such as the presentation of medals, which were often followed by tea and the Balmorals, for as many of the officers and men at the event that could be squeezed in.[58] He was not all cordiality and his wrath percolated down the system, in this instance to Cairnie 1/5th Seaforths, noting 'the Colonel and Adjutant were round this morning playing havoc, and passing on the row they got themselves from the Divisional General. The trenches are in a bad state and the fire-step has all to be revetted.'[59]

Harper's wrath was gently mocked in a parody of 'The Mountains of Mourne', by Lt.E.Alan Mackintosh of the same battalion:

> Oh, Mary the front is a wonderful place,
> Where a person can't fight without shaving his face;
> We're not frightened of shells, so I've found,
> But when generals come near we all get to ground.
> I met one in a trench, and some tea-leaves were there,
> And we got such a strafing it whitened our hair,
> So it seems we must swallow the leaves in our tea,
> Where the trenches run down from the Somme to the sea.[60]

Bewsher boasted that Harper 'understood the ways and means of defeating the German in a manner which was probably unequalled, and certainly never surpassed on the Western Front. Further he possessed such gifts as an instructor as enabled him to train his Division in these ways and means in a manner which set a standard to the British armies in France.' [61]

At the Battle of Loos, (Sept. 25th 1915) the 15th (Scottish) Division's instructions for the attack stated:

> 1. a)... the assaulting columns will be to go straight forward
> as far as possible to their final objectives.

b) Assaulting columns will not be entrusted with the tasks of occupying and consolidating positions [author's italics] . . . These tasks will be allotted to parties told off from Bde. Reserves.' [62] The 15th (Scottish) Division smashed the German defences, shared the capture of Loos with the 47th Division, crossed the summit of Hill 70 east of Loos, met the Germans last line of defence, two and a half miles from their start line, and, depleted and leaderless, retreated over Hill 70, where the remnants, with reinforcements, held off German counter-attacks.

Harper dictated that the first wave would take and consolidate the first objective, and prepare it for a German counter-attack. The second objective would be taken by fresh battalions leapfrogging the first wave, by then in defensive mode, and so on, until the final objective had been reached. Thus each stage of an advance was sustained by a well defended trench behind it, and phased advances would lessen the number of casualties suffered by any one battalion.

Bewsher claimed that Harper's plan was the key to the 51st's successes and that it became the normal form of attack used by most divisions in France. [63] Harper's *Notes on Infantry Tactics and Training* were written for IV Corps, when Harper was given command of it in March 1918, and would have been based on his experience with the 51st. In an assessment of Harper John Hussey enthused about Harper's tactical instructions, but referred Harper's Notes to General Sir David Fraser and Dr Paddy Griffiths, for even more informed opinion. The former found them 'practical and unambiguous', displaying a 'combination of firm principles with flexibility at junior levels of command', the latter thought Harper's style was like that of Canada's Currie and Australia's Monash, both generals of high repute. Dr. Griffiths thought that the Notes were even more sophisticated than those of Ivor Maxse, Inspector-General of Training in France from April 1918. Griffiths' most significant comment is:

'The constant theme is the maintenance of voice control over every man, by section commanders, while simultaneously thinning out the men as widely as possible. The theme is elaborated in remorseless detail for every subject tackled. . .

Harper has totally renounced any military theory that equates fighting power with maximizing numbers at key points. He is very careful to circumscribe the exceptional occasions when more (rather than less) men can help – and then he is keen to thin them out again as soon as possible'. [64]

Compared with the cavalier approach of other commanders, with consequent heavy casualties, the leapfrogging attack, coupled with thinned out tactics may have contributed to the ordinary soldiers' reported admiration of Harper.

The above raises the question of why there were no detailed methods of attack in the B.E.F. early in the war. Officers relied upon Field Service Regulation Parts 1 and 2 of 1909 which were written for the use of professional officers, which said that orders were 'not to be too detailed, instead leaving the man on the spot to use his own initiative.' [65] Delegation down to divisional and brigade level was a reality, and much local initiative was permitted, provided the orders to attack were carried out timeously. However, the expanding British Army was officered by increasing numbers of amateurs, who needed detailed orders: no one had any experience of deadlocked trench warfare, nor of its new weapons, and the B.E.F. was on a steep learning curve, and under pressure to achieve quick victories. This urgency and a lack of prescription meant the unnecessary forfeiting of many lives as commanders struggled to master the new arts of war.

. . .

Winter clothing was issued in October 1915 and C.S.M. Guthrie, 1/6th Black Watch, observed that 'the men are all delighted with their new fur coats, they look a wild lot when one sees them dressed in all shades and colours, the coats are very comfortable and warm, but they will have their drawbacks.' [66] As a home for lice the sheepskin jackets equalled the kilt.

St.Andrew's Day was celebrated by 1/2nd Highland Field Ambulance with the Maire and schoolmaster of Warloy in attendance. David Rorie 'gave them broth, 'saut herrin', 'biled hens' and a haggis-made by the skilled hand of our sergeant-major with 'Auld Kirk' (whisky) to wash the solids down; and for their edification our junior officers danced perfervidly (and more or less correctly) our national dances.' [67]

On 28th December 1915 the 51st left the Albert sector for six weeks rest and training and C.S.M. Guthrie, 1/6th Black Watch, was happy to 'have come back for over 20 miles and are now out of hearing or reach of the guns. So we will have a peaceful Xmas. . . The first day we did 13 miles & the second nearly as many, a good many of the boys found it very trying as the trench life makes them very unfit for travelling. . . we have been issuing all sorts of clothing and Xmas gifts to the men, plum puddings, raisins, currants, dates, sweets, cigarettes, dominoes, playing cards, xmas cards, shirts, socks, hoe (hose) tops, tunics, Kilts, boots etc etc. . . the younger lads are a bit disappointed we did not get to a larger place.' [68]

Hogmanay (New Year's Eve) was then Scotland's major winter festival and Captain Sutherland of 1/5th Seaforths 'brought in the New Year with

full Highland honours. When twelve midnight came, the pipers of the battalion formed up outside headquarters and marched through the principal streets of the village, and it was at once manifest from the numbers that turned out from their billets that few, if any, had gone to bed before the mystic hour that ushers in the New Year. Each barn had its own little sing-song, each Sergeants' Mess was also very much alive, while all the officers of the battalion, on the Colonel's invitation, were present at a dinner at headquarters.' [69] 1/5th Seaforths were at Molliens au Bois, north of Amiens.

Captain David Sutherland

When the celebrations were over work began, much of it on a training area near Fleselles Station, that had been prepared by 1/8th Royal Scots.[70] The pattern would have been the same for all the battalions as it was for the 1/6th Seaforths: 'starting from platoon drill, we gradually worked up to battalion and brigade practice attacks, while great care was taken to the training of the various specialists – such as bombers and machine-gunners. Bayonet fighting, musketry and gas helmet drill also had their fair share of time.' [71] In addition men of the 51st were used as labour, repairing roads degraded by winter weather, building railway lines, and moving stores.[72]

Many of the 'hostilities only' officers had never ridden a horse and were ordered to acquire the skill. Lt.E.A. Mackintosh, 1/5th Seaforths, found himself:

> 'painfully engaged in what I believe is called a canter . . . My horse rushed up alongside the Colonel, bumping me in a most unpleasant manner. The Colonel said: 'You're a junior officer; what are you doing here?' I replied, 'I'm not here on my own free will; you'll have to talk to the horse, sir! . . . and the next thing I knew I was away. . . past the football field. Every 'Fifth' man on the field immediately stopped his game, lined up and gave me a tremendous cheer as I rushed past. . . Stalk (2nd Lieutenant Robert Stalker*) passed at this moment, and seeing the streak of foam from the horse on my face shouted, 'For goodness' sake, stop him, Major, he's foaming at the mouth.' At this point Stalk's horse bolted too, and we had a hammer and tongs race up the hill missing the mess cart coming in the opposite direction by a fraction of an inch.' [73]

Training, sport and recreation characterised January. Second Lieutenant Cairnie 1/5th Seaforths recorded:

> '20-Jan-16
>
> Very bright morning. Battalion out route marching today. Had 'A' Coy bombers until 2 p.m. Threw the dummy test, and put 20 men through the live as well. Throwing pretty good.
>
> Harper had an accident with the Lewis Gun today, while demonstrating with dummy cartridges – Pte. Thompson 'B' Coy, being shot through the abdomen. Harper was very much cut up about it. [Pte Thompson* died as a result]
>
> The officers played a scrap team from 'A' and got beaten 3:1 but we hadn't put out a decent team. I was very off-form and quite out of condition.' [74]

The Comforts for Combatants Committee of Peebles' Red Cross had knitted socks for 1/8th Royal Scots and wrote to its C.O. complaining that men had returned on leave to Innerleithen without any socks. On 20th February 1916 Lt.Colonel Gemmil* explained that:

'During the month of December there were issued to B Company – the Company in which the men belonged who went home with no socks – 160 shirts and 156 pairs socks. In addition, the regimental wash house was kept going regularly, where the underclothes of each Company were washed, dried and ironed every ten days. . . It is of course, quite possible that men have gone home without socks, but if so, it is entirely their own fault. One cannot hold kit inspections with the same regularity as one would do in barracks at home. . . ' [75]

The C.O.'s evident satisfaction with a ten day washing cycle for underclothes says much about prevailing standards of personal cleanliness and the correspondence demonstrates the gulf in understanding between civilians and soldiers at the front.

On 6th January 1916 the Lancashire Brigade left for the 55th (West Lancashire) Division, leaving the 1/6th Cameronians behind. 1/4th and 1/5th Black Watch and 1/4th Camerons, all severely depleted, joined the 51st until late February. 1/4th Seaforths and 1/4th Gordons joined in January and 1/7th Argylls and 1/9th Royal Scots (Highlanders) in March. Haig, visiting the 51st, 'passed the 6th Battalion of the Cameronians. . . it was proposed to put the 6th Battn (Territorials) into a Highland brigade. The Battalion demurred and many said their grandfathers had fought against Highlanders. So the Battalion is under Divisional Head Quarters.'[76]

The 1/6th Cameronians came from Lanarkshire, old Covenanter territory. Such respect for tradition would not have been connived at later in the war. In reality the battalion was in the process of leaving to train as pioneers, and amalgamated with 1/5th Cameronians in May 1916.

Football was very popular. In January 1916 1/5th Seaforths played 1/4th Camerons and lost 3-1 but the Camerons had an edge as they had the 'advantage of football boots. Fight on the field and a Cameron player sent off.' [77] 1/8th Royal Scots played in the semi-final of the Divisional

Cup against the North Irish Horse, then the 51st's divisional mounted troops, 'but, after a good first half, the game became a farce and we eventually won by 13 goals to one.' Two days later 1/8th Royal Scots beat the Divisional Cyclists 7-1 'thereby winning the competition, having played nearly twenty matches without a reverse. Major-General Harper congratulated both teams on their success in the competition and presented a silver matchbox, appropriately inscribed, to each member of the Royal Scots team.' [78]

The rest ended on 6th March 1916 when the 51st began to move north in bitter cold and deep snow. In a two day blizzard from 9th to 11th of March the 51st relieved French troops at the southern end of Vimy Ridge: officers and men were unsure of their whereabouts until the storm abated. Captain Sutherland, 1/5th Seaforths, observed that 'a new trench cannot be dug without coming on the hastily buried dead, grisly hands stick out of the present trenches, while one machine-gun crew, in making a recess for their gun, tried four times before they found a spot clear of bodies.' [79] The entire area was under observation from the heights of Vimy Ridge and its spurs and the communication trenches from the villages of Maroueil, Anzin and Mont St. Eloi were a winding, weary two miles long.

1/9th Royal Scots war diary noted that 'the fire trenches and communication trenches were left in very bad repair by the French and an enormous amount of work was done in clearing them, making the parapet bullet proof, making firesteps and traverses, putting the fire trenches in repair and support line – Lewis Gun emplacements and Sniping posts were also made.' [80]

The area had been fought over by the French and Germans and was described by Private Anderson 1/9th Royal Scots as the Labyrinth from the fact that, owing to the numerous attacks and counter-attacks in front of Vimy Ridge, the ground is simply honeycombed with trenches and it would be quite possible to walk into the German lines, if it were not for the barricades erected across all the connecting saps. The sense of direction at night, however, is so upset that there have been several cases of working parties walking into the midst of the enemy, or shot if unable to answer the challenge.'

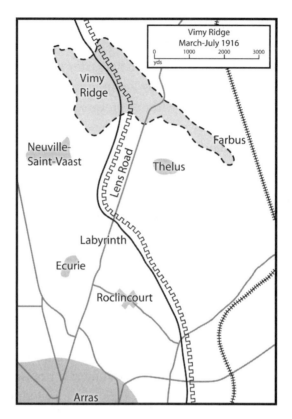

Vimy Ridge
March–July 1916

0 1000 2000 3000
yds

Vimy
Ridge

Neuville-
Saint-Vaast

Farbus

Thelus

Lens Road

Labyrinth

Ecurie

Roclincourt

Arras

Head wounds from shrapnel were common and the British adopted basin shaped helmets and Anderson wrote that 'practically all of the battalion have now been issued with steel helmets. . . The steel helmets give a greater feeling of security, although it is doubtful if they would be of much use against a direct hit. We find them handy, however, in protecting our heads from bumps against the roof-props, whilst descending dug-out stairs.' [81]

The Labyrinth was a warren of German mines and the French had created a thinly held outpost line, to diminish frontline casualties from mining. The outpost line was backed by support and reserve trenches. Harper continued this policy and for the next three months the 51st laboured on new and improved trenches. When the 51st took over there were signs of German domination, or of previous Franco-German 'live and let live'. On 1/6th Seaforths' first day in the line 'we found the German sentries to be very bold – they used to stand up in their trenches to look over the parapet, exposing themselves down to the waist. Some accurate sniping soon put a stop to this impertinence, and on the second day only heads were to be seen. Further accurate sniping soon taught the Germans that periscopes were safer, and periscopes were soon all that we ever saw of our friends the enemy.' [82]

1/6th Seaforths had rapidly decided to win moral ascendancy, but 1/4th Seaforths lost their commanding officer to a sniper on their first day in the line, and in less than two weeks his successor was sniped. The 51st drew on the civilian skills of its stalkers and ghillies, ran courses, organised snipers, and gained parity if not constant superiority over the enemy. Observers sketched the enemy trenches lines, identifying low parapets, loopholes and weak points where German soldiers might be exposed: these were issued to the snipers before they took their positions. On 18th March 1/7th Black Watch's 'snipers 'got going' from a newly constructed 'nest' today and claim to have shot one German. The enemy snipers were also very busy, but in other directions were less active. Killed one; wounded four. Weather fine.' [83] Sniper Sandy MacDonald* of 1/5th Seaforths was credited with 97 Germans.

Sniper Sandy
Tune: 'Sister Susie's sewing shirts for soldiers.'

SANDY MAC the sniper is a sniping from his loop-hole,
With telescopic rifle he is looking for a Hun.
If he sees a sniper lurking, or a working party working,
At once he opens fire on them, and bags them every one,
And when you come to our trench, by night-time or by day,
We take you to his loop-hole, and we point to him and say. . .

Chorus:
'Sniper Sandy's slaying Saxon soldiers,
And Saxon soldiers seldom show but Sandy slays a few,
And every day the Bosches put up little wooden crosses
In the cemetery for Saxon soldiers Sniper Saxon slew.' [84]

Mining was endemic and well organised. As the Germans assaulted the fresh crater their trench mortars and artillery fired to cut off reinforcements to the shattered British trench. The British counter bombardment would hit the German front line trenches and rear areas so that reinforcements could not reach the German's assaulting force, isolating them within the British front line, whilst the British infantry counter-attacked the Germans in the crater. The 51st held supplies of wire, posts, sandbags, and shovels in the trenches for use in captured craters and each battalion had a platoon whose task was to consolidate the crater when the infantry had recaptured it.

On the evening of 21st March 1916, on 1/7th Black Watch's sector, 'the enemy fired a mine near our front line and blew in 20 yards of trench. They kept up rifle, trench mortar & grenade fire for about an hour afterwards but no attack took place. Some French sappers were buried in the mine explosion. . . one man was found to be dead and another wounded. Our Lewis Guns opened fire to prevent the enemy sttacking. Casualties: wounded, other ranks, two. Weather dull.' [85]

Private James Rennie, 1/6th Gordons, was guarding a crater outpost and suspected that the Germans had glimpsed their periscope:

> 'They started bombing (with rifle grenades?) and by God Almighty, for a start they went over us and were hitting our front line. The boys were all in the dug-out, they didn't care, they let them go to it. They finally got closer and closer. We were right inside a mine hole . . . great big hunks of ground all piled up . . . we were on the edge of it. The bombs were coming over, they were going a little too far for a start, but then they shortened up the range and shortened up and shortened up and each bomb was just a little bit closer than the other and finally I says to myself, 'The next one is going to get us. . . ' We were sitting there shivering, our teeth chattering with fear, scared to death. . . So, the last bomb came over and landed right on top of the sand bags behind us . . . It scattered us with dirt and dust all over the place. And that was the last one they threw over, if they'd have thrown over another one a foot or so shorter it would have got the works.' [86]

Mining was frequent. On 28th March 1916 a mine exploded near a 1/4th Seaforths' officer:

> 'I am lying in a dug-out, reading The Motor Cycle, and wondering if I shall ever ride again, when there is a terrific

explosion. A mine has gone up! The timber supports in the dug-out sway to and fro, my candle goes out, and I am almost buried with dirt that falls from the roof. Almost as soon as I can struggle up and spit the dirt out of my mouth a voice at the top of the dug-out steps shouts; 'All out, with gas masks on!' I pull mine out of its satchel, grab my rifle and run up the steps. I could not smell any gas, but there were clouds of smoke from the mine, which, luckily, had gone up just in front of our front trench, filling a good part of it up, but most of our men were down in the saps. A tremendous strafing was going over from both sides – shells were screaming over and the air was alive with machine-gun and rifle bullets, bombs, etc., and star shells of all colours made the scene a very thrilling one. Thinking the Germans were attacking I jumped on the fire step, and a big bomb or shell bursting only a few yards in front of me put me on my back at the bottom of the trench. An officer coming along just then picked me up, and finding that I was not hurt told me to get down the trench to my right, as it was quieter down there.' [87]

By 10th April 1916 1/6th Argylls had been mined six times and had suffered so much that the battalion left the 51st in June to become the pioneer battalion of 5th Division. 1/6th Gordons, from 7th Division, replaced them.

There was heavy pressure on battalions to raid. G.H.Q. insisted that raids took place, to gather information, dominate No Man's Land and 'blood' inexperienced troops. While blooding new troops may seem merciless, 'the experience of almost all other wars is nearly unanimous in recommending such a policy.' [88]

Another reason for raiding was political, as the French were bearing the brunt of the war and thought the British slow in sharing its burden. The French wanted large scale attacks, which Haig resisted, as the New Armies were untrained and unavailable in sufficient numbers. Simply holding the line opened the British to French criticism, but 'raiding, however, provided a partial answer to this problem . . . Insofar as raiding prevented a worsening of Anglo-French (Franco-British) relations, it was a politically expedient measure.' [89]

Lt. E.A. Mackintosh 1/5th Seaforths led a raid on 16th May 1916: operational orders for raids involved artillery, trench mortars, Stokes mortars, machine guns and Lewis guns, snipers, telephone arrangements, and Royal Engineers. The kit to be carried was precisely laid:

> '. . . be equipped as lightly as possible. Identification marks removed. All the men will carry a haversack filled with bombs, slung in front of them, and tied round to prevent swinging about. Bayonet men will have magazines charged with 9 rounds, one in the chamber, twenty rounds in their pockets. . . each will wear a piece of white cloth on their arms at the shoulder . . . it is not anticipated that the raid will take more than 10 minutes.' [90]

This raid was in retaliation for the detonation of a German mine and raid on 28th April 1916, which had cost 1/6th Seaforths 5 officers and 62 other ranks, of which 15 were killed and 19 missing. [91] Mackintosh's raid succeeded, at the cost of four Seaforths' deaths.

Captain Ross, 1/7th Gordons, described the mood of the men of a 1/6th Black Watch raiding party under under Captain Herd, which turned up at 'the Elbe shelters close after 6 o'clock, in fiery eagerness to go 'over the top', and perhaps a little inclined to show my battalion, which was then tenanting the trenches, what the redoubtable Black Watch could do. It was a reasonable desire. In war egoism must count for more than altruism; it is the self-assertive who conquer.' [92]

Counter mining, mining, sniping, raiding and accurate artillery fire all contributed to the 51st's attempts to establish ascendancy. It was resisted by a skilful and determined enemy, who practised the same skills, and the 51st, like most of the B.E.F., endured the crushing labour and boredom of trench warfare, punctuated by sudden injury and death. Routine activity included digging listening posts in No Man's Land and bringing up supplies. Private Anderson, 1/9th Royal Scots, described the normal anxieties:

> 'A party of us was turned out one drenching night to dig a listening post in no-man's-land, about thirty yards from the German line. There was a lot of intermittent machine-gun fire, and we worked with a will digging ourselves in to afford

sufficient cover. The star shells held us up frequently, when we had to stand quite still, and hope we weren't spotted. A stray machine-gun bullet got one of our party through the knee, and we were scared stiff in case his yell gave our position away. The Germans heard all right, but their fusillade of bullets passed wide of us. We completed our job and, helping our wounded man along, returned cautiously in what we trusted was the right direction. No sounds could be heard from the trench before us, and we were compelled to lie flat in the mud, hoping to get some sign to let us know we were at our own lines. After a bit, getting fed up lying in the dirt our sergeant decided to risk giving a shout. Fortunately for us it was answered by one of our own sentries and we scrambled back to the shelter of the trench.' [93]

Anderson found bringing up supplies at night from Roclincourt hazardous:

'This is a hot spot for machine-guns. We can distinguish between the sound of our own and the enemy's guns, ours giving quick bursts in rapid succession, whilst the Germans' are more deliberate and of longer duration. Our ammunition dump is in cellars in the ruins of Roclincourt, and each night parties are engaged in bringing stores up to the firing line. We curse the full moon these nights as we can easily be spotted by the Germans while working at the village, and we have to run the gauntlet of their snipers and machine-guns which are concentrated straight down the Lens Road, over which we have to pass.

Even when it is pitch dark there is always firing along this which runs right across no-man's land. If the firing is heavy, we have to go as far as the ruins by trench, then, one by one, we dash across to the corner of a building on the opposite side of the road, after which we flatten against a wall and work our way to the entrance to a large courtyard. The first part of our journey is over, but we have to get back again several times to the trench with heavy boxes of ammunition.' [94]

On 21st May 1916 German artillery began an intense barrage on 25th (New Army) and 47th (London)(TF) divisions, on the left of the 51st, and the line fell to the Germans, who ended up facing the Highlanders in the same trench, separated only by barricades. The flank was strengthened by digging a new front line trench and deep dug outs in case of a repeat of the bombardment that had fallen on the 25th Division. Hard digging and heavy carrying, combined with a cold snap in June, brought on trench foot, and put the men under huge pressure.

To the south preparations were taking place for the Somme offensive, and on 1st and 2nd June the 51st extended its front to cover the 25th Division's disappearance. All the 51st's brigades were at full stretch, for 21 days out of 28. To conceal the 25th Division's removal the 51st was put into English uniforms. 1/5th Seaforths thought this was 'some Sassenach plot to strip them forever of the kilt, grumbled very much and protested to their officers.' [95] Nicholson would have contradicted this and stated 'that the men of the Highland Division wanted rid of the kilt, as it was conspicuous, heavy when wet and muddy, and a home for a myriad of lice. Harper agreed with them and G.H.Q. and Third Army stated that they were the only Highlanders who wanted to shed the kilt – the proposal was forwarded to the War Office, which refused its consent. The 51st got round the problem by accumulating 400 pairs of trousers per battalion as trench stores: 'for a long time a great many of our men had made for themselves breeches of oatsacks or sandbags, or else wore only the apron.'[96]

Captain David Sutherland refers to a 1/5th Seaforths' company going on fatigues which 'put off all their clothing except their boots and kilt aprons, and, thus lightly clad, they dug and shoveled for five or six hours while the rain fell in torrents. On coming off parade, this wise company hung their kilt aprons out of doors, gave themselves a good rub down, and went to bed... while the other poor unfortunates had either to search for dry underclothes or shiver in their wet garments.' [97]

All soldiers harboured body lice, known as 'Scots Grey' or 'cooties' and seven or eight yards of pleated kilt provided more lodging places for lice than trousers. The 'click' in the last stanza was the sound made as a lit candle drawn across a seam or pleat eliminated a louse. A 1/9th Royal Scot parodied Burns' 'To a Louse':

What Labyrinthine dug-outs too
Ye're making in oor kilts the noo
. . .
Ye hardly let me tak a doze.
For ye're parading right across
Ma back, ma neck, an' doon ma spine,
Thinkin' na doot, ye're daein' fine,
Sookin' ma bluid.
. . .
The mixture in this bottle here
Is bound tae mak ye disappear,
Nae mair I'll need tae mak ye click;
Ane dose, they say, will dae the trick
As share (sure) as death. [98]

Apart from Festubert, the 51st had not been in a major offensive, and many thought that they were being sidelined because they were territorials, or because they had failed at Festubert. Their G.O.C.'s surname and the HD initials on the division's badge, spawned the nickname 'Harper's Duds'. Despite the hardships of trench warfare, some still wanted to be part of a major engagement. All their training included attacking, with bayonets fixed, culminating in the occupation of the enemy's trenches. The 'Big Push' was due, the first major British effort in the land war, with the New Army present in great numbers. Optimism prevailed, both at home and on the Western Front. The importance of well trained and resourced artillery had been proved and the ammunition shortages of 1915 seemed to have been amply overcome.

The still innocent spirit of many was captured in another parody of the 'Mountains of Mourne', written in early July by Lt.E.A. Mackintosh, 1/5th Seaforths:

At Albert they've lately begun an advance
Which is going to shove all the Bosches out of France,
And we are all waiting and hoping some day
To meet with the gentlemen over the way.
And oh, what a state of delight we'll be in
When we're bombing our way up the streets of Berlin,
So I hope in a few months I surely shall be
In a train running down from Berlin to the sea. [99]

On 27th June 1916 the 51st began to introduce the 60th (2/2nd London) Division) to the trenches prior to it taking over the line on 14th July. At this time Brigadier-General Ross of 152nd Brigade was replaced by Brigadier-General H. Pelham-Burn, who, at thirty four, was the youngest appointment to that rank up to then. Ross reverted to the retired list, was later given an appointment in the UK, then command of 228th Brigade in Salonika. This has all the signs of a sacking – retired list, home defence troops, then Salonika, which was often used as a repository for less than good divisions and senior officers. Haig thought highly of Ross and his troops admired him. Peel and Mcdonald said 'his constant presence in the front trenches, his unfailing cheerfulness and contempt for personal danger, and his incessant attention to the welfare of the men he commanded had earned our unstinted admiration and esteem' [100] and that he left 'after an unfortunate difference with the Divisional Commander.' [101] The point of difference is unknown: it could have been over tactical or man management matters, or a clash of strong personalities.

On 14th July 1916 the 51st moved by lorry to Doullens-Lucheux-Baudricourt, then marched to Candas, where, on 20th July, they boarded trains to Mericourt, south west of Albert.

On Saturday 15th July, as the 51st moved to the Somme, a poem by Private A. MacFarlane, 1/7th Black Watch, appeared in the *Dunfermline Press*:

> Who is it mans the trench?
> And sticks it, wet or fine;
> Covered with blood or caked in mud?
> Seventh Black Watch every time!
> Grousing and swearing, but sticking,
> 'Game' to the call of 'Time',
> Still 'neath the
> light of the Very flare,
> Black Watch, every time! [102]

Private MacFarlane's pride in his regiment and battalion is apparent, but a newer sense of identity had developed at a higher level: as they moved to the Somme the officers were issued with:

> 'A few 'Donts' for the attack', the last piece exhorting: 'First-Last and Always – Don't forget you belong to the Highland Division and STICK IT OUT.' [103]

With a year's experience the 51st approached the maelstrom of the Battle of the Somme, which had begun on 1st July.

NOTES

1. E.A. Mackintosh *War the Liberator* 'Four and Twenty Bombers' (Murray 1918) p.112. Campbell and Green p.193.
2. Bewsher p.25
3. C.S.M. Alick Guthrie 1/6th Black Watch letter to his wife Chrissie 17.7.1915 (BWRA)
4. Bewsher p.29.
5. Bewsher p.2.9
6. DM Sutherland *The War Diary of the Fifth Seaforth Highlanders* p.27.
7. Tony Ashworth *Trench Warfare, Live and Let Live* (MacMillan 1980/Pan 2000) p.10.
8. Ian Hay *First Hundred Thousand.* (Blackwood 1915) pp.247-8
9. Brigadier-General F.P. Crozier *A Brass Hat in No Man's Land* (Florin Books Jonathan Cape1930) p.128.
10. Ashworth citing Crozier *The Men I Killed*, (Michael Joseph, 193) pp.21-22.
11. Bewsher p.29.
12. Malcolm p.25.
13. Malcolm pp.27-28.
14. Nicholson p.148.
15. Guthrie letter to Chrissie 14.7.1915.
16. Guthrie to Captain Alexander 1/6th Black Watch 10.8.15.
17. Malcolm p.25.
18. Ross pp.106-108.
19. Pte.John Greer, signaler, 1/6th A&SH, dairy A&SH Museum.
20. Wadham and Crossley p.33.
21. Ross p.107.
22. Greer, signaler, 1/6th A&SH, diary, A&SH Museum.
23. Guthrie letter 25.8.1915.
24. 152nd Brigade War Diary 26.7.1915.
25. David Rorie, *A Medico's Luck in the Great War* (Milne & Hutchison 1929) p.61.

26. Wauchope p.132.

27. Bewsher p.31.

28. Mackintosh, *A Highland Regiment* p.17; Campbell and Green p.74.

29. Peel and MacDonald p.13.

30. Bewsher p.34.

31. Cairnie diary 15.9.1915.

32. 152nd Brigade War Diary 1-11.9.1915

33. Cairnie diary 24.8.1915.

34. Sutherland p.29.

35. Cairnie diary 26.8.1915.

36. Mackenzie pp.91-2.

37. Greer diary.

38. War diary 1/5th Gordons 31.8.1915

39. Lt. Hugh A. Munro 1/8th A&SH Museum to his father Neil Munro 30.6.15.

40. Rev. H. Reid Chaplain 1/8th A&SH Museum 23.9.15 Letter to Neil Munro.

41. Private Vincent Collins letter to parents 1/8 A&SH, undated A&SH RHQ

42. Cairnie diary10.9.15.

43. Guthrie letter BWRA 5.11.1915.

44. Cairnie diary 29.10.1915

45. Guthrie letter 9.11.1915

46. War diary 1/5th Gordons 31.8.1915.

47. Bewsher p.39.

48. Haig diary 12.1.1916

49. Rorie pp.73-74

50. Sutherland p.39.

51. Guthrie letter 27.8.1915.

52. Nicholson p.256/Richard Holmes, *Tommy* (Harper Collins 2004) p.602. For several photographs of the Balmorals see http://digital.nls.uk go to Browse and Search and enter Balmorals.

53. War diary 1/8th Royal Scots 1-20.12.1915.

54. War diary 1/8th Royal Scots 1-20.12.1915.

55. *The Mouth of Hell* author unknown A&SH Museum.

56. Bewsher p.46.

57. Cairnie diary 28.9.15.

58. Nicolson pp.141-143.

59. Cairnie diary 9.11.1915.

60. Mackintosh, *War, The Liberator*, Page 96/Campbell and Green Page 134.

61. Bewsher p.47.

62. Stewart and Buchan *The Fifteenth (Scottish) Division 1914-1919* (Blackwood, 192) p.309 Appendix E.

63. Bewsher p.52.

64. John Hussey *'Uncle' Harper at Cambrai: A Reconsideration.* (British Army Review Number 117 December 1997) p.80.

65. Andy Simpson *Directing Operations, British Corps Command on the Western Front 1914-1918* (Spellmount 2006) p.6.

66. Guthrie letter 31.10.15 to his wife 1/6th Black Watch BWRA
67. Rorie, p.73
68. Guthrie letter 24.12.1915
69. Sutherland p.56.
70. War diary 1/8th Royal Scots 31.12.15.
71. Peel and MacDonald p.17.
72. Sutherland pp.58-59.
73. *John O'Groat Journal* 21.1.1916/Sutherland p.51; Campbell and Green p.101.
74. Cairnie diary 20.1.1916.
75. Letter to Peebles County newspaper March 1916.
76. Haig diary 12.1.1916.
77. Cairnie diary 26.1.16.
78. War diary 1/8th Royal Scots 3 and 5.3.1916.
79. Sutherland p.61.
80. War diary 1/9th Royal Scots 16-22.3.1916.
81. Anderson 1/9th Royal Scots: personal diary IWM.
82. Peel and MacDonald p.19.
83. War diary 1/7th Black Watch 18.3.1916
84. Mackintosh *War, The Liberator* p.114.
85. War Diary 1/7th Black Watch 21.3.1916.
86. Rennie recollections.
87. Haldane p.157 unattributed account.
88. Griffiths, Battlefield Tactics of the Western Front. The British Army's Art of Attack 1916-1918 p.61.Yale university Press
89. Ashworth p.84
90. 152nd Brigade War Diary 16.5.1916 TNA WO95/2861
91. Peel and MacDonald p.21.
92. Ross p.189.
93. Anderson diary.
94. Anderson diary.
95. Sutherland p.69.
96. Nicholson pp.145-146.
97. Sutherland p.40.
98. Anonymous soldier of 1/9th Royal Scots, in 'Twentieth Gazette' the organ of the 20th [Central Ontario] Canadian Battalion.
99. Mackintosh, *War The Liberator* p.96; Campbell and Green p.135.
100. Peel and McDonald p.23.
101. Peel and McDonald p.23.
102. 3032 Private A MacFarlane, 1/7th Black Watch The Dunfermline Press 15.7.1916.
103. 51st [Highland] Division, Circular Memorandum No.41 17.7.16 TNA.

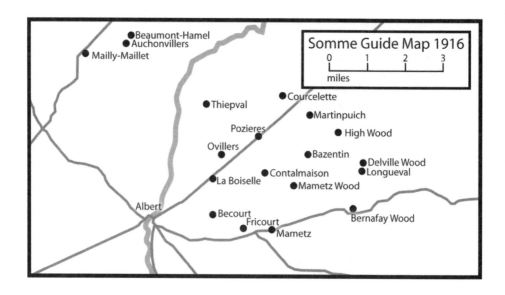

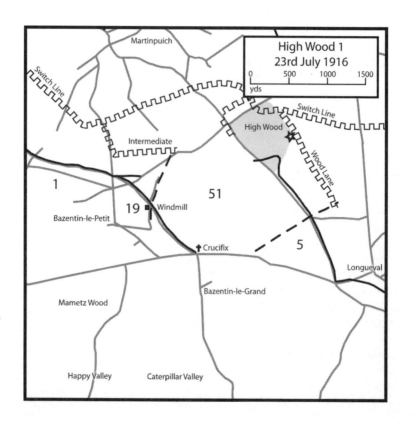

CHAPTER 3
FAILURE
High Wood

'Broken, broken, broken,
Is the pride of the Gael.' [1]

There had been disagreement over the tactics to be employed on the Somme front. General Rawlinson planned to deploy ten divisions of his Fourth Army along an 11.3 mile front, take the German front line, stop and consolidate, bring up artillery to destroy German counter-attacks, and to support attacks on the German second line. Haig thought that the plan lacked the element of surprise and was too cautious [2] and wanted the seizure of the German second line and a breakthrough. Rawlinson agreed to attempt more than he thought possible, which condemned the infantry to trying to penetrate too deeply, given that there were insufficient howitzers and howitzer ammunition to smash the German trenches and cut the barbed wire in both their first and second lines.

The men had been led to believe that the seven day bombardment that preceded the infantry assault at 7.30 a.m. on 1st July 1916 would dispose of the German front line defenders: it did not and on a 16 mile front the price was paid by almost 20,000 men killed and 38,000 wounded. Only on the southern flank, beside the French, who were successful, did the British hold parts of the German front line. Rawlinson's Corps Reserve was too far back, as it was only to move forward for the second phase, when the artillery had been brought forward and the captured German front line had been consolidated.[3] The chance of a deeper penetration was lost.

Rawlinson wanted his centre and northern corps to take the objectives they had failed to achieve on 1st July [4] but Haig over-ruled this and Rawlinson ordered his three southernmost corps to take Bernafray Wood, Mametz Wood, la Boisselle and Contalmaison, which were needed before an attack could be launched on the Germans' second line. These were taken by 14th July at a cost of 25,000 casualties. [5] By the 17th most of Delville Wood, part of Longueval village and the villages of Bazentin-le-Grand and Bazentin-le-Petit had fallen to the British. Cavalry had reached the line between High Wood and Delville Wood on the 14th of July, and on the 15th the 7th Division had entered High Wood, but was ordered to evacuate it. Thereafter it challenged the British for two months.

High Wood overlooked a British salient, and troops approached it through Happy Valley, south and east of Mametz Wood. Happy Valley was regularly harrowed by high explosive, air burst and gas shells. When shelling began the vehicles on the dirt road accelerated or diverted to escape the shelling, but the burdened infantry, trudging off road, could not escape. Bewsher paid tribute to the work of the RAMC who 'slowly pushed their wheeled stretchers from the Crucifix at Bazentin to the dressing station, heedless of the shell-fire and their own security. . . Happy Valley, with its stench of half-buried animals and men, will remain to all who knew it an ineffaceable memory.' [6]

Private Wrench, 1/4th Seaforths was there and recorded:

Private Wrench

'Old Fritz is shelling fearfully with tear gas shells. The air is stinking with it and it is terrible. We put on our gas goggles at first, but could not see with them and it was too dangerous getting in the way of excited and restless horses and mules of gun and wagon teams. . . some of us were nearly down beneath the wheels. So it was safer to put up with the watery eyes, painful as it was, for they nipped like fury.' [7]

On 22nd July the 51st relieved 33rd Division: five of its battalions had attacked High Wood on 15th July, and failed and on 20th July four battalions attacked and attained a foothold in the south west corner of the wood. The division was there from 15th to 22nd July.[8] Captain Dunn, Medical Officer of 2nd Royal Welch Fusiliers recorded the 33rd Division's relief by the 51st, who 'were a fine body of men, although the kilt is a costume that flatters.' [9]

154th Brigade completed the front line relief of the 33rd Division by 3 a.m. on the 22nd. It was then ordered to assault High Wood early on the 23rd as part of an offensive by three corps to seize Pozières Ridge. At 10 p.m. on the 22nd, on the 51st's right, two battalions of the 5th Division reached the crest west of Wood Lane, where the attack withered.

On the 51st's right were 1/4th Gordons whose war diary recorded the catastrophe:

'At 10.30 p.m. B Coy made a small attack on a strong point on right of High Wood which failed.' [10]

On the 23rd: At 12.30 am attack was made by Division on our left. (19th Division – author's note) At 1.30 a.m. our artillery lifted and the whole battalion advanced in lines of Coys, 'C' Coy and 'D' Coy leading. Our attack utterly failed. The wire in front of the German trenches was found to be intact and the ground so broken up with shell holes that in a few minutes all sense of direction was more or less lost. Coys. were reformed and the trench in wood and trench on SW and SE sides occupied by what was left of the Batt. Casualties were very heavy 12 officers and about 250 OR.

In the previous afternoon one Coy. of 4th Seaforth had been sent up to support us and at midnight another Coy. came up. From 6 a.m. to 7.30 a.m. our own artillery landed a considerable number of shells in and around trench on SE edge of High Wood causing about 40 casualties to 4th Seaforth and our L.G. (Lewis gun) team there.' [11]

On the left 1/9th Royal Scots war diary account is equally bleak:

'Inf.(antry) Assault began at 1.30 am. . . The assaulting Coys. were subjected to heavy shell fire while crossing open ground also to machine gun fire. . . The two Coys. lost touch with each other and also with Battns. on right and left. . . (6 named officers) were wounded and brought back. . . many of the N.C.O.s and men became casualties and the remainder of the two coys, having become split up, returned to the trench from which they had started. . . ' [12]

Fire from 1/9th Royal Scots' left had come from Intermediate Trench, about which they had no warning.

Ewing, historian of the Royal Scots, expressed a lingering doubt that 'officers and men of 1/9th Royal Scots who took part in the operation had, and still have, a suspicion that the assault was hardly expected to be successful, and that it was designed to prevent the enemy sending reinforcements to Pozières, where we did make a successful attack on the 23rd. It is highly probable that they were right in this conjecture, since all the arrangements had to be made very hurriedly.' [13] The engagement was part of the battle for Pozières.

The 51st's attack on High Wood was not a diversion. Zero hours varied all along the front, despite Rawlinson's original order for the attack to begin at 1.30 a.m. This reflects bad communications, an adherence to the delegatory principles of Field Service Regulations, and Rawlinson himself altering attack times. It is astonishing that neither the Corps Commander, Horne, nor Rawlinson made greater efforts to co-ordinate the attack. There were five XV Corps' divisions on a 5,500 yards front from south of Longueval to south of Pozières.

On the 51st's left 19th Division had been ordered by Rawlinson to attack at 12.30 a.m. to eliminate the newly discovered Intermediate Trench that had appeared in front of the Switch Line, their 1.30 a.m. objective. The 51st was not informed of this change of plan, [14] nor of the existence of Intermediate Trench, on its left. [15] On the left of 19th Division, 1st Division attacked at 12.30 to co-ordinate with the Australians. The 1st Australian Division took its first objective and most of its second objective.

Artillery suppression was already the proven key to success, but it was woeful on 22nd and 23rd July 1916. The artillery support for the 10 p.m. attack on High Wood by 1/4th Gordons began at 4.30 p.m. [16] As long as there was daylight aircraft could report on the accuracy of the guns, but it became hit or miss after dusk, and some of the batteries did not know of the attack until dusk had fallen. [17] These batteries could not register their targets, i.e. find the range by experimental ranging shots, and the trees in High Wood made the shrapnel barrage ineffective.[18]

Back in their trenches the remnants of 1/4th Gordons and 1/9th Royal Scots survived until they were relieved in the evening of the 23rd by 1/7th Argylls and 1/4th Seaforths. There was a gap in the British front between the 51st and the 19th Division and on the afternoon of the 23rd Captain Rowbotham of 1/8th Royal Scots (Pioneer) battalion with four men, in daylight, taped out a trench joining High Wood to the Windmill. On the nights of the 23rd, 24th and 25th 1/8th Royal Scots companies cut the trench, wired it and completed the British front line. [19]

When they had relieved the 1/4th Gordons, 1/4th Seaforths' snipers were forbidden to shoot on the 24th, the battalion's first day in High Wood:

'so as to give everyone a chance of locating his position and finding his way about. On the far side of the wood opposite us there was a footpath leading to a concrete block-house occupied by a German post, and all day the Germans sauntered up and down along this path. The following days, however, the snipers were allowed to shoot and claimed seventy-seven killed. Even if this number is exaggerated the fact remains that they had a lot of shooting all day, mostly in the centre of the wood, and still the Germans continued to walk openly and blindly across this corner until it seemed almost a shame to shoot them, it was so easy. One wondered if this awful bombard-ment they were constantly exposed to had so dazed them that they hardly knew and were careless of what they did.' [20]

On the 24th the new trench from High Wood to the Windmill was accurately shelled by the Germans. A German counter-attack on the 51st in High Wood, at 7.30 p.m. failed. The new trench was heavily bombarded again.

Private Wrench, 1/4th Seaforths, was carrying dispatches and guiding people in Happy Valley, also known as Death Valley:

'This was another hell of a day. Telephone wires cannot be maintained under such conditions, therefore a visual station has been established on a high position forward beside an old mill. So I had to journey there. . . it was an exciting journey to the visual station and I thought we would never get there. But coming back was even worse, and I was alone. Twice I threw myself into a hole just in time to escape a shell, one of which landed only a few yards away where other fellows were taking the same kind of shelter and they were all buried. They scrambled out and helped each other so I do not know how they fared, exactly, and did not want to see. But at the corner of Caterpiller Wood a motor car saved my skin again. Whoever drove up there in that car would never drive back in it again, I fancy. But through the smoke of that I heard cries for help for another poor man had got hit. He came staggering towards me, and had two ugly holes in his chest. I got his arm around my neck and helped him along to the field dressing station about half a mile back in a dug-out in an old quarry by the side of the road. The place was packed full of wounded, while outside on the ground were rows of stretchers with dead men wrapped up in blankets.' [21]

During the day on the 25th 1/4th Seaforths established three posts in the wood and connected and wired them during the night. Then:

'At at 9.20 pm, after preliminary bombardment Lt. Ross led a storming party against the N.E. corner of the wood. The attack failed completely. . . the party was greeted with a shower of grenades and a cross fire of M.G. Lt.Ross* was killed on the parapet. . . the casualties among the 50 men who took part were very slight – 2 men failed to be accounted for.' [22]

To deter further British attempts the Germans shelled the front lines and Happy Valley all night, mixing high explosive and shrapnel with phosgene, which caused less coughing than chlorine, so more was inhaled and it could be two or three days before its effects were fully felt.

Reflecting on 154th Brigade's failure in his report Brigadier-General Stewart concluded that 'the majority of all ranks need training for open warfare. Most officers are quite ignorant of the rudiments of the conduct of night operations. . . The necessity for reconnaissance of ground over which an attack is to be made is not understood. Failures in these respects were especially noticeable in the operations of 22nd/23rd July.'[23]

As most officers and men were war time enlistments and had been involved in trench warfare for over a year, this was an unsurprising conclusion, although the notion that successful reconnaissance could have been carried out in daylight on 22nd July, overlooked by a competent enemy, is absurd, and is an example of shifting blame, as some responsibility for the troops' skill levels lay with the Brigadier-General himself. He criticised the deployment of Lewis guns, the fact that the tyres came off the handcarts on which they were pulled, and that the handles broke. He suggested remedies for all his criticisms. [24]

The Corps Commander's policy of constant attack, when possible, continued. On 26th July 154th Brigade was relieved by 153rd Brigade, which was to renew the attack. The 153rd Brigade had three days to probe the area to their front, immediately to the south of High Wood. The crest ahead of them sheltered the German trench at Wood Lane from view. The area was dominated by the German redoubt in the south-east corner of High Wood, the key to the failure of many of the attacks. Corps Commander Horne reported his unhappiness with Harper to Haig, who wrote, on 27th July, 'I visited General Horne at Heilly (XV Corps). He thought that the 51st Divn. under Harper was a little slow, but that the Divisional Commander knew his work. They were opposite High Wood.' [25] Harper had been deprived of the opportunity to prepare his men for the attacks on 22/23rd July, and was planning to ensure a modicum of success.

Anticipating a successful attack sappers at Bazentin le Grand were to erect barbed wire in front of the newly captured position, but had no wire cutting pliers. Sapper William Fraser 2/2nd Highland Field Company:

Sapper William Fraser

'It so happened that I was the only man who knew where our advance stores were, I was detailed, along with another man, to fetch twenty pairs of pliers. The store was about a mile away and located in a gravel pit by the side of the main road. We had put the stuff there during darkness two nights previously, but I have never forgotten my experience in making that journey in daylight in full view of the German line.

We emerged from the deep dug-out and stood for a few moments until our eyes got used to the light. It was a very hot humid day, with the sun dimly visible through a cordite and fume-laden atmosphere. The route lay through shell-filled dust-laden fields. On our left, half a mile away on top of a ridge was the German front line and in front of us was the charred and battered remains of what was High Wood . . . all around us were thousands of British soldiers invisible in their shallow, newly dug holes and trenches. An eerie silence reigned and not a thing moved, except a few stretcher bearers with their human loads snaking their way towards a field station. Suddenly as we approached the store a shell screamed over. It landed dead on a stretcher team which I never saw again. Other shells followed and by the time we reached the store they were dropping in all directions – one had hit the store, half burying the tools. I seized a pick, smashed open a box of pliers, grabbed the required quantity and made off. Fortunately the ground was soft which deadened the effect of the explosions. Fifty yards from our dug-out we were spotted by a machine-gunner and had to crawl flat on our stomachs as bullets spattered around us. When we reached the inlet to the dug-out, men were waiting for us and hauled us in greatly surprised that we had survived. Torn, exhausted and bruised but otherwise unharmed, a mug of tea revived us and we were excused further duty for that night.' [26]

The attack took place on 30th July. 1/5th Gordons' war diary:

'From 4.30 p.m. till 6 p.m. our artillery fired on the German trench along the sunken road running SE from the eastern corner of HIGH WOOD (Wood Lane) and on the various strong points held by the enemy. During this period, the companies occupying the sapheads 50 yds. in front of the assembly trenches, and in the assembly trenches themselves, were heavily shelled by a German heavy battery. . . two platoons of A Coy were buried but dug themselves out. Casualties during this phase were about 50, 40 of which were in A Coy.

At 5.45 pm the leading wave left their sapheads and worked forward under cover of our barrage, the sapheads being occupied by the second wave. At 6.10 (zero) the first wave commenced the assault. On crossing the crest line they came under very deadly fire from rifles and machine guns in front and in the flanks. The German trench was very strongly held, apparently with a man to every yard of firestep, and appeared to be quite untouched by our bombardment.

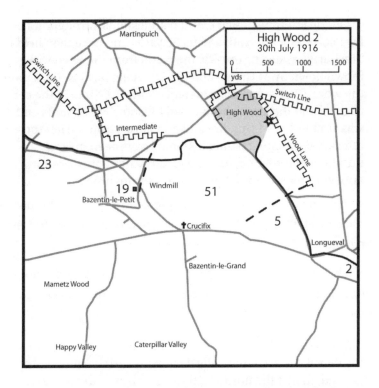

The first wave, in spite of very heavy casualties pushed on to within 50 yards of the German trench, by which time the ranks were so much thinned as to make a successful assault quite out of the question and the men were ordered to take cover in shell holes and in the long corn. . . News was received that the 6th and 7th Black Watch on the left and the 5th Division on the right, had also been held up, so a new fire trench was immediately started just on our side of the crest about 250 yards in advance of our original assembly trenches.'

The battalion's casualty summary, at the end of a most detailed and legible list of their names was killed: 3 officers and 87 other ranks; wounded: 10 officers and 224 other ranks; gassed: 11; shell shock: 3; missing 17. [27]

On 1/5th Gordons left, in the centre of the attack:

'The 6th Black Watch got hung up by heavy machine gun fire from strong point on East Edge of the wood where three machine guns were in action. They commenced to consolidate a line 200-300 yards in advance of their old line. This line is in contact with the Battn on left but not with the 5th Gordons on right. . .

'On the left the 7th Black Watch attacked on strongpoint at East corner of Wood advancing 50 yards and were then held up. The party assaulting outside the wood from the open was mown down by M.G. fire, and the attacking parties throughout the wood were stopped by grenades and M.G. fire. In the centre of the wood the attack progressed for some 60/70 yards and was stopped by M Gun fire and grenades. . . On the left the attack did not progress at all. Enemy were seen in large numbers in the wood, and the Artillery Barrage does not appear to have stopped the Germans from lining the trench.'[28]

The German trenches were not damaged much by the barrage. 1/7th Black Watch's 70 yards gain in the wood was lost due to German shelling, but the new line outside the wood held.

A fresh attack was ordered at 9.45 p.m. but the orders did not reach the attacking battalions in time and it did not take place. Harper's reported on the attack to XV Corps:

'I would suggest that the eastern and western strong points in the WOOD be systematically dealt with and the intervening ground; in fact the northern three quarters of the wood, should be searched by heavy artillery. It will be necessary to withdraw our troops in the WOOD , and an advance could then be carried out under artillery fire. . . I am convinced that before a further attack in the WOOD can hope to be successful the enemy's line in the WOOD must be made a burden to him by heavy artillery bombardment searching up and down the WOOD. He must in fact be completely demoralised and then only should an attack be made. . . ' [29]

XV Corps ignored his comments. [30]

On 31st July the battered 153rd Brigade was relieved by 152nd Brigade. On the previous day, after being shelled in Happy Valley, Lt.E.A.Mackintosh, 1/5th Seaforths, had distracted the men by asking if it was a Sunday and 'the strong voice of a sergeant was lifted up in the shaking lilt of an old Psalm tune.'

'He took me from the fearful pit
And from the miry clay,
And on a rock he set my feet,
Establishing my way.'

The Psalm ended; another voice said, 'I'll give you a grand one for this day, boy,' and once again the strong rough voices rang out through the wood, grim earnestness in every tone:

'Now Israel may say, and that truly
If that the Lord had not been on our side,
If that the Lord had not our cause maintained
When cruel men against us furiously
Rose up in wrath to make of us their pray. . .
Therefore our trust is in the Lord his name,
Who heaven and earth by his own power did frame.' [31]

This may have evoked memories of home, reinforceded identity and roots and reminded men of what they were defending. Luckily for 152nd Brigade the futility of piecemeal attacks on High Wood had been recognised, and:

'no advance on a large scale was contemplated by the XVth Corps during the next few days, but that every effort was to be made by energetic patrolling to locate definitely the enemy's positions, and also by means of sapping and advancing heads to push forward our line as far as possible, with a view to capturing HIGH WOOD and the WOOD LANE TRENCH preparatory to a subsequent attack on his SWITCH LINE.' [32]

On the 51st's right, on the night of 3/4th August, outside the wood, covered by a barrage, parties dug a trench 200 yards ahead of the front line, about 50 yards short of the fatal crest between the British and Wood Lane trench. This was garrisoned by dawn on the 4th, and then linked to the old British front line.

Entrenching a shattered wood was difficult, and digging amongst decomposing corpses in temperatures that ranged from 19C to 29C was disgusting. The Barratt Hydraulic Forcing Jack was deployed: it was assembled in a front line trench, from where it forced an iron pipe filled with explosive through the ground, theoretically parallel to its surface, at a depth of four to five feet. The charge was exploded to create a trench. It was known colloquially as a mole and was completely unsuited to High Wood, where the ground was interlaced with tree roots. Bewsher thought that 'the labour of carrying the pipes and ammonal up the line, and of working the task, proved incommensurate with the results obtained.' [33]

The 1/6th Gordons, on the left in High Wood, reconnoitred the enemy's positions, pushed out saps and connected the sap heads, and wired their front. [34] There was shelling and James Rennie, 1/6th Gordons, was near a sap running towards High Wood:

> 'We were sitting there one night after a strafe. . . in comes one of these guys out of the sap, and he's all worked up and he's hollering 'Krueger's deed, Krueger's deed, come on, hurry, Krueger's deed.' So what could we do but go up there . . . we get to the trench and ask him where Krueger was. 'Oh, Krueger's in there, Krueger's in there, he's deed by noo.' . . . We had to be careful that we didn't hit the poor soul underneath all this dirt. We got some dirt scraped off and we came to Krueger's head. . . we cleared the dirt away so that he could breathe. . . he talked a little bit and grunted a little bit. We finally got the dirt cleaned away and got Krueger out and shook the dirt off him a little bit. We asked him how he was. Oh, he was alright. . . but he thought he was sent for.' [35]

The key to the German defences was a redoubt in a hollow at the eastern corner of High Wood, which dominated most of the battlefield. It had resisted all attempts to eliminate it. On 5th August Brigadier-General Pelham-Burn suggested: 'that a tunneling Company should be employed to destroy by a mine the enemy's post at the E corner of HIGH WOOD. This was decided upon and work was immediately started.' [36]

The 51st was relieved in daylight on 7th August by 33rd Division, and no casualties were sustained, because the relief avoided the nightly German shelling of Happy Valley.

In his review of 152nd Brigade's time at High Wood Pelham-Burn was withering in his criticism of the artillery:

> 'No good results will ever be obtained until the question of co-operation between the Artillery and the Infantry is placed on an altogether different footing. The only connection between the front line and the Artillery on my Brigade front consisted of two F.O.O.s (Forward Observation Officers) at HIGH WOOD who, however, had no means of communicating with their own or any other batteries. However these F.O.Os. had strict orders never to report the fact of our own shells falling short,

which resulted in the fire of a Battery of 9.2 Howitzers being entirely thrown away for four hours in one afternoon and $1^{1}/_{4}$ hours on another, these shells falling onto our own trenches, 300-350 yards short of the hostile line. . . unless the fire of the Artillery is better directed we cannot expect to find the way clear for assaulting infantry. I may add that 12% of the Casualties sustained by this Brigade (Casualties from Gas excluded) are known to have been caused by our own guns.

I think that a system of Light Signals should be adopted to signify that our own shells are falling short.' [37]

The 51st was tired from a sustained period garrisoning the Labyrinth and was thown hurriedly into the battle, as were many divisions in this phase of the Somme battle. The deep sense of failure felt by the 51st is expressed in the reference, at the top of this chapter. Unlike Festubert, when the division knew that it was raw, it had come to High Wood with a year's experience of trench warfare. It went into battle with no time to reconnoitre, plan, rehearse or co-ordinate its attacks. Harper's harbouring of human resources ensured that whole brigades were not swallowed up in an attack: only two battalions out of four of 154th Brigade attacked on 23rd July, and three out of four in the 153rd Brigade attack on 30th July. 152nd Brigade was not required to attack, but to dig.

Captain Dunn, author of *The War the Infantry Knew*, noted that the 51st Division had only two-fifths of the casualties taken by the 33rd Division. [38] This could imply criticism of the 51st, although it is likely that the author simply included the statistics from the Official History as an incidental. The casualties in the Official History are: 22nd July to 7th August, 51st: 120 officers and 2000 men, [39] 15th July to 22nd July, 33rd Division 263 officers and 4932 men. [40] The 51st committed two battalions on 23rd July, a fifty man raid on 25th July and three on 30th July, just over five battalions. The 33rd Division engaged five on 15th July and four on 20th July, a total of nine battalions. [41] Having committed fewer battalions to the attack than the 33rd, the 51st was bound to have fewer casualties. The 33rd's attacks all took place in daylight, whereas the 51st's took place at night on the 23rd, which may have diminished the effectiveness of the German artillery, although it did not impair their riflemen and machine-gunners. Army and Corps' realisation that the 152nd

Brigade should dig and not attack was another factor that spared the 51st. The 51st served for just 16 days on the Somme whereas the average number of days for a division to be engaged on the Somme was 20.7. [42]

In a comment in a book on the Battle of the Somme from the German point of view an author asserted that the 51st's losses at High Wood gave it experiences which made it an élite formation in the latter half of the war. This conclusion is followed by the comment, in parentheses, that this was 'in its own estimation at least.' [43] No self-respecting division would underestimate itself, and the 51st was no exception. The comment did not presage any analysis of the Scottish psyche. 'Here's tae us, wha's like us, gey few, an' they're deid' (Here's to us, who is like us, very few and they are dead) is a toast that still enjoys some currency in Scotland. If that kind of braggart self-belief reinforced battalion and divisional pride, it was wholly justifiable in circumstances that demand much more of men than mundane civilian life.

The 51st learned the need for reconnaissance, good gunnery and better infantry/artillery co-operation. It had entrenched the gap between High Wood and the windmill at Bazentin-le-Patit, completing a new front line, and Pelham-Burn's suggestion that the German redoubt in the eastern corner of High Wood be mined contributed to its capture on 15th September 1916.

On the 8th of August most of the 51st's infantry were entertained near Méaulte by the 'Balmorals' and on the 9th moved by train via Longpré-Pont Remy to Blaringhem. On the 15th and 16th August the 51st relieved 1st New Zealand Division, which went to the Somme. The sector was between Chapelle d'Armentieres and the River Lys and was fairly quiet, although subjected to occasional artillery bombardment, raids, mortar and grenade attacks. [44] It was a breastwork line in a flat landscape which allowed movement immediately behind the line to be unobserved by the enemy. James Rennie, 1/6th Gordons, had to fetch water from a well, which was behind the breastwork, but the area was subjected to minenwerfers and 'we'd be watching for these things. . . you could hear them going off over the German lines. You'd watch them and figure out which way to run. . . you could run any way to the back . . . you could run all over the country as long as you kept behind the breastwork.' [45] Private William Couston, 1/7th Black Watch, found the trenches lively in other ways as 'the dug-outs were infested with rats – whoppers too. No food can be left lying around else it very soon disappears. They even eat through valise bags to get at the eatables inside.'[46]

The 1/6th Seaforths, 1/6th and 1/7th Gordons, and 1/7th Black Watch raided in this period. [47] James Rennie, 1/6th Gordons, took part in one:

> 'we were going to carry ammonal tubes. . . And they hook
> (push) them all together and shove them under the wire. So,
> we sneak through our wire and away we go with these
> ammonal tubes. We carry them up to the German wire and lay
> there very quietly . . . got to be damned quiet or you don't last
> long. You shove them under the wire, keep shoving and keep
> shoving. . . The field engineers, they explode these . . . Well,
> the bomb throwers, they're all laying up there with their faces
> blackened and loaded with bombs. They have a knuckle
> duster with a blade on it . . . you're armed to the teeth. And
> over you go, just shoot everybody you see. . . unless they have
> their hands up. . . let them have it. And you throw cans of
> gasoline in the dug-outs and another bomb to set fire to it.
> First thing you know there is smoke and fire. . . everyone is
> running and shooting and having a hell of a time . . . and you
> grab these prisoners and maybe one guy will be watching the
> prisoners while the other guys will be doing the shooting and
> raising hell. You get so long and then you go back, right away,
> quick you boost these prisoners over the top and drag them
> and run with them back to your own line, you see. Then, they
> start interrogating the prisoners and you get cleaned up and
> that's all you do for the night . . . You're allowed a few hours for
> yourself.' [48]

Bewsher records that on one successful raid by 1/6th Seaforths, chosen for inclusion in his divisional history by Harper, the men wore Dayfield body shields, which had grenade splinters sticking out of them when the men returned. [49] These shields consisted of four panels of metal joined together by steel strips, the whole covered in khaki cloth and worn over or under under the tunic.

Apart from raids, the artillery and mortars regularly destroyed the German breastworks, and Bewsher's view was that the 51st achieved ascendancy over the Germans in this activity, as there was little German retaliation. Bewsher thought that the time in the Armentieres sector was the 51st's best experience of trench warfare. [50] Although it was damaged Armentieres had good billets, and functioning shops, estaminets, tea-shops and restaurants. [51]

On 17th September Brigadier-General Hamilton took command of 154th Brigade, as Brigadier-General Stewart had been killed by shell fire three days earlier. [52]

On 25th September 1916 the 51st moved to Bailleul, Meteren and Estaires, where it spent five days before traveling by train to Doullens and Candas. On 1st October 1916 the division marched to Bus-les-Artois, Bois du Warnimont, Authie, Vauchelles and Thievres, joining XIII Corps, and relieved 2nd Division in the line near Hebuterne. The 51st was to attack Puisieux on a single brigade front, with the two following brigades leap-frogging, but legitimate anxiety about the well-defended German position at Serre, which had broken the British on 1st July, and over-looked the right of the 51st's planned advance, and the dire consequences to the 51st if it did not fall, ensured that the plan was shelved.

NOTES
1. Mackintosh. *Three Battles: High Wood War, The Liberator,* p.26/Campbell and Green p.167
2. Prior and Wilson p.146
3. Edmonds 1916, v. 1 Appendices pp.170-171.
4. *Fourth Army Op Order No 3 1/7/1916 Fourth Army Papers Vol.7* TNA.
5. Prior and Wilson p.187.
6. Bewsher pp.75 and 76.
7. Private Wrench 1/4th Seaforths, personal diary 22.7.1916 IWM.
8. Captain.J.C.Dunn *The War the Infantry Knew* (King Ltd, 1938, this ref. Sphere Books 1989) p.225ff
9. Dunn p.244
10. War diary 1/4th Gordons 22.7.1916.
11. War diary 1/4th Gordons 23.7.1916
12. War diary 1/9th Royal Scots 23.7.1916
13. Ewing Vol 1 p.308.
14. *19th Division's 57th Brigade's Preliminary Order No 22 for 23 July 1916,* point five of which outlines the procedure on the Capture of the Intermediate Line, was not listed as being copied to the 51st Division TNA.
15. Robin Prior and Trevor Wilson *The Somme* (Yale University Press, 2006) p.149.

16. War diary 1/4th Gordons 22.7.1916.
17. Terry Norman *The Hell That They Called High Wood* (Kimber 1984) p.163.
18. Bewsher p.78.
19. War diary 1/8th Royal Scots 25 and 26.7.1916.
20. Mss. Author unknown 1/4th Seaforths Q.O.H. Museum Fort George.
21. Wrench 24.7.1916.
22. War diary 1/4th Seaforths. 25.7.1916.
23. 154th Brigade report 20.8.1916 TNA.
24. 154th Brigade report 20.8.1916 TNA.
25. Haig diary 28.7.1916.
26. Lance-Corporal William Milton Fraser 2nd Highland Field Company/401st Field Company R.E. recollections.
27. War diary 1/5th Gordons 30.7.1916.
28. War diary 153rd Brigade 30.7.1916.
29. Harper to HQ XV Corps 31 July 1916 TNA.
30. Norman p.176.
31. Mackintosh, *War, The Liberator* pp.151-152/Campbell and Green pp.151-152
32. War diary 152nd Brigade 1.8.1916 TNA.
33. Bewsher p. 83
34. War Diary 1/6th Gordons 1-5.8.1916.
35. Rennie recollections.
36. War diary 152nd Brigade 5.8.1916 TNA.
37. Pelham-Burn 19.8.1916 TNA.
38. Dunn p.248.
39. Edmonds 1916 v.1 p.186 footnote.
40. Edmonds 1916 v.1 p.113 footnote.
41. Chris McCarthy *The Somme. The Day by Day Account.* (Brockhampton Press) 1998 pp. 50-79/War diary 1/4 Seaforths 25.7.16
41. Haig's diary
43. Christopher Duffy *Through German Eyes: The British and the Somme 1916* Phoenix 2007 p.196
44. Bewsher pp.85-87
45. Rennie recollections
46. Pte William Couston 1/7th Black Watch 28.8.1916 BWRA
47. Bewsher pp. 90-97
48. Rennie recollections (The tubes were Bangalore torpedoes, invented in 1912 by Captain McClintock of the Indian Army's, Bombay and Madras Sappers and Miners, and their use persisted into the Second World War) (see *Saving Private Ryan* opening sequences)
49. Bewsher p.95
50. Bewsher p.97
51. Bewsher pp.87-88
52. Bewsher p.88
53. Bewsher pp.98-99

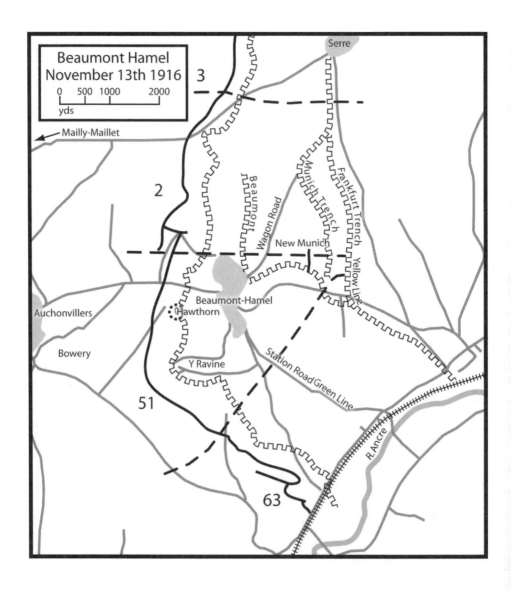

Beaumont Hamel
November 13th 1916

3

0   500 1000   2000
yds

Mailly-Maillet

2

Serre

Beaumont

Wagon Road

Munich Trench

Frankfurt Trench

New Munich

Yellow Line

Beaumont-Hamel

Auchonvillers

Hawthorn

Bowery

Y Ravine

Station Road Green Line

51

R. Ancre

63

CHAPTER 4

FAME
Beaumont-Hamel

'By the vengeance we took
In the bloody ravine,
By the men that we slew
In the mud and the rain,
The pride of the North,
Has arisen again.' [1]

The last phase of the battle of the Somme was to be an attack on Beaumont-Hamel and the Ancre heights, to pinch off the strong German salient which lay between the Albert-Bapaume road and Serre. II Corps was on the right, separated by the River Ancre from V Corps, which consisted of the 63rd, 51st and 2nd and 3rd divisions. On 17th October 152nd Brigade relieved a brigade of 63rd (Royal Naval) Division in the trenches at Beaumont-Hamel and the rest of the division moved to billets around Léalvillers, Forceville and Varennes. On 20th October 153rd Brigade moved in on the right of 152nd Brigade, and preparations began for the assault on Beaumont-Hamel.

Lance Corporal Thomson, 1/4th Seaforths, in his third winter of the war, wrote to his former headmaster at the Nicolson Institute, Stornoway:

'Night after night we are coming in in the small hours of the morning tired, wet, and hungry, and with only sufficient energy left to crawl like rats into our billets and sleep as only men dead beat can sleep.

Can you imagine the whole battalion on a 'fatigue'? Falling in at dead of night in some ruined village, numbering off in the dark, and then moving off in the mud, keeping touch as best one can, tripping over wires, and falling into shell-holes. I think myself, this is the most trying thing we have to do here for, with passing artillery limbers splashing one and parties coming and going jostling one, it is more than one can do to keep one's temper and one's nerves here are never what they should be.'

A survivor of High Wood, his innocence of battle long gone, he touched upon morale:

'. . . soon we will leave the shelter of our trenches and ferret the Hun out of his. We are all confident of success but a great apathy has set among us, and neither the prospect of success can make us enthusiastic nor failure leave us despondent. . . We are not complaining, for we realise what an honour we are accumulating for ourselves in putting up with hardships for ideals that generations to come will consider glorious. Still it is at times very difficult to keep smiling.'

Then, to prove that smiling was possible or to finish on an upbeat note:

'The boys are wonderful amongst it all – having a jest ready to the tongue even when the hand is blistered on the spade or the eye burns in the socket for want of sleep. In a few hours everything is forgotten and the villagers are treated to the sight of as merry a crowd of Tommies as could be seen on a Fete day in 'Blighty'.' [2]

The omens were bad: the dead of 1st July still lay before Beaumont-Hamel and the 51st's experience at High Wood suggested that it was about to suffer again. But V Corps' artillery support was formidable, with 'a field gun (or howitzer) to every 13.5 yards of front, and a heavy gun (or howitzer) to every 31 yards. . . the figures for 1st July are 21 and 57'. [3]

The artillery was to isolate the area to be attacked, and II Corps' artillery, south of the Ancre, was to lay down the kind of barrage that would precede an infantry attack, although none was planned. [4] On the left of V Corps the artillery of XIII Corps would fire on the approaches to the German front. The shelling began on 20th October, four days before the planned attack, to demoralise the Germans, and cut the wire, which was monitored by patrols and by photo-reconnaissance and 'maps were made daily, in which the portions of the enemy wire which could be observed were shown in one of four colours, a separate colour being used to denote the varying conditions of the wire – i.e. satisfactorily cut, partially cut, damaged, intact. . . these maps were passed on to the gunner officers responsible for the wire-cutting.'[5]

When German repairs to their wire were observed the 4.5 inch howitzers destroyed them, then Lewis guns and machine-guns were sighted on the gaps to fire on them at night, when German work parties would be repairing them again. Bangalore torpedoes were useful for wrecking repairs, and a 1/6th Gordons raid on 1st November broke through two rows of portable barbed wire knife rests, and returned without casualties. [6]

The 51st's machine-guns were placed on the Bowery, a small hill near Auchonvillers, from which they would lay down a barrage over the attackers' heads. The trajectory of a machine-gun bullet rises upwards then descends, and the vagaries of wind, weather, and wear on the gun barrels produce an elliptical 'beaten zone' of bullets, designed to pre-empt the Germans' long range machine-gun fire and their advancing reserves. This would be a new experience for the men and they were warned that although the bullets would sound as if they were within inches of their heads, they would be traveling many feet above them.[7]

Between 1st and 3rd November 1/8th Royal Scots built an R.A.M.C. dressing station, a soup kitchen, dumps, a railway, a bath-house and canteen; cleared five trenches, enlarged a dugout and made a second entrance and stairway to it.[8] Atrocious weather meant that 'Z' day, the planned day of attack, was moved from 24th to 30th October, then 1st, then 5th November, before being indefinitely postponed on 7th November. On the 10th it was scheduled for the 13th. The roads were so saturated that each division was restricted to four lorries per day, so the burden of moving supplies fell on the infantry. [9] 1/4th Gordons, in reserve, were well occupied:

'8/11 Wet. 330 O/Rs on various fatigues up in the trenches during day. Managed to get the whole Battn. bathed at Mailly before and after fatigues.

9/11 Dry today. 200 O/Rs on fatigues rest occupied in camp

improvements. Brigade warned Battn.to move to FORCEVILLE tomorrow morning and orders issued accordingly.

10.11 At 2.30 am Bde cancelled movement to FORCEVILLE 180 O/Rs on various fatigues. Rest cleaning up camp and equipment.

11.11 Dry but very dull.470 ORs on fatigues during afternoon and evening.

12.11 Dull. Preparing for the attack. 2 officers and 100 O/Rs detailed by Brigade as burial party. 1 officer and 16 O/Rs as a trench control party.' [10]

1/8th Royal Scots cleared trenches just sufficiently 'to enable men to pass right along it and stay in it for about 2 hours (Y/Z night) and then leave the trench over the parapet for the assault.' [11]

154th Brigade was in reserve and Private Wrench, 1/4th Seaforths, observed:

'It was a funny sensation to feel when the whole division of troops marched up past here for the stunt in the morning. They are the left division [2nd Division – author's note] and I think they are all well oiled, as they seem so happy about it. An extra rum ration does an awful lot to cheer men up a bit who are going into God knows what. Anyhow, little did they seem to care if it is their last long trail, and the way they were singing, and what they leave unsung about 'Mademoiselle from Armentieres' is nobody's business. . . excitement is high and suspense is great.' [12]

Operational orders in 153rd Brigade decreed that the men would be equipped with:

Greatcoat with skirts looped back
Full equipment (less pack) haversack on back
Iron ration, and the day's ration
Filled Water Bottle
4 bombs in his pocket
2 sandbags attached so that they cannot fall off

tin disk attached to haversack
Every alternate man will carry either a pick or a shovel in
proportion of two shovels to one pick
Men carrying wire cutters will have white tapes on their right
shoulder strap.' [13]

Burdened, and soaked through, 152nd and 153rd Brigades set out at
9 pm on 12th November to march five miles from Forceville to the
assembly trenches, a little cheered by a 45 minute stop between Mailly-
Maillet and Auchonvillers for tea, but subsequently less heartened by
the fact that 'numbers of aeroplane flares, very light pistols and
cartridges, phosphorous bombs & etc were distributed throughout the
different platoons'. [14] 'An extra breakfast ration was provided out of
canteen funds, consisting of tinned herrings or sausages: this was much
appreciated. In addition to above a ration of chewing gum was given to
each man and a packet of chocolate, the latter being provided out of
canteen funds.' [15]

When Sergeant W. Mitchell, D Company, 1/6th Black Watch, arrived
at the assembly positions:

> 'we got everything in order for jumping over. We had first to
> cut a few gaps in our own wire to enable men to get through
> without delay. In this operation we had no trouble at all. It was
> about the quietest night I ever had in the trenches. We had
> now everything arranged, so there was nothing more to do but
> wait patiently for 'Zero'. None of us slept much that night, but
> everyone was in wonderfully bright spirits. . . about 5 a.m. we
> had a hot drink served out to us. It was dignified with the
> name of 'rum-punch', but its actual character was the subject
> for some difference of opinion. 'It's rum with some tea in it,'
> said one man – 'Away, man, it's tea with a little rum.' Whatever
> the concoction may have been it put a nice heat into us.' [16]

James Rennie, 1/6th Gordons, witnessed a soldier break down, who. . .

> 'was just a kid, and he was bawling, he was crying and he was
> shaking. And we tried, well there was no use trying to talk to
> him, Christ, he couldn't hear you. And, Jesus Christ, here
> comes Paddy Burns, (Brigadier-General H. P Burn 152nd

Brigade) the brigadier... What the hell he was doing up there under these conditions, I don't know ... but, there he was. And, by God, he patted the lad on the back and says, 'You come with me.' And he took him by the hand and away he went. He was no bloody good there, he may well have been down the line someplace. Christ, he was only going to get killed anyway. He was just scared to death...'

Although the young soldier was treated with compassion twenty men of the 51st were condemned to death by courts martial and four were shot. With approximately the same

Brigadier-General Pelham-Burn

number of months of active service 9th (Scottish) had two shot and 15th (Scottish) ten. [17]

Daily morning barrages since 20th October had accustomed the Germans to them ceasing without a subsequent attack, and because of the postponements a greater volume of explosives had fallen on the Germans than had been originally planned.

The attack was on a broad front. On the extreme right II Corps battered the German flank. On V Corps' front the 63rd, between the River Ancre and the 51st, approached Beaumont-Hamel from the south west and west. North of the 51st were the 2nd and 3rd Divisions, facing Serre. V Corps' left was to be protected by XIII Corps' 31st Division, attacking north of Serre. Because the 51st's divisional boundaries narrowed to an apex containing Beaumont-Hamel, its flanking divisions, the 63rd and 2nd, were to continue the attack beyond the 51st's advance. The 51st's prime objective was the Green Line, which embraced Beaumont-Hamel and Station Road to its south-east, and, at the tip of its diminishing front, a length of Frankfurt Trench, designated the Yellow Line.

Hawthorn Crater, created on 1st July and occupied by the Germans, was on 152nd Brigade's front. At 5.45 a.m. on 13th November the detonation of a 30,000 lbs ammonal mine disposed of a platoon of the

German III/62nd Regiment. Simultaneously the British barrage fell on the Germans, although 25% of the field guns fired fifty yards short of it, to prevent the Germans moving into No Man's Land to establish improvised defensive positions. Six minutes after zero the creeping barrage began, at a rate of 100 yards every five minutes, followed by the infantry. [18] It was dark when the barrage lifted, and as well as having their vision impaired by darkness and smoke filled mist, progress was hindered by water filled shell holes and glutinous mud, so that achieving the planned yardage per minute was difficult. Starting out in sodden clothing the weight of the mud slowed the men. Bewsher:

> 'Let two teams dressed in battle order play football in the dark on a ploughed field in clay soil after three weeks rain, and the difficulties of the attacking troops might then in some measure be appreciated.' [19]

On the right of V Corps the Royal Marine Light Infantry of 63rd Division made good progress and kept in touch with 1/7th Gordons who were on the extreme right of the 51st: the Gordons' two companies stayed close to the lifting barrage, and stormed their objectives, by-passing the east end of Y Ravine. By 6.45 a.m. they had reached the German third line and with elements of Royal Marine Light Infantry followed retreating Germans uphill towards the north, took 40 prisoners, then consolidated on Station Road.

The link-up with 63rd Division was not without its troubles. A jaundiced 1/5th Seaforth reported:

> 'The 51st Division has a grudge against the Naval Division, which was on its right, and especially with a man of peace in that Division, who for the nonce had seemingly become a man of war.

One battalion officer, dressed for the attack in private's kilt and tunic, was, with a small party, marshalling 600 prisoners for leading to the rear, when this padre, with a stronger party, rushed up and demanded that the prisoners should be handed over to him.

On the officer demurring, the padre, so the story goes, knocked him into a shell-hole and took the prisoners to the Naval Division.

> 'On a protest being lodged, the Naval Division offered to go halves, but as we could afford to be generous, they were told to keep them.' [20]

1/7th Gordon's left companies and 1/6th Black Watch were held up for several hours by machine-gunners and riflemen in Y ravine. Some of 1/6th Black Watch skirted the northern side of Y ravine and moved on. Sergeant W. Mitchell, D Company, 1/6th Black Watch, was one of them:

> 'it was so misty we could barely see ten yards in front of us, but we knew which way to go, so we started creeping forwards, and as the barrage lifted we made for the enemy trenches. We had little difficulty in getting over his wire, and as he had noticed this with his flare lights, he started bombing us, causing some casualties. Our other platoons meanwhile had got through on the left, and working along the trench they came across the Hun about the same time as we got through ourselves. It was our turn then. We cleared the trench of all that was left, and leaving a number of men to see that no occupants remained in the dug-outs, moved forward towards the second line along with another company. The Germans put up a little more resistance there, but we captured the trench after a bit of a struggle, and took a great number of prisoners, especially from their dug-outs. By this time my company had only one officer left, and owing to the darkness in which the attack began, some of the companies got a bit mixed up. That did not hinder us any, however, as we all knew our final objective, and with a few hurried orders we moved forward to take the third line. It was at this time that I was slightly wounded. . . but could see our men entering the village of Beaumont Hamel.' [21]

1/4th Gordons were committed from divisional support to tackle Y Ravine, bombing from either end. Soldiers of 1/7th Gordons and 1/6th Black Watch who had earlier been surrounded in the centre of Y Ravine by Germans who had emerged from their deep dug-outs, stood their ground until they were rescued by 1/4th Gordons' bombers, and elements of their own battalions.

North of Y Ravine, 152nd Brigade had different problems. To the south of Hawthorn Crater 1/5th Seaforths were held up by uncut wire and 1/6th Seaforths were sent to help. On their left 1/8th Argylls took punishment from machine-guns, but their flanking companies moved forward, captured the guns, and advanced to the enemy's third line.

An anonymous soldier of 1/8th Argylls amalgamated his experience with that of others:

'. . . alone in the mist am I now, in so far as actual sight of human beings is concerned. . . I can't see five yards. No doubt 'A' Company are in the midst of a stern struggle, just a few yards to my right. The Germans are putting up a determined resistance with much bayonet work, rifle firing, and bombing. . . overhead the screaming shells and hailing bullets are making, still, their infernal din, while ahead is a wall of flickering flames, flashing in and out with reddish flares, as if the thousand furnace-doors of Hell itself are being flung open. . . Still, a cheerier idea, they are also guiding lights. . . our artillery has done its wire-cutting well, for very few strands of German wire have I seen, although a part of 'A' Company have suffered through coming across a thick belt of it, forty yards long, hidden in a sunken portion of No Man's Land. Forward then! Jump a trench-count 'One' (should have counted 'Two') (the first line trench was unrecognizable)

'B' Company are in this trench, the second German line, and are having a rough time of it with bombs very much to the fore. Ably and courageously led by Lieut. McKellar* of 'A' Company, they are wearing down the opposition with the aid of those same Mills bombs that caused such chafing on the march up. They will clear up this particular nest of hornets, but, alas, will lose their leader when the fight is at its last gasp. This will not be, until a few of 'C' Company will have jumped over the trenches and will have been shot at from some of those dug-outs now behind us. But more of 'C' are coming on, will take part in this game and, infuriated by this shooting of their comrades in the back, will 'attend promptly' to the thirteen Germans on the losing side. ['attending to' is a synonym for killing regardless of whether or not they had surrendered] There'll be some bayonet work. Being to the left of all this I can't see it, and, in any case, am busy counting 'Two' while taking a flying leap over a trench which appears to be ten to fifteen feet deep. See no one in it, as I scramble to my feet again, should have stayed in that trench, for it's 'C's' objective but, through miscounting, go on. Fear I'm behind time, so break into a run. Run hard into that wall of smoke and flame, thinking it must be lifting from my objective. . . I haven't found my (presumed) objective yet. Won't find it either, for here the German fourth line has been blown in by our high explosive shells. Fancy those ground-bursts are going on around me now that I can see new shell-holes actually being made as I pass through that inferno of a barrage. I get through it, right to the other side, where dawn is breaking. Then discover from the downward slope that I have come too far, and must return through the barrage. Lose my feeling of elation – get the 'wind up' in fact – imagine every second that I shall have one of those H-E's splattering through my chest. . . get back as fast as the shell-holes will permit. . . drop back at last into my objective 'C' Company's line, near the dug-out I had passed on my way forward. Find 'C', all that is left of them, busy digging out firesteps on the German side of the trench. Feel very weary, but, with the inspiration of a few cuss-words from our platoon officer, soon begin digging a firestep for myself. . . ' [22]

1/8th Argylls' Commanding Officer's battle report confirmed that men were close to the barrage: 'Two of the company officers reported to me that their men halted; one 15 yards from the barrage and the other 20 yards.' [23] There is no condemnation, this simply records over-enthusiasm tempered by self-preservation. He also reported that some of the men threw away their picks or shovels in the excitement of the advance or in the heavy going.

The prevailing lack of communication is evidenced in the 153rd Brigade War Diary at 10.15 a.m:

'152nd Bde report they have the N [orth] end of BH and probably South. They have about 200 prisoners. It seems fairly certain that 7 Gordons are in 2nd and 3rd German trench and possibly 5th Gordon are in Station Road, 6 Black Watch still obscure. Parts of front German line are still held by the Germans. 1 battn. of 154th Bde being sent up as reinforcements. It is decided to bomb out detachments of Germans in front line and try to clear up position of troops.' [24]

All 153rd Brigade's runners were killed or wounded by Germans still holding out in their trenches. [25]

By 10.30 a.m. the 51st was on its main objective (Green Line), but Germans who had been by-passed in the mist, hiding in dug-outs, and those in the south-west ruins of Beaumont-Hamel, caused problems. At 10.30 two tanks were sent to help clear the village but they accumulated so much mud that they stuck on the German front line. A Scottish officer of one of the tanks dismounted his Hotchkiss machine-guns and joined the infantry in consolidating the Green line. [26]

No attempt was made to advance to the fifth objective (Yellow Line) as many of the men tasked for that had been involved in the battle for the fourth objective (Green Line), numbers had been reduced, and the barrage had outstripped the infantry and to advance without it would have invited unnecessary casualties, and predictable failure.

Paul Maze, a French N.C.O. liaising with the British Army, made his way through barbed wire and destroyed trenches to Y Ravine. The visibility was bad and he could hardly see the bottom of the gully. He could hear bombs exploding then found cheery, cigar smoking, loot-laden Scotsmen coming out of a dug-out, who told him that: 'the bastards are still all over the place in between our troops.' Maze went underground and found Highlanders in a small room, some wearing German helmets, which seemed to amuse their prisoners. [27]

On the left of the 51st, 2nd Division wallowed in mud, and lost the barrage, yet some men reached Frankfurt Trench before retiring to Beaumont Trench, where they consolidated. The division was not in touch with the 51st's left. On 2nd Division's left 3rd Division's assault was a disaster. It bogged in the mud, the gaps in the German wire were few, the following battalions got confused with the leading battalions, and the infantry lost the barrage. [28] Some fought their way to the German support line, and others reached the German reserve line, and even the fourth objective (Green Line), but all were driven back or wiped out. By 6.30 am it was clear that no progress could be made and a later decision to press the attack was cancelled. By the end of the day the 3rd Division was back on its start line.

On the left of 3rd Division 31st Division's 92nd Brigade was to protect 3rd Division's flank and two battalions formed a temporary salient, which would be eliminated when the 3rd Division advanced. There being no advance by 3rd Division the men of 31st Division retired, their two battalions short of 800 casualties. [29]

Amongst victorious, happy looters at Beaumont-Hamel was James Rennie, 1/6th Gordons:

> '. . . the Germans had fancy helmets with the spike on it and pajamas. . . we were collecting revolvers and field glasses and spiked helmets and junk like that. We used to take them back and sell them to the non-combatants, like the A.S.C. men.'

Rennie and his friend Jimmy Hope awaited reliefs, and when they arrived, they were given permission to go back.

> '. . . away we went, Hope with his sandbag full of souvenirs and me with my sandbag full of souvenirs. . . We would run a little ways, black dark, you know, darker than hell. And wire and everything there. We would run a little ways and duck. . . I remember I got a bullet through my water bottle and my field dressing . . . I'm laying in a shell hole . . . and finally we take off again. And we're pretty well getting out of range of the smaller guns, but, Jesus, some of them coal boxes come over . . . Dig a hole and put this house into it. So two or three of them came over and we were getting close to the road and they were shelling the road . . . And then the machine-gun bullets are going. . . So finally I get up and run and I says 'To hell with the souvenirs' and drops them and I go down the road. Jimmy Hope, he says, 'Oh, hell, I ditched mine a while back. To hell with it. I'm the only souvenir that counts for anything here.' We finally got back, minus the souvenirs.' [30]

At the end of the day 'B' Company 1/8th Royal Scots 'went up to consolidate GREEN Line – East of BEAUMONT HAMEL' and in the night 'one platoon of 'A' Coy went up to consolidate the GREEN Line with 1/1 Field Coy: 2 platoons of 'C' Coy.' [31]

Although it had been planned to attack the Yellow Line on the 13th

Private James Rennie

it was decided to attack it at 5.45 a.m. on the 14th. 1/7th Argylls, who had been sent up on the 13th to reinforce 152nd Brigade, misinterpreted a message on a bad telephone line and thought that the attack had been cancelled: it was merely postponed and when they did bomb their way into Munich Trench, they were too exposed in its flattened remnants, and pulled back to Leave Alley. [32]

Two platoons of 1/8th Royal Scots had been sent forward to consolidate Munich Trench. Finding it occupied by the enemy 'Capt. Mitchell therefore decided to dig a new trench about 200 yards west of MUNICH Trench. . . CAPT. MITCHELL received word that this trench would be used as a 'jumping-off' place by the attacking troops the following morning. Instead of cutting a fire step, therefore, he cut steps up over the parapet.' [33] 1/9th Royal Scots noted that 'in co-operation with 8th Royal Scots and 7th A & S Hdrs he (Captain Cowan) dug the 'NEW MUNICH TRENCH' and remained there, occupying it with his company until the following morning.' [34] Bewsher attributed the new trench to 2/2 Highland Field Company and one company of the 1/8th Royal Scots.[35] Regardless of whether a captain of the 1/8th or 1/9th Royal Scots initiated the trench, a lot of urgent collective effort was displayed.

At 9 a.m. on the 15th an attack on Munich and Frankfurt Trenchs took place in co-operation with the 2nd Division, which was on the left and 500 yards behind the two companies of 1/7th Argylls that attacked from New Munich Trench. The barrage moved at fifty yard lifts and 1/7th Argylls noted:

> 'The artillery barrage opened short and fell on our jumping off trench but despite that the Coys advanced meeting with heavy bombing and M.G. fire. They advanced across MUNICH TRENCH and some bombers and part of 'D' coy entered FRANKFURT TRENCH and proceeded to bomb outwards. They bombed two dug-outs full of Germans and killed many others but as the attacks on the right and left had failed they got no support and eventually had to retire, our Lewis Guns, covering this movement. We consolidated the NEW MUNICH TRENCH which was still the most advanced part of the British line.' [36]

Harper's response to a Corps enquiry laid some blame on the 1/7th Argylls, before attacking the artillery plan:

> 'The failure of the attack of the 51st Division was undoubtedly due to the impetuosity of the attacking troops. They had previously been trained to watch and keep close under the barrage.' [Then Harper justified them:] 'At the same time they had been trained in 100 yard lifts as the normal, and it was this 50 yard lift arranged as stated in para. 5 to agree with the 2nd Division which was the cause of the trouble.' [37]

In this response Harper told Corps that even if the 51st had captured Frankfurt Trench its success would only have possible had the 2nd Division been alongside the 51st when the attack took place. He suggested that joint command of the forces committed would have been helpful. 2nd Division's two battalions on the left got lost in the mist, ended up behind 1/7th Argylls, then fell back to Wagon Road, having suffered heavy casualties.

Fifth Army responded to Harper's note on 18th November by recognising that their orders had put too much onto the divisional commanders and did 'not exercise sufficient control over the operation' and that it 'would probably have been better to have given the divisions a definite hour for reaching and leaving the intermediate objective. The action of artillery and infantry would then have been co-ordinated from Corps headquarters.' The same failure to control battles at Corps and Army existed in November as it had at High Wood in July, although there appears to be a slow dawning that Corps ought to control the artillery and battles more closely. In a pompous response to Harper's remarks on the yardage of the artillery lifts V Corps wrote:

> 'it is not clear why the infantry should have been <u>trained</u> to think that 100 yd lifts are normal. It is only necessary for the infantry to know that they are to keep close to the barrage; they need not worry about timings. Nothing has ever been <u>laid down</u> about 100 yard lifts, although they may have been found to be convenient in most cases.'

Is Harper being criticised for training his men? 'They need not have to worry about timings' speaks volumes of some individual's attitude to the infantry. Fifth Army then asked by whom the artillery 50 yards lifts were ordered. The signatory of the document wondered if this was a V Corps order – Corps did not know. [38]

The 51st held the line until 17th November and provided fatigue parties, salvaged, and buried the dead. The 51st had requested V Corps that a:

> 'special burial party to be attached to the Division . . . As this was not forthcoming, 154th Infantry Brigade detailed a party of 2 officers and 100 other ranks from 1/4th Bn. Gordon Highlanders. . . on the 14th inst most of this party were employed by A.D.M.S carrying wounded from the battlefield. The remainder commenced burying bodies at 'Y' Ravine, where three small cemeteries had to be established, owing to the difficulty of carrying bodies through very thick (mud) under shell fire. . . Bodies were collected and carried on the AUCHONVILLERS-BEAUMONT HAMEL Road and Light

Railway, and thence conveyed by transport and trucks back to AUCHONVILLERS and MAILLY Military Cemeteries, where trenches had been dug in readiness. . . The Brigade holding BEAUMONT HAMEL supplied two parties per day of 1 officer and 20 other ranks to work in conjunction with the Divisional Burial Party.' [39]

Often men buried their own companions or close relatives. Amongst those buried at Maillet Wood was Sniper Sandy, Alexander MacDonald, 32, of 1/5th Seaforths. Nineteen years old 2nd Lieutenant Norman Collins, 1/6th Seaforths, was in charge of a burial party. Having buried their own dead at Maillet his party was detailed to clear the men who had died on the 1st of July, which was an extremely unpleasant task. [40] They were: 'sprinkled with quick lime and buried on the battlefield as it was impossible to remove them for burial.' [41]

'The flesh had been devoured from the bones by rats, which swarmed in thousands, and made their homes in the empty trunks. Six hundred and ninety six of these skeletons were buried on the front of the 152nd Brigade alone.' [42]

On the 15th Rorie, of 1/2nd Highland Field Ambulance, explored a German dug-out:

'On descending about forty steps one was in a large floored and timbered chamber some fifty feet long; and at the further end a second set of steps led to a similar chamber, one side of each being lined with a double layer of bunks filled with dead and wounded Germans, the majority of whom had become casualties early on the morning of the 13th. The place was, of course, in utter darkness; and, when we flashed our lights on and the wounded saw our escorts with rifles ready, there was an outbreak of 'Kamarad!' while a big bevy of rats squeaked and scuttled away from their feast on the dead bodies on the floor. The stench was indescribably abominable: for many of the cases were gas gangerous. Any food or drink they had possessed was used up, and our water bottles were soon emptied amongst them.' [43]

Officers and N.C.O.s struggled to account for their men:

'From O.C. A Coy.
To Adjutant 1/8th A&SHdrs.
Reference attached.
2754 Pte. MacArthur C. of the same platoon states that on the
morning of the 13th Nov. 2794 Pte.Sinclair D.* was shot
through the right temple while speaking to him. This occurred
in the enemy front line and he is certainly dead.
3403 Pte.Grubb F. corroborates this statement.' [44]

The immediate post-battle return gave the casualties as: officers 30
kia, 78 wounded, 3 missing: men: 494 kia, 1381 wounded, 194 missing, a
total of 2,180. [45] Bewsher's total was 123 officers and 2355 other ranks
killed, wounded or missing. [46] and the Official History states nearly 2,200
officers and men. The 2nd Division, on the 51st's immediate left, lost
nearly 3,000 men, and gained little ground, and the 3rd Division, to its
left, lost 2,400, for no gain. [47]

The enemy on the 51st's front was the 12th Division. A German
enquiry, rightly, attributed the defeat in part to the false sense of security
generated by the numerous days of bombardment without attacks, the
mist, which made accurate German artillery fire difficult, and the quality
of the 12th Division, which was deemed to be unreliable, and allowed
itself to be surprised. The divisional commander had not taken a grip
on the battle and German First Army headquarters had taken control of
it. [48] The accusation that the defenders were taken by surprise has to be
balanced against the closeness with which elements of the 51st followed
the barrage into the German trenches. The 12th Division was recruited
from Polish Silesia, and there may have undertones of racism in the
scapegoating.

The 153rd Brigade's assessment concluded that: 'the mist on the
whole helped the attack', that 'zero hour was too early and the darkness
caused loss of direction', that 'the bombardment over a long period
undoubtedly deceived the enemy and he had given up expecting an
attack', that 'the front of our attack was too extended for the number of
men available. . . and if the element of surprise had been lacking the
attack might easily have failed'. The summary said that: 'all reports testify
to the accuracy of our artillery fire: also to the effectiveness of our

machine-gun barrage at the beginning of the action.' Communications had been difficult: 'Up to 12.40 p.m. there was a complete lack of information owing to so many runners being killed by snipers left in portions of the German line'. 'Y ravine was a much more serious obstacle than was anticipated, and its capture reflects great credit on the troops.'

The brigadier ended the report by writing: 'the success of the operation was due mainly to the determination, courage and resource of the Regimental officers and men. It was a soldiers' battle throughout . . .' [49]

The V Corps Commander, Lieutenant General Fanshawe wrote:

'It is evident from the newspapers that all the world looks on Beaumont-Hamel as one of the greatest feats of arms in the war, and to those who know the ground it must ever be a marvelously fine performance.' [50]

Harper, speaking in 1922 said:

'Here was a fortress defended by every artifice of which the Boche was a past master. It had several lines of defence connected by subterranean tunnels, and each line defended by several belts of barbed wire. When the Division proceeded there the place had been attacked on at least two occasions, and it still remained intact. When I went to those Divisions that had attacked in order to try to get some tips, I was told, 'You have not a dog's chance.' As you know it rained continuously for several days before 13th November. In fact we carried out a raid two or three days before, and the men were so involved in the mud that they could not get on and could scarcely get back. Yet Beaumont Hamel was taken, you might say, with almost automatic precision. We took nearly 3,000 prisoners and that in spite of very little progress being made on our left. This was the same Division that had fought bravely at Festubert. It had taken over the Labyrinthe from the French, which was really over a Boche mine-field, for mines were blown up practically every night. And yet it lost hardly a single trench. It was the same Division that had fought at High Wood on the Somme with great loss. The reason was that everywhere else we were pitchforked into other people's battles, whereas at Beaumont Hamel the Division was able to prepare and fight its battle in its own way.' [51]

An anonymous survivor of the battle is alleged to have summed it all up: 'Onywey, they winna ca' us 'Harper's Duds' noo.' [52] The 51st had made its reputation as an élite division, a reputation for which it would pay a heavy price.

The 51st garrisoned the line until it was relieved by the 7th Division on 24th November. The much depleted division was billeted in the area Arquéves-Rancheval-Hedauville-Varennes-Forceville-Léalvillers until 25th November, when 153rd Brigade marched to Ovillers Huts, followed by 154th moving next day to Aveluy, and 152nd to Bouzincourt and Senlis.

On 27th November 153rd Brigade took over Courcelette from the Canadians, who had captured it. The Germans overlooked the British and safe movement could only take place at night. The land was so featurless and devoid of formal trenches and wire entanglements that both sides' runners and ration parties sometimes strayed into each other's lines. The dead and litter of the Somme battles were scattered across the swampy landscape, and ropes were issued as trench stores, to hoist trapped men from the mud. The front line was a succession of watery shell-holes, some of which were linked by the remains of trenches. There were no communication trenches and duckboard tracks were laid across the waste land to enable the men to reach the front.

On 30th November Sapper William Fraser, 401 Field Company, R.E., 'went out to Courcelette to make road' and expanded on his diary entry after the war:

> 'Our duty was an attempt to construct roads to the front, but in the end we were baffled. The ground was honeycombed with shell craters up to twenty feet deep and full of water and as we made the roads the transport slipped off them and hundreds of horses and men were drowned. . . We spent Xmas and New Year in this terrible place.' [53]

For 1/6th Black Watch:

> '. . . the trenches were mere pits often waist deep in mud, into which the men sank, their boots sometimes sucked off by the wet clay. It was impossible to get hot food up to the front line – and it was equally out of the question to change socks in these

mud holes. Only those who went through this particular experience can have any idea of the misery of it, and it was of but a slight consolation to know that the Germans, a hundred yards in front, were in the same plight.' [54]

The men could not stand up in case they were shot. The duckboards and boxes on which they stood or sat frequently submerged, and there were no latrines. The men in the reserve line had access to a few dug-outs, and the reserve battalions occupied rudimentary shelters which were useless against shells. The field artillery sank in the mud and shells were brought by pack-horses, which could only carry eight rounds. The gun pits had to be constantly baled out. Depleted and physically and emotionally exhausted by Beaumont-Hamel, resistance was low, and illness flourished.

'Old wounds reopened, as they did in the days of scurvy. In December dysentery appeared. The wastage amongst troops became serious, and a general air of depression settled down over the Division. In fact, General Harper once confessed that he had never seen a man smile east of Pozières.' [55]

On 28th December 1916 Harry Lauder's son, Captain John Lauder, 1/8th Argylls was killed. There has been controversy about this death and it was suggested that he was shot by his own men. A veteran of the 1/8th Argylls was asked by his nephew, a Scottish author, if the rumour was true and: 'he said nothing and just looked at the ground.' [56] This account was not supported by letters received by Harry Lauder from officers of 1/8th Argylls. [57]

By 6th January 1917 1/6th Black Watch:

'had dwindled to 17 officers and 426 other ranks. . . the two companies in the front line [were brought up to] a strength of fifty each; thus one hundred men held over a thousand yards of line, the fighting strength of the Battalion being under two hundred rifles. . . Illness rheumatism and trench foot brought on by being for days under wet, sodden conditions had caused more losses than were suffered by the Battalion in the Battle of Beaumont Hamel.' [58]

Behind the lines sappers and pioneers laboured to improve living conditions and communications. 1st January 1917 1/8th Royal Scots' war diary summarised the previous days' labour. 'C' company was at work on a light railway,

'the ground over which it was laid was nothing more or less than a succession of shell holes full to the lip with water. This part of the line is about 3000 yds in length and since its completion has proved very serviceable as a means of getting material and stores of all sorts forward to a point which cannot be got to by horse or motor transport. It is calculated that 20 Tons go forward every day.'

'B' Company was constructing 16 man shelters in the banks of sunken roads, and had been repairing a road which 'was very much broken up by shell fire and has still to be repaired almost daily on this account... a log road is being made towards COURCELETTE.' 'D' Company erected huts at both divisional and brigade headquarters then were allocated the cutting and drainage of a communication trench, which was 'finally given up by order of the division.' Detached parties of the battalion were digging dugouts for gunners, machine-gunners and the RAMC, and 24 men were at a Royal Engineers sawmill. [59] The army struggled to overcome near impossible conditions. A kitchen was set up near the front line brigade's headquarters, dispensing hot soup to reliefs going up or down the line and to working parties. It was shelled on most days, repaired by working parties, and carried on. The master chef was an old Hussar who 'made no complaints. His services to the Division on this, and, indeed, many other occasions were invaluable.' [60]

Normally men cooked on coke braziers or makeshift fires, which were impossible at Courcelette, so they survived on biscuits, cold tinned meat and water. Hot food containers could not be carried through the mud, and eventually Tommy cookers, which burned solidified alcohol smokelessly, were issued to heat the tinned rations. There were insufficient of these so 1/6th Gordons' Quartermaster created his own flammable mixture of rendered fat, paraffin, dubbin and scraps of sandbags and four by two (rifle cleaning cloth), which was issued in tins and enabled the Gordons to brew two cups of tea per day. 1/6th Gordons suffered half the cases of frost bite endured by other units in the Brigade by supplying dry socks and whale oil every night. Rubbed on the feet the whale oil was reputed to prevent trench foot. [61] Thigh length rubber boots did not go well with the kilt, for their upper edges chafed the tops of the men's bare thighs, causing sores which rapidly became infected, and prolonged wearing of rubber boots softened the feet and trench foot ensued. Kilts were temporarily abandoned in favour of 6,000 pairs of trousers. [62]

The men were so debilitated by front line duty that the time spent there was reduced from 5-7 days to 2, with a day of complete rest before and after being in the front line. Buses came to Pozières to transport the men to their shelters. Muddy, unshaven, exhausted, chilled and sodden, some would collapse at the roadside in the rain and instantly fall asleep. When the 51st handed over to the 2nd Division, on 12th January, duckboard tracks had been laid, shelters existed for reserve battalions, one belt of wire had been erected at the front, salvage had been collected and most of the dead had been cleared away. Bewsher believed: 'That the sickness and wastage was not greater, and that the whole conditions of life materially improved, was mainly due to the enterprise, energy and endurance of the three field companies and the 8th Royal Scots.' [63]

The 51st moved to Marieux/Beauquesne/Puchvillers/Rubempré then marched via Bernaville and St. Riquier to Buigny-St. Maclou, near Abbeville. The accommodation was poor, there were few training areas and it was the coldest winter of the war, with temperatures as low as minus 24 degrees.

1/4th Seaforths' 'billets were in ramshackle clay and straw walled barns through which the cold winds found a ready passage. . . the buildings would have been ideal summer quarters but they provided little shelter from the severities of winter. But the men were too pleased to be out of the line for a time to be discontented. They were, in fact, supremely happy. Early in the morning when a bitter wind was blowing and the thermometer was below zero, you would see them going to the nearest pond or streamlet and, stripped to the waist, wash as cheerfully as if they were in the heat of summer.'

The New Year's dinners to companies were served in the neighbouring village of Le Crotoy on 30th January and the Officers entertained General Harper, Brigadier-General Hamilton and Officers of the Divisional and Brigade staffs and of the 7th Argyll and Sutherland Highlanders.

All through this time, the cold remained intense. 'The estuary of the Somme was packed with great blocks of ice and might have been the Arctic Ocean itself, but the icicles on the Sergeant-Major's moustache attracted even more attention from the men.' [64] 1/7th Argylls were in some discomfort as 'fully eighty percent suffered from severe chilblains on the knees.' [65]

The 51st marched for six days from these billets to Maroeuil, Ecoivres, Bethonsart, Acq and Frevillers, west of Vimy Ridge, where they had been stationed in the Spring of 1916. The marching conditions were appalling, with icy roads which slowed up the troops, the transport, and the field kitchens, and made finding a warm place to rest overnight virtually impossible. The 1/4th Seaforths had some good luck which 'brought us to easy distance of the only colliery working in France. Fuel was at a low ebb but the Quartermaster and Interpreter took a lorry and returned with it full of coal, and so solved the fuel problem for the battalion. But the colliery was an interesting commentary on the condition of things. It was crowded with limousine cars, taxis from Paris, farm wagons and every kind and description of vehicle.' [66]

NOTES

1. Mackintosh. *War The Liberator, Beaumont-Hamel. November 16th, 1916 p.* 26/Campbell and Green pp.168-169
2. L/Cpl A Thomson 2399 D Company 1/4th Seaforths Letter. 10.10.1916 Museum nan Eilean, Stornoway.
3. Miles 1916 v. 2 p.478 footnote.
4. Miles 1916 v.2 p.478.
5. Bewsher p.100.
6. Bewsher p.107.
7. Bewsher p.104.
8. War diary 1/8th Royal Scots 1,2,3.11.1916.

9. Bewsher p.105.

10. War diary 1/4th Gordons 8-12.11.1916.

11. War diary 1/8th Royal Scots 10,11.11.1916.

12. Private Wrench 13.11.1916.

13. War diary 153rd Brigade 23.10.1916 Operational Order No.149 WO 95/2871 TNA.

14. Bewsher p.110.

15. War diary 51st Division 1.11.1916 to 30.11.1916. TNA.

16. Wauchope v2 p.151.

17. James Rennie recollections and David Tattersfield Stand To! Western Front Association: August/September 2008 p.12.

18. Miles 1916 v. 2 p.479.

19. Bewsher p.114

20. Sutherland p.86. (A 1/6th Seaforths' party, 'much reduced in numbers was obliged to hand over its prisoners to a contingent of the 10th Royal Dublin Fusiliers.' Miles 1916 v.2. Footnote p.493. Could this be the incident to which Sutherland refers? 10th Royal Dublin Fusiliers were in the 63rd Division.)

21. Wauchope v.2 pp.150-152

22. *At Beaumont-Hamel with the 8th Argylls* Anon. Doc 16062 A&SH RHQ.

23. Report CO 1/8th Argylls 18.11.1916 A&SH RHQ.

24. War diary 153rd Brigade 13.11.1916 10.15 a.m.

25. Bewsher p.116.

26. Bewsher p.117.

27. Paul Maze. *A Frenchman in Khaki* (Printed and bound by Antony Rowe Ltd) pp.194-8.

28 Miles 1916 v.2 p.498.

29. Miles 1916 v.2 p.501.

30. Rennie recollections.

31. War diary 1/8th Royal Scots night of 14-15.11.1916.

32. Bewsher p.118.

33. War diary 1/8th Royal Scots 14.11.1916.

34. War diary 1/9th Royal Scots 14.11.1916.

35. Bewsher p.118.

36. War diary 1/7th A&SH 15.11.1916.

37. Harper to Corps 18th November 1916 TNA.

38. Fifth Army to V Corps 25.11.16 S.G. 72/86 ref 51st Division, pp.1-2 TNA.

39. 51st Div General Staff report on arrangements for clearing battlefield. TNA.

40. Norman Collins, Ed. Richard van Emden *Last Man Standing*. (Pen and Sword) 2002 p.108.

41. 51st Div. General Staff report on arrangements for clearing the battlefield TNA.

42. Bewsher p.124.

43. Rorie p.113.

44. 1/8th Argylls' file A&SH RHQ.

45. Casualties to units of 51st (High) Division during operations 13th to 17th November, 1916. TNA.

46. Bewsher p.123

47. Miles OH 1916 v 2 footnotes pp.512- 513.

48. Duffy p.259-260.

49. Brigadier-General Campbell commanding 153rd Bde 20.11.1916 TNA.

50. Bewsher p.125.

51. Rorie pp.104-105.

52. Bewsher p.126.

53. Lance-Corporal William Milton Fraser, 2/2nd Highland Field Company/ 401 Field Company R.E. Diary 30.11.1916 and recollections.

54. Wauchope p.154.

55. Bewsher p.129)

56. Lorn MacIntyre (telephone call with the author 2007)

57. Trevor Royle, *The Flowers of the Forest* Birlinn 2006 p.111

58. Wauchope p.156.

59. War diary 1/8th Royal Scots 1.1.1917

60. Bewsher pp.131-2

61. MacKenzie p.207

62. Bewsher p.131

63. Bewsher p.135.

64. Unknown author 1/4th Seaforths QOH RHQ records.

65. Morrison p.26.

66. Unknown author 1/4th Seaforths Q.O.H. RHQ records.

see also Arras guide map on page 40

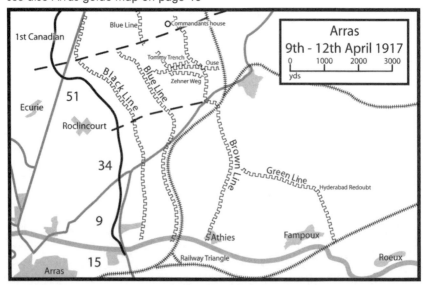

Chapter 5

ATTRITION
Arras and Roeux

The steady grim despairing ranks,
The courage and the pain.
The bodies of my friends that lie
Unburied in the dew.'[1]

A Spring offensive was being planned when the 51st relieved the 9th (Scottish) Division on 11th February 1917 near Roclincourt. Haig and Joffre had agreed that the German salient, between the Ancre and the Scarpe, would be attacked by the British at Arras and by the French east of Soissons. On the British right Gough's Fifth Army would attack on the Ancre and on its left, the assault would be by the Third and First Armies. The capture of Vimy Ridge would allow the British to overlook the Lens-Douai plain, and reduce the likelihood of a successful German attack on Arras.

On 22nd February 1917, whilst these plans were being laid, the Germans began to withdraw to the Hindenberg Line, which they had been preparing all winter. Rear-guards, booby traps, delayed action mines, trees felled across roads and blown bridges slowed the tentative Allied pursuit. The Germans reduced their front by 25 miles, [2] saved 13 or 14 divisions and shortened their lines of communication. An outpost zone about 600 yards deep faced the Allies, behind which was the Hindenberg Line, sited on the rear of slopes, with concrete dug-outs and triple barbed wire defences, each ten to fifteen yards deep. Telephone cable was buried, light railways laid and an infrastructure of supply and reinforcement was established.

The British attack on 9th April was designed to divert German troops from the French front, where Joffre had been replaced by Nivelle, who would launch his war-winning attack on 16th April.

121

The Third and First Armies were to attack from Croisilles, east south east of Arras to Givenchy, at the north west end of Vimy Ridge. The Third Army, from right to left: VII Corps; VI Corps; XVII Corps (4th, 9th, 34th and 51st Divisions); the First Army: Canadian and I Corps. 44 out of the 120 infantry battalions committed (36.6%) were Scottish (12 each in 15th and 51st; 9, including the South African Scottish in the 9th; 6, including 4 Tyneside Scottish in the 34th; 3 in the 3rd; one in the 30th and 1/1 London Scottish in the 56th.[3] Even allowing for a percentage of these battalions not being Scottish born, this was an over-representation that contributed to Scotland's loss of 3.1% of its adult male population in the war against the rest of Britain and Ireland's 1.6%. Of those mobilised Scotland had 26.4% killed against the rest of Britain and Ireland's 11.8%.[4]

Experience had taught the need to retain a cadre, a minimum reserve, around which to reconstruct battalions after a battle. Either the C.O. or Second in Command, Company Commanders or their Second in Command, were to be left behind: not more than two company officers, and not more than 20 officers per battalion, excluding the Medical Officer were to be committed to the attack. In each battalion 2 company sergeant majors, 10 signallers, 12 runners, 1 gas, 1 bombing, 2 Lewis Gun, and 3 other instructors (e.g in dug-out construction) were to stay behind. In each company a sergeant, a corporal and a lance corporal, and in each platoon a rifle bomber, a scout/sniper and two Lewis Gunners were to be left behind. If a battalion was at full strength, 108 men would be in reserve. [5]

Ancient caves and passages spreading east from Arras had been extended by tunneling companies to house large numbers of troops, allowing them to emerge near or in the front line, without the risks of moving through trenches. There were underground generating stations, a light railway, cooking and medical facilities. The weather on Easter Monday, 9th April, 1917, was bad. The night had been cold, and snow, sleet and rain fell on the waiting troops. In the assembly trenches they were miserable and cold, and in some they were knee-deep in liquid mud.

On the right the VII Corps' left hand divisions, the 56th and 14th, made nearly two miles progress. By the end of the day the right and centre divisions of VI Corps, the 3rd and 12th Divisions, had advanced two miles, whereas 15th (Scottish) on the left had advanced nearly three. XVII Corps was north of the River Scarpe with 9th (Scottish) Division on its right: it reached all its objectives, allowing 4th Division to pass through it and take Fampoux and the Hyderabad Redoubt, three and a half miles from the start line. The Germans were in disarray and it was realised that cavalry could have exploited the situation, but the cavalry were too far back, and the chance was lost. [6] 34th Division was in the centre, and succeeded on its right and centre. On its left its 103rd Brigade took their first objective easily but when the leapfrogging troops went through towards the second objective 'they were disorganised by troops of the 51st Division first crossing its front and then falling back through it.' [7] By the end of the day the left of 34th Division had not passed the Blue Line.

The 51st's task was complicated: on its right, a rightwards shift to the flank was required to capture the first objective (Black Line) and on the left, its second objective (Blue Line) did not correspond with the Canadians' Blue Line 'so that the left of the 51st Division would have, by a separate operation, to swing up in order to link with it'.[8] Although the Official History states that there were no tanks allocated to the 51st [9] Bewsher asserted that two tanks allocated to assist the 51st were out of action and never reached the leading infantry. [10]

On the right 152nd Brigade attacked with 1/6th Gordons on its right and 1/6th Seaforths on its left, and despite heavy casualties both battalions took the Black Line. Passing through these battalions to attack the Blue Line 1/8th Argylls and 1/5th Seaforths were delayed by machine-gun fire and lost the barrage. 1/8th Argylls then withdrew its first wave to the New Black Line, delaying the eventual capture of the Blue Line. By the end of the day these battalions were halfway between the Blue and Brown Lines.

On the left, 154th Brigade's attack was led by 1/9th Royal Scots and at 5.30 a.m.:

> 'The barrage opened and the Battn. attacked and by 7.30 a.m. had captured its objective, touch being kept with 4th Seaforth

Hrs. on left and 6th Seaforth Hrs on right. The line was consolidated and carrying parties organised to take SAA [small arms ammunition] and other stores to BLUE LINE which had been taken at 8.30 a.m.' [11]

1/4th Seaforths, on the left of 154th Brigade, emerged from tunnels and took the German front line without difficulty:

> 'but heavy fighting occurred further on and in C.T.s (commun-
> ication trenches). Two platoons detailed for this operation
> proved insufficient and the remaining two platoons were led
> forward by their Officers. About 50 Germans had collected in an
> area which was out of the barrage table and fought hard till the
> Canadians worked round their rear. Two officers and 11 men
> were killed at this point.' [12]

This was in the Labyrinthe, familiar to the 51st in 1916.

Passing through the first wave, 1/7th Argylls and 1/4th Gordons took the Blue Line, but failed to attain the Brown Line. Reports show how protective authors and diarists were of their own people. Bewsher did not identify the battalion which erred, but wrote: 'that the officer of the 154th Brigade who had reported he was holding the Brown line was really in Tommy Trench, several hundred yards west of the Brown line, which was still occupied by the enemy.' [13]

Harper's account identifies the battalion which made the mistake, but does not name it:

> 'The right Battalion of this Brigade were not so fortunate, as
> they were held up by Machine Gun fire and lost the barrage.
> Despite this hostile fire they pushed on, but swung round to
> the right with the result that when they reached the BLUE
> LINE they found that they were occupying some of the
> frontage of the 152nd Brigade. This left a gap between them
> and the left battalion, but this was taken a little later by two
> companies of the 153rd Brigade who were coming up in rear
> to consolidate the BROWN LINE which formed the final
> objective.' [14]

1/7th Argylls had drifted to the right, thinking that they were crossing two subsidiary support lines and settled in the third, believing it to be the Brown Line, the Point du Jour line. [15] Their history made no reference to the loss of direction but says that: 'the system of the enemy's trenches there was very elaborate, and because of the damage done to them by our guns, definite locations could be identified only with great difficulty.'[16]

Private Wrench, 1/4th Seaforths, runner for 154th Brigade H.Q., touched on the conditions which made navigation difficult on the 9th:

'But as usual the rain and sleet is coming down in lumps and it is so difficult to get in touch with the battalions in their new positions. The tape lines are already broken with shells or buried in the mud and landmarks are nil. What an unholy mess.' [17]

1/7th Argylls' war diary indicates the reason for its C and D companies' deviation: when it had crossed the Blue Line,

'near the top of the hill they found the 152nd Brigade on their right were held up near the BLUE LINE and our companies experienced very heavy machine gun and rifle fire from the direction of ZEHNER WEG. They swung round attacked and captured three lines of trenches there taking two machine guns and some 70 prisoners including one Regimental Commander and all his staff.' [18]

1/4th Gordons, on their left, who had to keep in contact with the Canadians, sent their A and C companies to help their B and C companies take the Blue Line. Having done that these two companies swung too far to the right, except for one platoon which 'managed to keep direction however and under 2/Lt.Gauld reached objective on BROWN Line and established connection with Canadians on the left. The 7th A & SH on our right were responsible for direction. They lost direction however and pushed on to ZEHNER WEG (in 152 Brigade area) C Coy and 3 platoons of A Coy following.' [19] 1/4th Gordons rightly blamed 1/7th Argylls, but were guilty of a rightwards drift themselves.

This error created a gap, and left the Canadians' right flank in the air: 2nd Lt. Gauld subsequently rejoined his own battalion, and enlarged the gap: meanwhile Lieutenant MacNaughton, 153rd Machine Gun Company, reached the Brown Line on the 9th with two machine-gun teams, and only withdrew early on the 10th when Germans started to re-occupy it. [20]

1/7th Argylls war diary for the 10th begins: 'The 4th Gordons on our left had lost touch with the CANADIANS on the left and patrols found our BROWN LINE objective . . . to be strongly held by the enemy.'[21] Was this an attempt to divert attention from 1/7th Argylls' misdirection, or simply an admission that they now knew that they were not in the Brown Line? Private Wrench's diary for 10th April highlighted the lost opportunity:

> '. . . all over the new front with Capt. Durie (B.M.) [Brigade Major] today. . . two officers of the 4th Gordons joined us there. . . It was the 7th Argylls held up at this place yesterday and in trying to get around the position went off their objective, thereby leaving a gap in the line just over the ridge. This was the cause of the advance not sweeping right down all the way to Gavrelle which was according to plan. However, we four went on a regular tour of investigation of these very trenches still held by Fritz though we did not see a soul anywhere. Then we got out on top and a rifle bullet spat past us. Then another as we ducked into a shell hole. Now the rookie officer had to show how brave he was and got out on top to have a shot at anything or nothing at all in response, and in the direction from which the their shots came, 20 or 30 yards away. The damned fool was only asking for trouble and he nearly got it too.' [The Gordons' officers left them and Durie and Wrench dodged bullets until they found cover in the sunken road to Thélus, near the Commandant's House.]

> 'The dead are lying everywhere mercilessly butchered and there isn't a single person in all the world who can be held to blame. One young fellow of the Seaforths is stretched out as if he had just lain down to rest. Another head is completely battered in with the butt of a rifle. One other has his helmet broken and embedded in his skull, and in another place a Seaforth and a German are lying dead together with their fingers locked around each other's throat. Dead are also down

in the shell holes in positions too awful to mention. Some are only visible beneath the water and sometimes a pair of heels can be seen projecting from others.' [22]

1/7th Argylls' navigational error has been attributed to the loss of all its best officers, and insufficient briefing of all the officers, [23] yet their war diary notes only the chaplain wounded (but remaining on duty) on the 8th, three officers wounded on the 9th, and one wounded and missing on the 10th. [24] The 51st was accused of bad staff work, and it was suggested that Harper refused to admit an error.[25]

Harper noted: 'On the morning of the 10th, the 154th Brigade were able to correctly establish their position with the result that a report was received stating that they did not hold the BROWN LINE but occupied TOMMY TRENCH in mistake for it.' [26] This indicates bad or non-existent communications between 1/7th Argylls and 154th Brigade, exacerbated by the battlefield conditions and the hazards faced by runners carrying messages, who would be directed from Brigade HQ to seek 1/7th Argylls on the Brown Line, not in Tommy Trench.

Other units had strayed on 9th April. Lieutenant Colonel Croft, 11th Royal Scots, 9th (Scottish) Division:

'When our turn came to cross No-Man's-Land we found the most appalling mix-up of the division. Even at that early hour there were Highlanders [of the 9th's Highland Brigade – author's note] who had wandered on my left, and also South Africans. Most of my people were too much to the right, and it was all that one could do to get them back into their proper place in time for the advance on our second objective.' [27]

On the left of the 51st 1st, 2nd, 3rd and 4th Canadian Divisions, the Canadian Corps, attacked the main summit of Vimy Ridge. 1st Canadian achieved its objectives, but its right flank was exposed by the 51st's meanderings. 2nd and 3rd Canadian divisions both attained theirs, but the Corps' left flank was threatened by 4th Canadian's problems at Hill 145, where the C.O. of 87th Battalion C.E.F. had decided not to have his battalion's first objective shelled, in order to capture it undamaged. [28]

Machine-gun fire wiped out half his battalion, and suppressed the supporting 75th Battalion C.E.F. The Canadians did not take Hill 145 until the afternoon of the 10th, and the Pimple, which was to be taken after the capture of Hill 145, did not fall until the 12th.

On the 10th, on the right of the 51st, 1/5th Gordons, in co-operation with 34th Division on their right, attacked and took the Brown Line. When Harper learned at 10.30 a.m. that 1/7th Argylls had not taken the Brown Line he ordered them to take it but their attempts to bomb up Tommy and Ouse trenches failed because the Germans had reoccupied that sector of the Brown Line. The ever aware Private Wrench noted: 'The Argylls made three unsuccessful attempts to occupy that gap in the line (yesterday, 10th) even tho' we went through it unchallenged.' [29]

On the 11th the heavy artillery pounded the wire protecting the Brown Line, preceding an attack by a 1/7th Argylls' company, 1/9th Royal Scots and a 1/4th Gordons' company. When the barrage lifted at 5 a.m. patrols found that the Germans had gone. By 5.45 pm 1/9th Royal Scots had begun consolidating it and had contacted 1/7th Argylls on their right and the 1/4th Gordons on their left. [30] On the night of the 11/12th the 51st was relieved by 2nd Division.

Harper had departed from the Corps' order to use three brigades in the attack: he had deployed two brigades, each reinforced by a battalion from the third brigade. Whether this was a factor in the 51st's troubles is open to debate. The 51st's battle was not an unqualified success. The gap that it created on the Canadian 1st Division's flank hindered uniform success on the northern sector of the front, but the fact that the 51st's Blue Line objective and the Canadians' New Blue Line objectives were not continuous raises questions of planning and co-ordination above divisional level. The Canadian debacle on Hill 145, caused by forfeiting artillery support, was less forgivable than 1/7th Argylls' slow realisation of their true whereabouts, and the consequences created a longer delay in accomplishing the final objectives (the Pimple) than occurred on the 51st's front. The failure to exploit the success of the 9th and 4th Divisions was to have more serious consequences than all of the above, as it allowed the Germans to consolidate their line, and presaged the miserable months of April and May.

On 2nd May 1917 Harper congratulated 48 N.C.O.s and men who had been awarded the Military Medal for bravery on 9th to 11th April. Under a column headed 'Regiments' the numbers of their battalions were absent: the awards were shared by (The Sutherland and Caithness Highland) Seaforth Highlanders, (Morayshire) Seaforth Highlanders, (Banff and Donside) The Gordon Highlanders, and (The Argyllshire) Argyll and Sutherland Highlanders. [31] This recognised and reinforced the strong sense of local identity which characterised the Highland battalions. The 51st's first V.C. had been won by No.645112 Sjt. William Gosling, R.F.A:

Sgt. William Gosling

'For most conspicuous bravery when in charge of a heavy trench mortar. Owing to a faulty cartridge the bomb after discharge fell 10 yards from the mortar. Sjt. Gosling sprang out, lifted the nose of the bomb, which had sunk into the ground, unscrewed the fuze and threw it on the ground, where it immediately exploded.

This very gallant and prompt action undoubtedly saved the lives of the whole detachment.' [32]

(Sergeant Gosling had joined the 3rd Wessex Brigade R.F.A. in 1914. In 1917 he was serving in the 51st Divisional Ammunition Column, resupplying the mortars, when he won his V.C. The *Daily Sketch* in 1964 reported that former Sergeant Charles Fou(w)ler of Sevenoaks claimed that another man and Gosling had tossed a coin as to who would deal with the live fuse – Gosling lost the toss – and won a V.C. [33] After the war Gosling tenanted a farm at Wroughton, Wiltshire and had a shop. He was a major in the Home Guard and died on 12 February 1945 at the age of 52.)

After the initial successes of 9th April, and the next day's smaller advances, the battle stagnated, and attrition followed. Nivelle's offensive

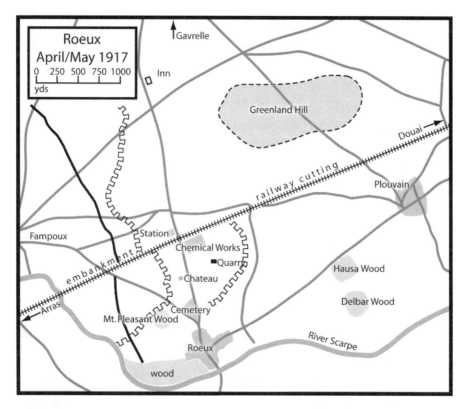

Roeux
April/May 1917
0 250 500 750 1000
yds

Gavrelle

Inn

Greenland Hill

Douai

railway cutting

Plouvain

Fampoux

Station

embankment

Chemical Works

Quarry

Chateau

Hausa Wood

Arras

Cemetery

Delbar Wood

Mt. Pleasant Wood

Roeux

River Scarpe

wood

failed and war-weary French soldiers mutinied. Haig concluded that he had to keep attacking, to relieve pressure on the French. The 51st went into the line at Fampoux on the night of 15th-16th April. It faced Mount Pleasant Wood, and another sloping wood that rose from the River Scarpe. Behind these lay the village of Roeux, a chateau, the soon to be notorious Chemical Works, a station, and an inn 1500 yards north of the station – all of which were protected by strong German outposts. East of Roeux were Delbar and Hausa Woods, on the southern side of the dominating problem, Greenland Hill, 'a knoll with gentle slopes and a flat top – just 30 feet higher than the surrounding ground.' [34] The Arras-Douai railway line approached it on an embankment from the west, then cut through it. Greenland Hill gave the Germans superb views of the British lines and they were subjected to rifle, machine-gun and artillery fire: there was little cover for the British artillery and the Germans constantly shelled the infantry. [35]

On 11th April an attack by 10th Brigade, 4th (Regular) Division, with the Chemical Works and Greenland Hill as its objectives, had been obliterated, with 1,000 casualties out of 1600 participants.

On 12th April 9th (Scottish) Division attempted to take the line of the Roeux-Gavrelle Road from Roeux to the Inn: it suffered many casualties from shelling before it even reached the front line, held by 4th Division; thereafter machine-gun fire prevented 9th Division's South African Brigade on the right gaining more than 200 yards, and stopped its 27th Brigade gaining any ground at all. It was rumoured in the 9th Division that South Africans had reached the Chemical Works – they had, and the 9th Division 'buried South African dead whom we found lying there at the end of May.'[36] 'The action . . . was calamitous. The firing of the heavy guns during the day never rose to the intensity of a bombardment, and the large collection of buildings round the Station remained quite intact, only one shell being seen to fall near the Chemical Works.'[37]

The River Scarpe was on the 51st's right and rear, into which it could be driven by a successful German attack. The plan was to push over Greenland Hill to Plouvain, encircling the Germans between Plouvain and the Chemical Works. [38] On 23rd April 1917, the 51st's objectives were: the Black Line, running west of the Roeux-Gavrelle Road; the Blue Line, which included the western side of Roeux, the Chemical Works and the Roeux-Gavrelle Road; the Brown Line ran from the Chemical Works to the Plouvain-Gavrelle Road; the Red Line included a German trench protecting Hausa and Delbar Woods (now Le Lac Bleu) and the station at Plouvain. These colourful flights of fancy then embraced Plouvain itself, with a Pink Line.

The attacking battalions were to emerge from a narrow front, and spread out on a wider frontage. The Germans did not have many dug-outs, and were fighting from shell-holes and battered trenches, and shrapnel was to be used, but there were insufficient guns, and the attack was executed too hurriedly. [38] Zero was at 4.45 a.m.

The 154th Brigade was on the right, led by 1/7th Argylls and 1/4th Gordons. 1/7th Argylls were held up by machine-gun fire for ninety minutes in and around Mount Pleasant Wood, and the wood near the

Scarpe. Most of their officers had been lost at the railway bridge over the Roeux-Fampoux road, but the battalion persisted.

> 'Finally our men, who were now led for the most part by N.C.O.s, advanced firing from the hip and employing Lewis guns in the same manner. A tank came up to hasten matters and the enemy began to retire. The Agylls pushed on into the village, followed by the tank, which did excellent work in chasing snipers out of the houses.' [39]

The tank, C7, commanded by Second Lieutenant Victor Smith, had been delayed by wounded lying on the road at an aid post under the railway arch at Fampoux. The combined force fought its way into Roeux village. . .

> 'where the tank repeatedly put 6-pdr shells through the windows of houses occupied by the enemy. [40] The Germans were ubiquitous. 1/7th Argylls' bombing parties began to clear the houses and a considerable number were cleared but the houses and gardens seemed to be connected as the Germans cleared from one seemed to appear in the next while machine-guns were active from many of the upper stories.' [41]

On their left 1/4th Gordons' two leading companies took some of the Black Line, but were held up in front of the Chemical Works: 'where a party of Germans with a machine-gun held out until much later.' The right supporting company found no enemy in the Black Line.

> 'A platoon of this Coy. appears to have lost direction towards the right and gone right through Roeux at 19D [map ref corresponding to crossroads in centre of Roeux] for at least 15 minutes. No one appeared on the right or left of the platoon and the commander decided to withdraw as he was being heavily fired on by machine-guns and snipers from all sides. . . he withdrew . . . Just west of MOUNT PLEASANT WOOD this platoon took 25 prisoners. . . Part of this company appears to have accompanied a tank into ROEUX village, where it remained for some time holding the line of the tramway track.' [42]

In Roeux, tunnels interlinked the positions and the houses, so that Germans re-emerged from buildings and dug-outs that the Scots had cleared. 1/4th Gordons' Sergeant Albert Anderson recalled that the Germans had fixed bayonets, and that no quarter was asked and none given. *[43] The desperate nature of close combat was confirmed by 'the fact that on the steps of Roeux Cemetery a Prussian and a sergeant of the Argylls were found grappled in death – the Prussian with his teeth in the Highlander's wrist the Highlander with his in the Prussian's throat. They had been killed by a shell.'[44]

On the left, 1/4th Seaforths, from support, helped 1/4th Gordons through the Black Line and thereafter: 'a small (1/4th Gordons) bombing squad from the right two companies appears to have worked its way forward along a communication trench as far as the Chemical Works-Roeux Road, where it held on for some time.'[45] This war diary report does not note that another tank, C22 had arrived late: it had been hit by armour piercing shells, and it had taken its wounded back, before returning with a diminished crew. It made its way up a communication trench in support of 1/4th Gordons, wiping out the last machine-gun post in the Chemical Works. [46] Eighteen years old Private James Mackay of Aberdeen, of 1/4th Gordons, was in his first battle and impressed by the noise, and by some of his platoon who were catching and returning German 'taddy-masher' (Tattie masher – potato masher) grenades. [47] 1/4th Gordons held for a short time, and later 'the 4th Seaforths (in reserve) at one time got past the Chemical Works, when brought up, they were finally compelled to fall back on the BLACK LINE.'[48] At Roeux the Germans had counter-attacked and had driven 1/7th Argylls and 1/9th Royal Scots back to the western edge of the village.

The 153rd Brigade on the left had equally mixed results. 1/7th Black Watch on its right could not reach the Black Line because of machine-gun fire. A company of the left battalion, 1/7th Gordons, took the Black Line, and its follow-up companies passed through it to take the Blue Line. Other elements of 1/7th Gordons were stopped between the Black and Blue Lines.

Behind the leading battalions were 1/6th Gordons and 1/6th Black Watch, on the right and left respectively, and later in the day 1/6th

Seaforths (152nd Brigade) reinforced the 153rd Brigade and moved north of the railway line to the Black Line. 1/6th Gordons passed through an enemy barrage which they thought 'was heavy, but the Battalion did not suffer greatly, except in one case where a platoon of 'B' Company was almost wiped out.' [49] Captain Hutcheson of 1/6th Gordons, in command after its C.O. had been badly wounded, at 9.30 a.m. established posts round the Chemical Works. With no reinforcements, and faced by an imminent counter attack Hutcheson made a sensible decision and withdrew his men at noon to the British front line, leaving a strong outpost in a quarry, which held its ground all day and took part in an advance later that evening. [50] It must have been a long afternoon for these men.

Elements of 1/6th Seaforths, sent to help them, approached from the north of the railway embankment, and attempted to link up with the 1/4th Seaforths and others at the Chemical Works. When they crossed the railway they were held up by heavy fire from the Chemical Works, and concluded that their colleagues had withdrawn from it.

The Germans counter-attacked and: 'the enemy artillery fire was very intense and shelled the CHEMICAL WORKS and ROEUX when their own troops were in these places, subsequently lengthening (their range) to the BLACK LINE and the Sunken Road from which Coys started.' [51]

The Germans emerged from the Chemical Works' tunnels to sow confusion behind the British. With the loss of most of the 51st's officers, it was a soldiers' battle. The Germans flung in counter-attacks from about 9 a.m., appearing over Greenland Hill in extended lines. Completely exposed to British observation they were cut down by artillery and machine-gun fire. Later German attacks suffered the same fate, but nightfall enabled the Germans to retake the Chemical Works.

The 1/4th Seaforths failed to retake the Chemical Works. Two battalions of the 34th Division were lent to Harper to sustain the 51st against German counter-attacks.

Private Wrench of 1/4th Seaforths waited to guide Northumberland Fusiliers of the 34th Division to the front:

'. . . the German barrage down in the valley and further forward is terrible. Their planes are up everywhere and all the time and are never challenged, which is awful at such a time when co-operation from our 'wonderful' air force could at least keep the Germans from spying around here and causing so much havoc on this side. There is never a single machine of ours to be seen except one which is now sticking tail up on top of the ridge across the valley, just the other side of Fampoux.'

Later in the evening Wrench sought out Lt.Colonel Unthank, C.O.,1/4th Seaforths and joined him, and Lieutenant Scott, his assistant adjutant, in a wooden hut, so that the C.O. could write a report for Wrench to take back to Brigade H.Q.

'A terrific blinding flash with a most awful explosion sent me sprawling on top of the Colonel and Scott down on his back beneath us, the shack a smash on top. [Scott was wounded and the Colonel went to find stretcher bearers. There had been a party of twenty five men outside.] Some of the poor fellows were so badly wounded tho' I do not know if any were killed outright. . . I can never forget this awful scene as long as I live. . . other shells burst and inflicted further wounds on those already wounded and it was pitiful to hear them calling in their agony, 'For God's sake help me' and 'For the love of Christ put me out of my misery,' and to feel so utterly helpless. . . it was some time later before the colonel returned with stretcher bearers and then we proceeded to search among the wreckage of the shack for the colonel's notebook with the report we (brigade) were still waiting for.'[52]

At the end of the day the 51st held the Black Line south of the railway, a few buildings north of the station and a line of trench running south to north, east of the Roeux-Gavrelle road. The formula of infantry following a barrage onto sparsely held German front lines had been proved to be successful, but it presupposed an identifiable trench line, and the ability of the infantry to keep up with the barrage. At Roeux the barrage was thin compared to that of the Germans and on the ground the Germans occupied shell holes and had well camouflaged and sited strong points. Ignorance of the precise whereabouts of the attacking troops, and bad communication, made close artillery support of the attackers impossible. Where German counter-attacks were clearly observed, the artillery played a major part in stopping them. The 51st had taken the Chemical Works and Roeux, and had failed to hold them. They were neither the first nor the last so to do.

The 34th (New Army) Division took over from the 51st, and on 28th April mounted a two brigade attack, north and south of the railway line, just as the 51st had done. At the end of that day the 34th Division was back at its start line. On 11th May the 4th (Regular) Division took Roeux and the Chemical Works.

The 51st had moved back on 25th April to Chelers, Acq, Tinques and Ternas, west of Arras to recuperate and absorb replacements. Trench warfare afforded few opportunities for soldiers to fire aimed shots, and the hand grenade and bayonet had become the weapons of choice for close combat, so training focused on musketry. The 152nd Brigade's competition was won by 'A' Company 1/5th Seaforths, with a score of 242 out of a possible 600 points. The average score in the competition was 159 and 'D' Company of the 1/6th Gordons scored 90 points. [53] These low scores contrast with the remarkable marksmanship of the regulars of 1914.

On 12/13th May the 51st relieved the 4th Division, which had established itself in the centre of Roeux, and on the eastern edge of its cemetery: the rest of the front line was 300-500 yards east of the Chemical Works, and 600 yards east of Roeux Station. Moving forward into his first action on the night of the 12/13th 2nd Lieutenant Alex Humble 1/8th Argylls recalled:

> 'Reached the Chemical Works which had just been captured
> . . . stench here something fearful; dead Germans lying in
> hundreds – shell still bursting all round – the enemy has got
> the wind up! I am getting my baptism of fire and no mistake
> . . . faced with the problem of holding with two and a half
> platoons a line previously held by a whole company. The only
> thing was to keep every single man on the firestep the whole
> night.' [54]

On the morning of the 13th Humble discovered that there was a 350 yard gap between his troops and the railway on his left, and that they were not in touch with the Dorset Regiment. Half his platoon, lost the previous evening, arrived, having waited for daylight to find their way. He was ordered to move forward at 10 p.m. and dig an oblique switch trench from A Company 1/8th Argylls, ahead and to the right, to link up with C Company's line. At dawn two platoons and A Company were left isolated without any water or rations. The whole area was heavily shelled, and on the 13th the Germans shelled the east side of the village, which they had evacuated. The 51st moved forward cautiously and established itself in shell holes near the road running from Roeux to the north, 750 yards east of the Roeux-Gavrelle road. 1/5th Seaforths were on the right, and 1/8th Argylls on the left, with their flank on the railway line, with some of their supporting troops north of it. Because few casualties were incurred grim soldier humour named it 'The Meatless Day'. [55]

The 14th was relatively quiet, but on the 15th, from dawn until 9.15 a.m., German guns pounded the 51st. Bewsher wrote:

> 'Shells were bursting in the brigade area at the rate of one 5.9., two 4.2's and two 7.7's in every seventy yards of the front. In addition, a number of 8-inch howitzers were freely employed ... the casualties... were not excessive. The three battalions in the front area were estimated to have lost a total of 450 men...' [56]

The casualty toll may not have been excessive, but Humble 'lost about half the strength of our company by shell splinters and shrapnel and still we are kept in this dangerous position without supports or reinforcements.'[57] Only men in the line of shell holes east of Roeux and the Chemical Works, unseen by the Germans, were spared the shelling.[58] Assuming a German attack the 51st's artillery shelled the Germans west and to the rear of Hausa and Delbar woods.

1/6th Seaforths, in support of 152nd Brigade, were to relieve 51st Brigade, 17th (Northern) Division, north of the railway, to create a single command in the railway sector, a potential weak spot. Because of the morning's heavy shelling 1/5th Seaforths were to be replaced by 1/6th Gordons, and 1/8th Argylls by 1/6th Seaforths. Some of the relieving troops were subjected to gas shelling and at 3.15 a.m. on the 16th, before the reliefs were completed, a major enemy barrage began and the Germans attacked beside the river and the railway line. They attained the west side of Roeux Wood, but their outflanking attack beside the Scarpe was frustrated by 1/5th Seaforths.

On 1/8th Argylls' front Lieutenant Humble:

> '. . . had scarcely dozed over when the word was passed around that the enemy were coming at us in strong numbers over the parapet. There they were – thousands of Germans – about 25 yds away. I had not time to join my own platoon so took charge of about 30 men round about, including a machine gun which had been sent up to strengthen our line. Men kept very cool and opened good rapid fire and the enemy were falling fast and soon hesitated and lay down in shell holes in front. . . What happened to the Dorsets? [supposed to be in contact with
> 1/8th Argylls on their left, at the railway embankment, but being replaced by 1/6th Seaforths] Managed to hold up the frontal attack but Germans got round our flanks round our support line and came at us from the rear and front at the same time. Now begin to see that it was a hopeless job – our men on the left broke and made off towards the rear. . .
> I stuck it out with about ten men until the enemy were about 10 yds away from me and then decided that we would have more chance of our lives if we scattered and got into shell – holes. We did this and I went off at a left incline; by doing this I hoped to run up against the Seaforths who, I knew, were supposed to be coming up to relieve the company originally on our right. Pushed from shell-hole to shell-hole and saw about 10 men coming towards me, in the darkness I could not see who they were, but I hoped they were some of our men; however they turned out to be Germans, I lay down in a shell-hole and fired 8 rounds with good result at them. This put the wind up them a bit as they all lay down. . . I decided to push on. . . one bullet got me just below the knee and as it was causing me pain I lay down again, and before long a German came creeping up but I silenced him with my remaining

round – I now knew I was at their mercy as I had no ammunition left. Crawled on a bit to get rid of this dead German and
was soon surrounded and had to give in. . . they took all my
equipment . . motioned me towards their own lines. . .
managed to escape my guide [or rather sentry] as it was still
dark, so crawled into a shell-hole to wait till daylight . .dressed
my wound with a Field Dressing and then hid myself as much
as possible. What suspense! Seemed to wait for ages amidst an
inferno of shells and bullets; how I was not killed is indeed a
mystery. At last dawn came, I crawled out to get my bearings –
but once more bad luck – half a dozen Germans were walking
straight for me, so once more I found myself in German
hands.' [59] [Humble spent the rest of the war in Germany.]

Germans advanced along both sides of the railway and the defenders
were pushed back, but a 1/6th Seaforth company, led by Acting
Lieutenant Dow of Elgin, threw all its grenades, then repelled them in a
bayonet charge. Dow's company was eventually forced out of its front
line trench but he and his survivors recovered part of it. His neighbouring
company, on his left, led by Lieutenant King, poured flanking fire on the
enemy, and held its own front. Lieutenant Dow* was shot in the lung.

The Germans forced their way along the railway embankment,
outflanked and retook the Chemical Works, and the buildings north and
south of the station. A German move south from the Chemical Works
appeared in the rear of 1/8th Argylls, and a company, led by Captain
Mactaggart, charged and dispersed them. Mactaggart had a hand
smashed by a shell splinter, lost an eye to another shell, and led his men
until he was fatally wounded in the abdomen. [60] Later in the evening
Lt. Dane of 1/4th Seaforths was leading his company to attack the
Germans in Colombo Trench when he heard a Scottish voice from the
trench – 1/8th Argylls still held it. 'They had managed to keep the enemy
at bay, the men facing to front and rear alternately.' [61]

Meanwhile Lt.Colonel Campbell, 1/8th Argylls, counter attacked
Germans who had penetrated north of the railway. With a handful of
officers, including rifle grenade expert Captain Pollard, the Germans
were grenaded from their shell holes and shot as they ran. Having
recovered their ground, Campbell saw that 1/6th Seaforths south of the

railway were being attacked head on and on their left and ordered them to attack the Germans, while his party gave covering fire from the railway embankment. Then he and his diminished party joined the 1/6th Seaforths digging in east of the Chemical Works.

South of the Chemical Works a counter-attack was mounted by 1/6th Gordons, 1/5th and 1/6th Seaforths, and others led by Captain Donald Clarke M.C.,* 1/6th Gordons. Lieutenant Innes was in charge of a 1/5th Seaforths' party helping sixty tunnellers to build dug-outs behind the Chemical Works when the enemy appeared two hundred yards away. The tunnellers scavenged rifles and bayonets, and led by Innes, wearing his Burberry trench coat and carrying a stick, went over the top with Clark's counter-attack and drove the enemy off.[62] Returning from the battlefield a staff officer enquired if they were the tunnelling company, to which someone replied, 'Tunnelling be damned, we've been over the bags.' [63]

The 51st regained the previous British front line, with the exception of some trenches straddling the railway, which were being heavily shelled, and they found the line still garrisoned by men of 1/8th Argylls and 1/5th Seaforths who had moved in on the 13th, the 'Meatless day'. By-passed by the advancing Germans, they had stood their ground, stopped two frontal attacks, one in columns and another in extended line, and thereafter had not been attacked again.

Although it was innacurrate, word arrived at 152nd Brigade H.Q. that the Chemical Works had been retaken by the Germans and that 1/5th Gordons were to recapture it, aided by the artillery. Lt.Colonel Campbell, in the trenches east of the Chemical Works, withdrew his men to prevent them being caught by their own shells. Then it was decided to concentrate 1/5th Gordons' attack north of the railway, in co-operation with 51st Brigade, 17th (Northern) Division. 1/5th Gordons recovered the lost ground, then were forced out of it, partly because 1/7th Border Regiment (51st Brigade) was given too little time to move forward. 'This was an unfortunate ending, but the operation had otherwise been strikingly successful. The ground recovered by the fresh German division thrown in with the object of retaking Roeux and the Chemical Works represented only a fraction of the British gains, and it was dearly bought.'[64]

1/4th Seaforths consolidated the area.

> 'In the main street of Roeux the German dead lay in hundreds; almost every step was over a dead enemy. In dug-outs and cellars, on floors and in the beds lay dead Germans, some in a horrible stage of corruption, especially those that had been gassed. The stench in Roeux was vile. Our troops were busy for the next ten days succouring the enemy wounded who lay out in the open. The stretcher bearers, cheeriest and bravest of men, risked the enemy fire to bring them in . . . one poor fellow in particular had been out about ten days with a very bad wound, which was appalling to behold, being gangerous and covered with flies, and giving off a most offensive smell. He had long since finished what rations and water he had had with him, and for drink had, in his misery, resorted to nature to alleviate the thirst that tormented him.' [65]

Allenby, commanding the Third Army, wrote: 'Convey to 51st Highland Division my congratulations on their great gallantry at Roeux and the chemical works.' The Corps Commander sent: 'Heartiest congratulations to you all on fine work on 16th and 17th May 1917, and especially on General Burn and 152nd Infantry Brigade, whose tenacity and pluck saved an awkward situation. The Division may well be proud of their latest achievement.'[66]

Pelham-Burn of 152nd Brigade issued a special order: 'In an action where all did so well, it is invidious to mention any special unit or detachment, but I would make an exception in the case of the Headquarters of the 1/8th Battalion Argyll and Sutherland Highlanders who, led by Lt.Colonel Campbell personally, vigorously attacked a party of the enemy who had broken through our line and turned the flank of our position, killing some 25 of their number and capturing 50 others, thus restoring the situation.' 1/8th Argylls began their defence of Roeux with 25 officers and 850 men, and came out with 5 officers and 200 men.[67]

On the 16th, 153rd and 154th Brigades took over the front and were shelled. Private Wrench, 1/4th Seaforths, was near a large munitions dump when it was hit:

'I thought we were all sent for as the crash that followed shook the whole place to the bottom of these dug-outs. The big howitzer there was caught in the explosion and smashed to pieces. An officer of some other unit was sitting astride the muzzle of the gun at the time writing a letter and was simply torn apart. Sergeant Christie* and Cpl Davie Gray (D.R.)* (despatch rider), and Harry Moffat* (A&SH) Pigeon man, were killed and Corporal Bill Chalmers (D.R.) badly crushed. They occupied a little dug-out near the entrance to the pit and got the full force of the concussion. [Next day]: We carried these bodies down to the cemetery beside the signal box at Fampoux, but oh, how unrecognizable they are. What a mess to make of anyone. The remains of the officer were collected in pieces and put into a sandbag. Well, there they lie and for them the war is certainly over. Perhaps they are lucky. [He moved to the rear later that day]: What a difference in the air back here now. The hedges are white with hawthorn and the trees are beautiful. The south bank of the Scarpe is a glowing mass of different colours and compared to the putrified atmosphere further forward, the perfume here is almost intoxicating.' [68]

The 51st was relieved by the 9th (Scottish) Division between 31st May and 2nd June. A 9th Division officer provided a succinct assessment of the 51st's defence of Roeux and the Chemical Works:

'We had taken over from the 51st Division who had just previously covered themselves with glory by utterly defeating a heavy Boche counter-attack – none of your imaginary affairs when the S.O.S. goes up at the appearance of two men and a boy, but a really good effort on the part of the Boche under a heavy barrage in broad daylight. The Boche got through too, which made no difference to those Highlanders, who just went on fighting back to back until counter-attacks mopped up the intruders. It was comforting to see the number of Boche dead lying about, but in that broiling summer sun the stench was too awful. We got them under as quickly as we could. . . ' [69]

The cost of April and May's battles to the 51st was a total of 6,377 casualties, of all ranks, killed, wounded and missing. [70]

Out of the line Bewsher thought that the Balmorals equalled other divisions' troupes of entertainers but asserted that everyone believed that 'our Gertie' was second to none.' [71] 1/4th Seaforths recovered from the squalor and misery of Roeux:

> 'For two weeks dull care was cast aside. The sun shone brightly, and everyone forgot there was a war on. Billets were very good and the villagers were cheery and most hospitable. There was the necessary minimum of training, but special attention was given to musketry. Discipline is a necessary quality in fighting troops. In the attack there is perhaps a short period when actual control is and must be absent. But in defence the moment control is lost, the fight is lost. Continuous periods in the line always weaken discipline and it is therefore necessary to remould a battalion at the first opportunity. Some days were so hot that companies paraded in shirts and kilt aprons only, resulting in a spectacle as attractive as the most lithe limbed beauty chorus on any revue stage.' [72]

The men had several weeks pay to spend, but the survivors of 1/4th Seaforths were most popular with the shopkeepers, for while they had been in Fampoux a shell had blown a cache of gold louis d'ors from a hiding place, each worth thirty francs! [73] Rest and recreation worked wonders with 1/6th Gordons:

> 'Good billets, excellent fare, bathing concerts and boating restored the body and refreshed the mind. A German document was captured at this time, giving, as a warning to German soldiers, a list of the most to be feared British troops. In this list the first place was given to the 51st Division.' [74]

NOTES
1. Mackintosh, War, The Liberator Victory and Failure. Arras April 9th, Roeux April 23rd 1917 p.13/Campbell and Green p.193
2. Falls 1917 v.1 p.110.
3. Falls 1917 v.1 p.203.

4. Jay Winter *The Great War* (Allen Lane) 1996 p.75, quoted in Niall Ferguson *The Pity of War* (Penguin) 1998 p.299.

	%age killed of those mobilised	Age 15-49	Of male population
Scotland	26.4	10.9	3.1
GB and Ireland	11.8	6.3	1.6
France	16.8	4.0	3.4
Average of all nations	13.4	4.0	1.0

5. Instructions issued by Lt.Col Dick Cunnygham General Staff 51st (Highland) Division 10.3.1917 TNA.

6. Falls 1917 v.1 p.229/Croft pp.116-117.

7. Falls 1917 v.1 p.253.

8. Falls 1917 v.1 p.234.

9. Falls 1917 v.1 p.234.

10. Bewsher p.155

11. War diary 1/9th Royal Scots 9.4.1917.

12. War diary 1/4th Seaforths 9.4.1917.

13. Bewsher p.157.

14. Harper Account of Operations carried out from 9th to 12th April 1917. 27.7.1917 TNA.

15. Falls 1917 v.1 p.235.

16. Morrison p.26.

17. Wrench 9.4.1917.

18. War diary 1/7th A&SH 9.4.1917.

19. War diary 1/4th Gordons 9.4.1917.

20. Falls 1917 v.1 p.236.

21. War diary 1/7th A&SH 10.4.1917.

22. Wrench 10.4.1917.

23. Kenneth Macksey *The Shadow of Vimy Ridge* (Kimber) 1965 p.78.

24. War diary 1/7th A&SH 10.9.1917.

25. Falls 1917 v.1 Page 25; Macksey p.78.

26. Account of Operations carried out from 9th to 12th April 1917, Harper 27.7.1917 TNA.

27. Lt.Col. W.D.Croft *Three Years with the 9th Division* (John Murray) 1919, pp.112-113 (On 12th September 1916, a fine but dull day, in daylight, the 1st Guards Brigade took its first objective, thought it was on its third objective, sent back a messenger pigeon to report being on the third objective, and was ordered to hold on until the next day. Ref: Robin Neillands *The Great War Generals on the Western Front 1914-1918.* (Robinson) 1999 p.284.

28. G.W.L Nicholson *Official History of the Canadian Army in the First World War: Canadian Expeditionary Force 1914-1919.* (Duhamel, Queen's Printer,Ottow). 1962 p.259.

29. Wrench 11.4.1917.

30. War diary 1/9th Royal Scots 11.4.1917.

31. Routine Order No.781 2.5.1917 Harper TNA.

32. The London Gazette 14.6.1917.

33. Gerald Gliddon *V.C.s Handbook 1914-1918* (Sutton Publishing) p. 75.

34. Edmonds 1918 v.4 p.328.

35. Bewsher p.161.
36. Croft p.120.
37. John Ewing *The History of the 9*th *(Scottish) Division* (John Murray) 1921 pp.203-4.
38. Bewsher p.162.
39. Morrison p.28.
40. Falls v.1 1917 p.395.
41. War diary 1/7th A&SH 23.4.1917.
42. War diary 1/4th Gordons 23.4.1917.
43. Jonathan Nicholls *Cheerful Sacrifice* (Leo Cooper) 1998 p.177.
44. Fred.A. Farrell *The 51*st *Highland Division War Sketches* Introduction, Neil Munro p.24.
45. War diary 1/4th Gordons 23.4.17
46. Macksey p.114.
47. Nicholls p.181.
48. Nicholls p.181.
49. War diary 1/6th Gordons 23.4.1917.
50. War diary 1/6th Gordons 23.4.1917
51. War diary 1/9th Royal Scots 23.4.17
52. Wrench 23.4.1917.
53. War diary 152nd Brigade 17.5.1917.
54. Lt.A.Humble 1/8th A&SH personal account A&SH RHQ.
55. Bewsher p.175.
56. Bewsher p.177.
57. Humble.
58. Bewsher p.177.
59. Humble.
60. Bewsher pp.181-182.
61. Haldane p.208.
62. Sutherland pp.116-117.
63. Bewsher p.186.
64. Falls 1917 v.1 p.515.
65. Haldane pp.208-209.
66. Bewsher p.187.
67. Malcolm pp.41-42.
68. Wrench 24 and 25.5.1917.
69. Croft pp.125-126.
70. Falls v.1 1917 pp. 559-560.
71. Bewsher p.191.
72. Unknown 1/4th Seaforths QOH RHQ p.110.
73. Haldane p.206.
74. MacKenzie p.122. This is the earliest reference to a 'most to be feared' list.

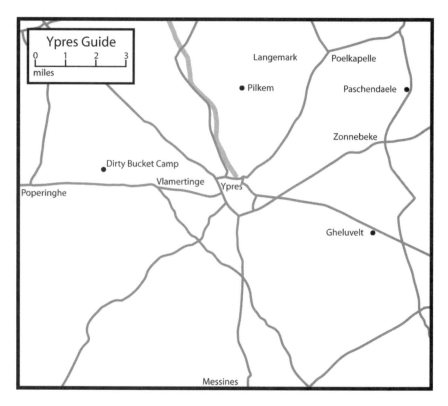

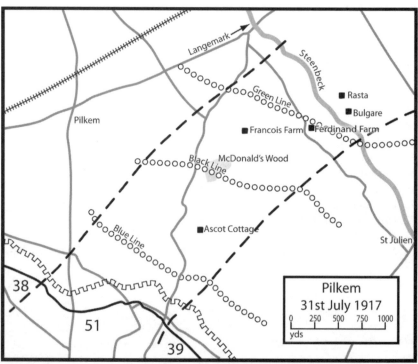

Chapter 6

ENDURANCE
Third Battle of Ypres

Buchan! Ye're bare an' bleak an' cauld like the coast around ye,
Wi' its auld grey rocks.
Nae a tree or a burn or a hull or a buss tae hap ye
Fae the winter's shocks!

But ye're nae sae bare an' bleak an' cauld as the plain o' Flanders,
Wi' its shell-scarred skull.
And och! I wad rise an rin tae whaur the fish-wife wanders,
And the hungry gull. [1]

From Arras the 51st moved to the villages of Tilques, Houlle and Nordausque, round Eperleques, near St. Omer, arriving on 7th June.

Ypres was a battered town in the south-west corner of Belgium where, in 1914, the Regular Army had foiled the Germans' attempt to take the Channel ports in the First Battle of Ypres. In the Spring of 1915, despite using chlorine gas, the Germans had failed in the Second Battle of Ypres.

Ypres is embraced by a concave ridge to its east and from the outskirts of the town the land rises approximately 70 feet to Passchendaele Ridge. The German lines were on the west of the ridge, two to four miles from Ypres. Part encircled, and overlooked by the Germans, the British were always exposed. Logic might have decreed straightening the line to reduce the number of troops needed to hold Ypres, but it had become an icon of British resistance, and if the new line had not held, the Channel ports might have been lost, and such a withdrawal would have been unacceptable to Belgium, clinging to its last corner of territory.

Haig had long wanted to attack at Ypres, and with the French Army in a parlous state there was a need to draw the Germans from the French front, and tactical benefits in taking the ridge.There were wider strategic reasons: German submarines were taking a heavy toll on the merchantile marine, jeopardising the Allies' ability to sustain the war. Breaking through at Ypres could close the U-boat bases at Zeebrugge and Ostende.

Whilst the 51st was moving north to join the Fifth Army a preliminary to Third Ypres took place at the south of the ridge, at Messines. Sir Herbert Plumer had commanded the Second Army in the Ypres Salient for two years, and Messines Ridge had been undermined. Following a bombardment from from 26th May until 6th June, at 3.10 a.m on 7th June, nineteen massive mines blew Messines Ridge apart in a noisome accumulation of body parts, shattered equipment and trenches, driven skywards in pillars of fire and smoke. Nine divisions took the ridge, with shocked Germans surrendering easily, but counter-attacks were mounted and by 14th June the new line had stabilised. Rolling up the German defences from the south might have been a sequel, but Haig was committed to attack east of Ypres.

The 51st was in XVIII Corps, commanded by Lieutenant-General Sir Ivor Maxse. In a lecture to the 51st's officers he said that Guards' march discipline was unequalled, and, soon after, two Guards' battalions marched through the 51st's area, one going to the front and another returning from it. In 1/4th Seaforths there was a voluntary frenzy of cleaning and polishing and the adjutant realised that the men wanted to rise to the Guards' challenge.Their C.O. insisted that the battalion must march ten miles, in full marching order, so, in muggy weather, it marched fifteen miles, without anyone falling out, through all the villages occupied by the Guards. [2] An example of esprit de battalion!

Pursued by XVII Corps for his account of the April battles, Harper made his excuses, promised an abbreviated report and asked a staff officer at Corps:

> 'If it would not cause inconvenience, there are two men I
> rather want to get back from the Corps School: one is Sergeant
> J. Illingworth, 1/6th Gordon Highrs., Lewis Gun Sergeant, who
> was sent before the Lewis Gun School was part of the 3 Corps
> establishment; the other is Private F. Sagar 1/4th Seaforth
> Highrs. who is a Runner, who the Battalion Commander is

very anxious to have back. As you know, we have had to replace a great deal, and we should like a few old faces. Please remember me affectionately to your General.' [3]

It is a measure of the intimacy of the 51st that its battalion comm-anders felt able to approach Harper with such specific requests, and of Harper's understanding of the needs of his battalion commanders for continuity of experienced personnel.

The 51st had six weeks to absorb drafts and there were good ranges and ample training space. Instruction manuals, circulated as early as May 1916 by Fourth Army, had called upon the troops 'to rely constantly upon the exercise of initiative by their officers and N.C.O.s or, if none of those are at hand, their own.' [4] By 1917 platoons had different functions, fighting, mopping up stray Germans who had survived the leading platoon, support and carrying. By 1917 the platoon was the battlefield tactical unit, divided into rifle/bayonet men, bombers, rifle grenadiers and Lewis gunners.

Bewsher records that the 51st had mastered the art of attacking behind a barrage and in consolidating captured positions. He asserted:

'the Divisional commander, therefore, next concentrated on training the platoons how to overcome local resistance by the aid of their own fire power. Each platoon was taught that, if it came under the fire of a machine-gun or a pocket of riflemen, it was useless to lie halted in the zone of hostile fire, and that by engaging the enemy frontally by one or more sections the remainder under cover of their fire could work round to the flank and overcome it.' [5]

Bewsher claimed all of this was Harper's own initiative, but it is more likely that Harper was passing down the Army's best practice.

There were large scale rehearsals.

'At St.Momelin the very contours of the chosen sector had a marvelous resemblance to our morsel of the Ypres salient … The imitation attacks were always preceded by a human barrage, composed of the pipe band complete with pipes, drums, and bugles, oddments of the transport, and signalers equipped with flags. This motley party produced the creeping barrage, and the efforts of the pipers and drummers who frantically emulated the scream and burst respectively of shells (which all had heard) were worthy of the cause. . . each man soon came to know the river Steenbeck and his own route to it as thoroughly as if the Lossie or the Findhorn [rivers near Elgin in the battalion's recruiting area] were to be his objective. . . replicas of the battlefield were constructed in miniature; actual pictures of places of interest on the forthcoming journey were produced and promised.' [6]

As well as training the 51st garrisoned breastworks north of Ypres. The support line was a few earthworks and some fortified farm houses, and the reserve line was fortified farms. All the battalion headquarters, reserve companies and support troops were in dug-outs on the banks of the Canal d'Yser.[7] The canal was decribed by Captain David Sutherland, 1/5th Seaforths, as:

'. . . a succession of dirty stagnant pools crossed at frequent intervals by high wooden bridges for horse traffic and by low lying bridges, supported on beer barrels, for pedestrians, while here and there it has been filled up with great earthen mounds, the high banks of the canal have been leveled, and on these earthen bridges rails have been laid, and at night little trucks, drawn by oil engines, pull supplies across. . . here as soil we have dirty blue clay where water is met at 3 or 4 feet. The result is that dug-outs have to be built up instead of down. . . The ordinary dug-out here is therefore a built-up structure, depending for safety on rows of logs or steel bars and some feet of earth and sand-bags on top, and is absolutely useless against direct hits. The canal banks are full of these shelters and an unlucky direct hit on one of them has been known to cause one of our battalions a loss of 20 killed and 10 wounded.'[8]

Casualties were routinely suffered and in a tour of the trenches between the 7th and 10th July 1/6th Gordons reported that 'ten men were killed and 21 wounded. On the night of the 9th/10th an exceptionally heavy bombardment of our positions in the support area took place. The Germans attempted a raid on the Battalion on our left, and put a barrage in our trenches. The raid was unsuccessful.'[9]

A change in rations indicated an imminent attack. 1/4th Seaforths remembered that 'there were issues of strawberry jam! Very hot fighting was expected, for the rations were unusually good; there was butter, jam, vegetables, fresh meat, and even chocolates and good cigarettes. The pill was well sugared!' [10]

On the eve of battle James Rennie, 152nd Machine-Gun Company, relaxed at Dirty Bucket Camp, near Vlamertinge, west of Ypres:

> 'We were alone in the camp. Me and this fellow Green. . . he had an 'under and over' table, you know where you put down your penny and it will be under seven or over seven. And I had one or two sous left and he had two or three sous left. . . 'Well,' he says, 'We'll play with what we have anyway.' . . . and finally I finish up with almost a franc. . . the boys started wandering back and getting into the camp and someone produced a 'Crown and Anchor' cloth. So we starts playing Crown and Anchor. . . Finally I finish up with sixty four francs. That's quite a lot of money. So next day we're going 'over the top'.
>
> I bought goodies . . . Peak and Frean biscuits. . . no chocolate bars. So I picked them up and spread them out among the boys and we had dinner and headed up. . .
> oh, about 5, 6 o'clock we were heading up the plank road to go into Ypres. . . And we had a 'fall out' and the paper kid came along. 'Paper, paper, Daily Mail, paper, Daily Mail.' So I says, 'By golly, kid, give us a paper.' . . . 'Here you are, kid,' and I gave him the wad of money I had. I never liked going into the line with any money. . . no one is going to rob me when I'm dead. I'll give it to him while I'm alive. So the kid, he threw his papers in the air and he let out a yell and he's down the plank road like he was shot.' [11]

Distracted by gambling, replete with biscuits, and with pockets emptied in a spirit of fatalism, James Rennie made his way to the front.

The 51st had rehearsed the journey to the assembly trenches, with and without gas masks: the movement took place after 8.30 p.m., when enemy air observation was impossible. Tapes marked the overland routes to the start of the communication trenches, experienced guides led the battalions and 'a hot meal was issued at the place of assembly, and soup and tea were issued from hot food containers at the positions of deployment.' [12]

The barrage had begun on 22nd July, with 2,299 guns and it was calculated that four and three quarter tons of shells fell on every yard of the enemy front, completing the ruination of drainage systems which had kept the land cultivable before the war. The ground was broken and pockmarked, trees were splintered and uprooted, and streams crossed the line of advance. The German outposts were backed by three lines of trenches or breastworks, and behind these was a battle zone sown with concrete bunkers, planned for mutually supporting machine-gun fire. Many of these escaped air reconnaissance and the barrage. The Germans' counter-attacking troops were at the rear of the battle zone. At 3.50 a.m. on July 31st 1917 the artillery progamme altered to include a creeping barrage, progressing at 100 yards every four minutes. It rained.

On the right II Corps were held up, became embroiled in Shrewsbury Wood, lost its creeping barrage, communication broke down, and the advance halted. One brigade's advance was slowed by losing its way and reporting that it was in Glencorse Wood when it was in Chateau Wood (shades of 1/7th Argylls at Arras?). The left division of II Corps reached its second objective but had to be withdrawn owing to flanking fire. Only 19 of the 48 tanks deployed with II Corps arrived at the front, where they fought: 'with great gallantry.'[13] XIX Corps' divisions were successful. In XVIII Corps the 39th Division was on the right, between the left of XIX Corps, and the 51st. The 39th Division reached its objectives and some troops crossed the Steenbeck.

The 51st's first wave, from right to left, were 1/5th Seaforths, 1/8th Argylls, 1/7th Gordons and 1/7th Black Watch. They followed the creeping barrage to the Blue Line (1st objective), and the German posts were eliminated. Bewsher claimed that: 'as infantry fighters they completely outclassed the Germans, and by using their Lewis guns and rifle grenades with considerable effect they promptly swamped every party of the enemy which opposed them.'[14]

Once the Blue Line fell, 1/6th Gordons, 1/6th Seaforths, 1/5th Gordons and 1/6th Black Watch were to leapfrog to take the Black and Green Lines. The Blue Line had been in shell holes and remnants of trenches, but the Black and Green Lines were reinforced by fortified farmhouses and by concrete pill boxes, some of which had escaped shelling, and were harder nuts to crack.

1/6th Gordons' War Diary recorded:

'from 4.10 a.m. onwards, our Front Line was heavily shelled, and this trench very much knocked about, but Companies moved out into No Man's Land, and thus avoided loss.

At 4.20 a.m. 'A' & 'D' Companies moved forward in three waves as per programme and passed through the BLUE LINE (already captured by 1/5th SEAFORTH HIGHLANDERS)... The whole moved forward under the barrage at

5.13 a.m... A Machine-Gun in action between ASCOT COTTAGE and the BLACK LINE was dealt with by means of Rifle Grenades. About twelve of the enemy were killed or captured here... The Platoon of 'D' Company was therefore pushed off to the left to get in touch with the 1/6th SEAFORTH HIGHLANDERS. This platoon captured a Machine Gun in this part of the BLACK LINE. Machine Guns were also active from MCDONALD'S WOOD and effective fire was directed on it by this Platoon. These Machine Guns were finally destroyed by a Tank...' [15] 1/6th Seaforths described the tank, G50, of G Battalion: 'on its sides was painted 'Gordon' in white letters. Like an elephant at play, the machine moved forward, clumsy and uncouth, doing inestimable damage to the enemy's morale and performing wonders with our own. Gathered in their pill-boxes the terrorised Germans must have unanimously voted for discretion... and clusters of weeping Germans gave up their arms and offered all they possessed to be spared.' [16]

'... the capture of McDonald's Farm... was a good example of infantry and tank co-operation.' [17]

[1/6th Gordons'] 'advance continued to a position 500 yards in front of the BLACK LINE where the Company was re-organised preparatory to moving forward to the GREEN LINE under the

barrage. . . the GREEN LINE was reached at 7.50 a.m. . .
Consolidation was commenced 250 yards south of the
STEENBECK under observation by hostile aeroplane.' [18]

As 1/6th Gordons approached the Steenbeck, easily forded when the
weather was dry, they were raked by machine-gun fire from a position
sixty yards beyond it. On his own initiative Private McIntosh, aged 20,
crossed the stream and earned a V.C. His citation read:

'No.265579 Pte George Imlach
McIntosh, Gord. Highrs. (Buckie,
Banffshire)

For the most conspicuous bravery,
when, during the consolidation of a
position, his Company came under
machine-gun fire at close range. Pte.
McIntosh immediately rushed
forward under heavy fire and reaching
the emplacement, threw a Mills
grenade into it, killing two of the
enemy and wounding a third.
Subsequently entering the dug-out he
found two light machine-guns which
he carried back with him. His quick
grasp of the situation and the utter

George V awards
Private McIntosh his VC

fearlessness and rapidity with which he acted, undoubtedly
saved many of his comrades and enabled the consolidation to
proceed unhindered by machine-gun fire. Throughout the day
the cheerfulness and courage of Private McIntosh was
indomitable, and to his fine example, in a great measure, was
due the success which attended his Company.' [19] [McIntosh
survived the war and became a Flight Sergeant in the RAF in
the Second World War. Died 20th June 1968, at Aberdeen.]

1/6th Seaforths found the German resistance hardening as they
passed the Saxons in the outpost line and met the 3rd Reserve Guards
Division. 1/6th Seaforths' Sergeant Edwards* (32) won the V.C:

'No 265473 Sjt. Alexander Edwards, Sea. Highrs. (Lossiemouth)

For most conspicuous bravery in attack, when, having located a hostile machine-gun in a wood, he, with great dash and courage, led some men against it, killed all the team and captured the gun.

Sergeant Edwards

Later, when a sniper was causing casualties, he crawled out to stalk him, and, although badly wounded in the arm, went on and killed him.

One officer was now left with the company, and, realizing that the success of the operation depended on the capture of the furthest objective, Sjt. Edwards, regardless of his wound, led his men on until the objective was captured. He subsequently showed great skill in consolidating his position, and very great daring in personal reconnaissance.

Although again twice wounded on the following day, this very gallant N.C.O. maintained throughout a complete disregard for personal safety, and his high example of coolness and determination engendered a fine fighting spirit in his men.' [20]

1/6th Seaforths stopped a German counter-attack before it reached the Steenbeck, then crossed it and captured strongpoints at Maison du Rasta and Maison Bulgare. Two platoons of 1/8th Argylls reinforced them, along with a Stokes mortar team. These positions could not be held as they were isolated and outflanked and the Steenbeck behind them had become a torrent which could block a later withdrawal. 1/5th Gordons were also on the Green Line, and had taken two major blockhouses with the co-operation of the 1/6th Black Watch and troops of the 38th (Welsh) Division on their left.

1/6th Black Watch were a slow in keeping up as they had been heavily shelled in their assembly area, and suffered the the division's highest casualty rate. But the battalion moved forward and:

'. . . good progress was made despite stubborn resistance from numerous enemy 'pill-boxes'. Here a tank provided invaluable assistance, dealing more effectively with the hidden machine gun nests than the ordinary infantry was able to do.

D company advanced and collected at the Gun-pits at Ferdinand Farm, where Colonel Booth, making a personal reconnaissance, found between thirty and forty men assembled. With two sergeants he proceeded over the Steenbeck and after inspecting the position, established four posts, which were afterwards placed under the command of Second Lieutenant Drummond*. Numerous small parties reported to this nucleus until the force holding the bridge-head was about 50 strong.

Attempts were made to further strengthen the position beyond the Steenbeck.' [21]

A mounted squadron of King Edward's Horse was sent to patrol beyond the Steenbeck, but was halted by machine-gun fire within sight of the stream. The dismounted survivors joined some 1/6th Seaforths near Maison du Rasta. Towards 3 p.m. the enemy massed near Lange-marck and counter-attacked unsuccessfully several times. Further enemy reinforcements were seen, and they attacked at 3.45 p.m., 4 p.m., 4.30 p.m. and 6.05 p.m. [22] These attacks menaced the exposed 1/6th Black Watch outposts across the Steenbeck.

'The plight of the mere handful of the 6th whose lot it had been to push forward into that advanced position was momentarily becoming more desperate. Ammunition was running short. A Welsh regiment on the left had fallen back. There was no connection on the right. What was to be done? There was nothing for it but to withdraw, temporarily at least. Word was passed for the men to make, one at a time, for the German Gun-pits on the other side of the river. Those who came through bear witness that it was one of the most terribly exciting moments of their lives. Stumbling through the mud, falling, rising, pressing on, while the enemy, barely 100 yards away, stood up and took deliberate aim at them – one of the memories of the Great War which no length of time will ever blot out.

'In one of the enemy's abandoned 'pill-boxes' at the Gun-pits, 'Company Headquarters' was established. The position, one which dominated the Steenbeck, was consolidated. Another counter-attack on the part of the Boche proved unavailing, being broken up mainly by a destructive barrage from the other side. Patrols were put out to prevent the river being re-crossed, but no further attempt was made to renew the struggle . . . it is doubtful if the gain of it was commensurate to the losses sustained and the heroism displayed.' [23]

Throughout the evening and into the night 'the merciless rain beat down and the ground was transformed into a maze of bogs and brooks. Darkness came before all the wounded had been evacuated: there was a scarcity of stretchers, so severe had been the losses. The patience of the wounded who bore this cruel inevitable exposure was beyond all praise . . . few of the men had any sort of overhead cover, and the misery of that night, 31st July – 1st August, is inexpressible.' [24]

[1/6th Gordons reported that] 'under the heavy rains the ground, which was a mass of enormous shell craters, was reduced to an indescribable condition. The positions which had been consolidated were from one to two feet deep in water: a message received from Captain Hutcheson at this time well illustrated the spirit which animated the men. It ran as follows: 'Posts are all about two feet deep in water, but spirits high.' [25]

Proof of the power of mind over matter, although it is doubtful if such optimism prevailed amongst exhausted men, fearfully awake, or amongst the sodden owners of punctured bodies, awaiting help. Some of the wounded crawled into shell-holes to avoid enemy fire and were drowned as water levels rose. The 153rd Infantry Brigade Report said, 'early on the 1st August much difficulty was found in obtaining bearers, and 50 men of those who had been in the attack on the BLUE LINE had to be detailed to assist.' [26]

On the afternoon of 1st August the Germans counter-attacked, and were dispersed by Lewis-gun fire, but in the evening, when 1/4th Seaforths moved forward ro relieve 1/5th Gordons and 1/6th Black Watch an enemy barrage fell, and it was reported at 9 p.m. that the Germans had crossed the Steenbeck. The relief was postponed, two companies of 1/5th Gordons formed a defensive flank and within three-quarters of an hour the situation was stabilised and the relief continued. A party of 1/4th Seaforths was ordered to recross the Steenbeck on 2nd August:

'I went forward and dug in about forty yards in front. The thing was a terrific gamble – a pure gamble with death. If we'd been spotted we'd have been blown to blazes and shelled out of it. Luckily I found an old communication trench fitted with corrugated iron shelters, the only one of which not blown in was about forty yards from the bridge . . . luckily we were in ground that had been shelled fairly heavily, and so our holes weren't conspicuous; and our boys camouflaged their trenches quite nicely. . . I almost stepped on top of one of my chaps before I saw him. He'd dug down about six feet, leaving a platform at each end of his hole to fire from, had spread his new earth about and stuck it full of thistles and sods, camouflaging it beautifully. . . we lay low during the day and kept good watch during the night, but weren't troubled at all, luckily for us.

We had two days there and then went back to our original positions; and getting out was even worse than getting in, for the mud had been stirred up to the consistency of treacle. However, we managed it. . . my company officer told me he's putting my name forward [for a medal]; but I don't for a minute expect to hear anything further about it. . . what I did was just the ordinary and there was nothing exceptional in the doing of it. The doing was simple. It was the gamble element that was awful, and I'm still feeling the strain and reaction.' [27]

1/6th Gordons were relieved by 1/9th Royal Scots. As they made their way back:

'. . . the roads were knee deep in mud, and heavy rain was still falling. A man of 'A' Company fell into a shell hole filled with water – far from being discouraged he immediately commenced to quack like a duck, and the remainder of his platoon, following his example, quacked their way cheerfully back to camp.

On arrival, hot soup and rum punch were served out to the men, and these, together with a dry shirt and socks, enabled all to sleep soundly. The state of the camp in which the battalion now found itself was very bad. Tents pitched in a sea of slippery mud which in many places was knee-deep, made cleaning up and reorganizing a matter of some difficulty. In addition, the continuous rain made it impossible to get their clothing dry.' [28]

152nd Brigade's Report of the battle cited 1/6th Gordons' 'quacking' soldier: 'as an example of the spirits of the men who had been without sleep for close on 60 hours, during which they had fought most severe battle and had marched 14 miles, in addition to being soaked to the skin.'[29]

On the left of the 51st the 38th (Welsh) Division used three brigades and reached the Steenbeck at 12.30, two hours after the 51st had crossed it. On the extreme left of the British attack, the Guards Division used elements of its three brigades to cross the Steenbeck. On their left two co-operating French divisions took their objectives. Bewsher referred to the battle:

'. . . as the neatest and cleanest performance which the Division had carried out. It was delivered against the Germans while their fighting efficiency was unimpaired, and while their numbers were still unappreciably diminished. . . the success was so complete that, even when the battle was over, nothing which was an improvement in the plans of attack suggested itself.' [30]

Not everyone agreed with this assessment, for there were short-comings in casualty evacuation and a 152nd Brigade machine-gun officer complained that 'the lack of stretcher bearers with my Machine Gun Company was felt and in future engagements I would recommend that some personnel from a Field Ambulance be attached to each company. There is a natural inclination amongst Battalion stretcher bearers to look after their own first.' [31]

Nor was communication perfect, although Bewsher states that telephone wires were laid fairly rapidly to new forward battalion headquarters in fortified farms, the 152nd Brigade Report recorded that 'a signal dog was allotted to the 6th Gordon Highlanders and was taken to the GREEN LINE by them. Here it was duly released with message attached and was with difficulty persuaded to start on its journey homewards. Eventually it left and was seen safely crossing the BLACK LINE. Two days later it reached its objective minus its collar.' [32]

The 51st had made one of the deepest penetrations of the day, and had ceded only the outposts east of the Steenbeck. The 51st deployed only two brigades, where other divisions used three, which suggests a high degree of training to achieve the most benefit from the smallest necessary number of men. 152nd Brigade's Report Summary recognised:

> '. . . the care and trouble taken by Battalion Commanders and others to perfect the training of their men, left little doubt as to the ultimate issue of the fight. . . the value of training given to the men was revealed again and again in the course of the fight by the way in which the machine-guns in concrete emplacements were engaged from all sides by Lewis Guns, rifle grenades, and riflemen, and finally rounded up without losing the barrage.' [33]

153rd Brigade reported under the heading: 'Advance of Small Parties. (Dribbling) The advantages of this form of attack against strong positions was repeatedly proven.' [34]

The 51st's casualties in killed, wounded and missing from 152nd and 153rd Brigades on 31st July to 1st August were 52 officers and 1516 men[35] – a total of 1568, or 63% of the 2478 casualties recorded at Beaumont-Hamel. Given that the weather in both battles was atrocious, and that the Germans were in well prepared positions and were not surprised, the lower number of casualties can be attributed to more flexible tactics, the increased initiative of junior commanders, and more heavy artillery than had been available at Beaumont-Hamel for pulversing the German wire, positions and supply routes; and larger machine-gun barrages.

This phase of the Third battle of Ypres is known as the Battle of Pilkem Ridge.

Despite the quagmire and rain, and the limited successes on 31st

The Volunteers, precursors of the Territorial Forces.

13 November 1916, 152 Brigade attacks Beaumont-Hamel. (*Drawing by Fred A Farrell*)

1/7th Gordons clearing Y Ravine. (*Drawing by Fred A Farrell*)

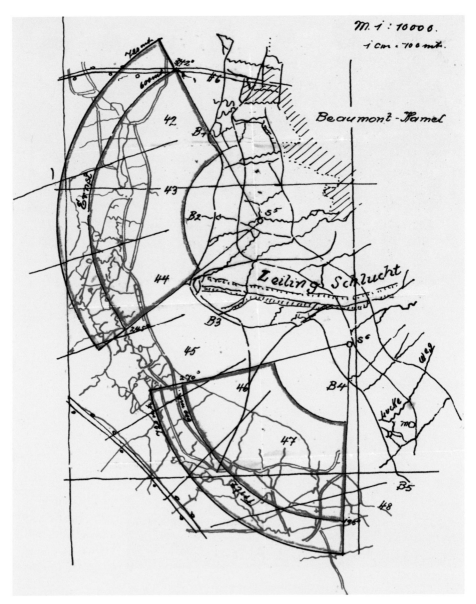

Above: Captured German map, Beaumont-Hamel. Lieutenant Cairnie, 1/5th Seaforths.

Below left: Highland Division insignia.

Below right: Post-war badge.

Above and below: Black Watch at leisure in barracks. (*Estate of Thomas Lindsay*)

Shelled building.
(*Estate of Thomas Lindsay*)

Left: Troop transport.
(*Estate of Thomas Lindsay*)

Below: Bedford. A Company
5th Seaforth Highlanders.

1/7th Black Watch
on Flesquières
Ridge. (*Estate of
Thomas Lindsay*)

Goose Observation
Post. (*Estate of
Thomas Lindsay*)

Black Watch recruit
in barracks. (*Estate of
Thomas Lindsay*)

Happy Valley – the road to High Wood with Mametz Wood on the left.

Mametz Wood and the 38th Division Memorial on the route to High Wood.

Newfoundland Park, part of the Beaumont-Hamel battleground.

Serried ranks of the Division's casualties from the Battle of the Ancre, Mailly Wood Cemetery.

Right: Summit of Flesquières Ridge.

Below: Flesquières Chateau.

Above left: The High Wood Cross Memorial, now above Y Ravine, Newfoundland Memorial Park.

Above right: The Division's Memorial above Y Ravine, with the Cross of Sacrifice in Hunter's Cemetery in the centre background.

Below left: The Seaforth Highlanders Memorial, Sunken Road, Fampoux.

Below right: A close-up of the Seaforth Highlanders Memorial.

July and 1st August, the need to relieve the French made continued attack necessary. An attempt to take the Gheluveldt Plateau on 10th August failed, owing to the 'energetic and resolution of the counter-attacking Germans.' [36] An attack planned for 14th August was postponed because of bad weather until the 16th.

On the 16th the unfortunate II Corps on the right attracted intense German barrages and six German counter-attacks: on the left the XIV Corps penetrated a mile on a 3000 yard front and captured the village of Langemarck. The conditions in which this battle was fought were worse than in the Battle of Pilckhem Ridge. Gough:

> 'informed the Commander-in Chief that tactical success was not possible, or would be too costly, under such conditions, and advised that the attack should now be abandoned. . . he told me that the attack must be continued.' [37]

Unimpressed by Gough, and by then committed only to a battle of attrition, with no prospect of swinging through to the Belgian coast, Haig delegated the capture of the Gheluveldt Plateau to Plumer's Second Army. Plumer chose 20th September for the attack. Subsidiary attacks on 22nd and 27th August failed. The weather was dry for the three weeks before the attack, which made the movement of men and materials easier. Activity took place after dark, when shattered roads were repaired by filling in the shell holes, levelling, and laying nine foot wide plank roads, which were invariably shelled and had to be repaired. Plumer planned four 1500 yard bounds, each separated by six days. The intervals would allow field guns and supplies to be brought forward for the successive phases. The men would attack on a front of 3000 yards, a reduction of the 6800 yards proposed by Haig. On this front Plumer would have an exceptionally heavy concentration of artillery. Gough's Fifth Army, of which the 51st was part, was involved in the 20th September attack, the Battle of the Menin Road.

It rained during the night.

On the 20th the infantry followed the barrage. In the Second Army, on the extreme right the 19th and 39th Divisions reached the third objective and 41st and 23rd Divisions took all of theirs with the exception of the area around Tower Hamlets. Next to them 1st and 2nd Australian Divisions fulfilled their day's objectives.

On the Fifth Army's right 9th (Scottish) took its objectives. The 55th (West Lancashire) Division did not – it had lost 135 officers and 3,720 other ranks on 31st July, and its replacements had come slowly, and 1000 men had been so late in arriving that they were left behind.[38] The 58th (2nd/1st London) Division was a second line Territorial Force division, which contained two 3rd line battalions, an inauspicious combination for their second major engagement. They did well, and achieved all their objectives.

The 51st had garrisoned the line from the 20th August and knew the terrain. Like others in September it had been subjected to the Germans' latest chemical novelty, mustard gas which was delivered by shells, blistered exposed skin, caused temporary blindness, and serious exposure killed. It lingered on clothing, weapons and the ground, maintaining its efficacy for days. Kilt wearers were especially vulnerable to it.

On 6th September 1/5th Seaforths had launched a futile raid on Pheasant Trench, which was to be taken on 20th September. They were stopped in No Man's Land and had to wait until nightfall before they could withdraw. Of 103 men involved 20 were killed, 20 wounded and 9 missing, a 47.5% casualty rate for an estimated total of less than 30 German casualties and minimal information. Bewsher's uncritical inclusion of this raid reflects the acceptance of high casualties as the price of trench warfare. [39]

Haig had travelled to meet the Corps HQs of the Fifth Army on 18th September. He was critical of V Corps artillery arrangements and:

> '. . . directed General Birch (my artillery adviser) who was with me to go into the details of the artillery plan with Fifth Army . . . I next visited General Maxse Commanding XVIII Corps – Generals Harper (Commanding 51st Division); Fanshawe (Commanding 58th Division) explained their plan of attack. All very thorough and satisfactory. Brigadier General Fasson the CRA was as usual very clear in his explanations.' [40]

The 51st's attacking brigade had practised for five days on a full scale replica of the battlefield, and its battalions had honed their fire and movement skills. The artillery support on the Fifth Army's front was less intense than that on the Second Army's front, but was impressive compared to the meagre efforts of 1915 and early 1916. The 51st's artillery support expended the following:

'The 22 18-pounder batteries supporting the brigade attack in the 51st Division's sector fired 67,000 rounds between noon on the 19th and noon on the 20th; the six 4.5 inch howitzer batteries fired 14,000 rounds during the same period; the 12 6 inch howitzer batteries fired 5,561 rounds between 5.30 a.m. and 9.35 a.m. on the 20th, and three batteries of 9.2 inch howitzers fired 685 rounds. In addition to 60-pdrs. And other medium and heavy artillery, 16 trench mortars fired 2,700 rounds.' [41]

Thirty two machine-guns laid a barrage on enemy strong points as the attack went in. [42]

The infantry was preceded by a creeping barrage which progressed at 50 yards every two minutes until the first objective, then at 50 yards every four minutes to the last objective. A hundred yards ahead of this fell another creeping barrage. A combing barrage preceded the creeping barrage by 200 yards, focusing on pill boxes, strong points and communication trenches: this was stiffened by shelling by 6 inch howitzers and 60-pounders. Falling beyond that, on the main German routes to the trenches, and on their possible assembly points for their reserves, were shells from heavy howitzers and 60-pounders.

Most of these shells fell on a front of just 1500 yards, widening at the last objective to 1900 yards, in an area 1500 yards deep. It was anticipated that the Germans in the outpost line of shell holes and trenches would succumb quickly and that taking the defensive zone of pill boxes and fortified farms would be slower, as there was no guarantee that the artillery could destroy all these positions.

154th Brigade, which had not been involved on 31st July, attacked. Two companies from each of its attacking battalions led, 1/9th Royal Scots on the right and 1/4th Seaforths on the left. On their attainment

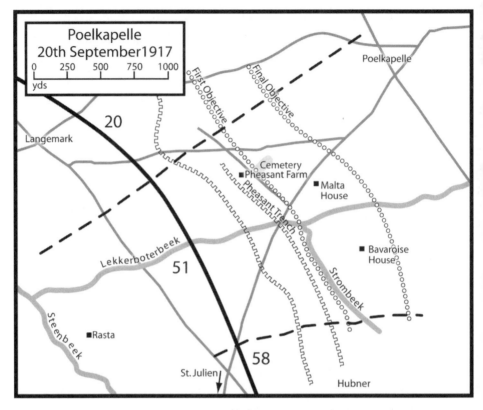

Poelkapelle
20th September 1917

0   250   500   750   1000
yds

20

Langemark

Poelkapelle

First Objective

Final Objective

Cemetery
Pheasant Farm
Pheasant Trench

Malta House

Lekkerboterbeek

51

Strombeek

Bavaroise House

Steenbeek

Rasta

58

St. Julien

Hubner

of their first objectives the 1/7th Argylls and 1/4th Gordons would pass through them and 1/8th Argylls and the 1/5th Seaforths, from the 152nd Brigade were positioned in the rear to reinforce 154th Brigade if it became necessary. These two battalions had been in the first wave on 31st July.

It rained heavily in the night, created mud, filled shellholes, and widened streams, marshes and pools. Bewsher described these as 'the normal conditions of the Ypres salient in those days, and the men were learning to expect nothing less.'[43] Twelve tanks were allocated to the 51st.

1/9th Royal Scots suffered 11 wounded as they moved into their assembly positions:

'Assembly was made difficult by heavy rain which fell about midnight 19/20th. . . Zero hour was 5.40 a.m. at which hour the barrage opened and the men got well away close up to the barrage. By 6.45 A.M. PHEASANT TRENCH on the right including all adjacent strong points was captured and consolidated.

Considerable opposition from strong points was speedily overcome. Touch was kept with the Battn. on right (2/8th LONDON REGT Post Office Rifles) throughout from the start. On the left. . . the attacking waves of B Coy were stopped by heavy machine gun fire and returned to our lines. There they were quickly reorganised. . . and again advanced and captured the trench, being assisted very greatly by the action of the section commander on the right flank of the Company who – on finding the enemy still holding the trench to his left – worked along it. The second waves (C and D Coys) passed through and reached the STROOMBEEK with very slight opposition except on the extreme right of C Coy where they came under enfilade rifle fire from HUBNER FARM which was strongly held. Fire was opened by rifle and Lewis gun on this point to support the advance of 2/8th LONDON REGT. who successfully captured the farm, after which right Coy (C) established a post where party from 2/8th LONDON REGT. was met.

The battalion was established on the line of the STROOMBEEK by 8.10 a.m., the company on the left (D Coy) having suffered somewhat severely before reaching it and in the vicinity of PHEASANT TRENCH – The 7th A & S Hrs. were all well up to the leading wave at the STROOMBEEK in artillery formation and passed through in good time to catch up the barrage. The remainder of the day until well on in the evening was uneventful – the Enemy put down heavy barrages intermittently on the line of the ST JULIEN-LANGEMARCK road during the day, his first barrage opening about six minutes after zero.[44]

1/4th Seaforths on the left had to fight to take their portion of Pheasant Trench, but by '6.10 a.m. CEMETERY and PHEASANT TRENCH reported captured, large numbers of Germans killed; very few prisoners taken.'[45] 'Very few prisoners taken' suggests little desire to take prisoners, or that the Germans had fought to the death, and 150 German bodies were later counted in the trench.[46]

1/7th Argylls, having passed through 1/9th Royal Scots reached the final objective, as did 1/4th Gordons, who by then had six platoons of about ten men each and three officers left. Both battalions had been shelled as they had advanced, and had to fight to reach their objectives.

Whereas the 51st was in touch with the 58th Division on its right, the opposite situation prevailed on the left, where the 20th Division had failed to take most of its first objective.This allowed the Germans to enfilade the 51st and 1/4th Seaforths and 1/4th Gordons formed a 1000 yards long protective flank.

At 11.45 a.m. and 12.30 p.m. the Germans counter-attacked on the 51st's left, and these attacks were repelled. A 1/8th Argylls' company reinforced the flank and other Argylls were disposed elsewhere along the line. Of twelve tanks allocated to the 51st only D44 arrived on the Poelcappelle Road, near Malta House, and broke down. It became a company headquarters, three of its Lewis guns and 200 rounds of ammunition were given to the infantry, one Lewis gun was kept in the tank, and the tank's six pounder was manned. Around 5 p.m. a counter-attack supported by a concentrated barrage 'of unusual intensity'[47] on 51st's left took place down the Poelcappelle spur, a gentle slope leading into the 51st's position. This counter-attack was held by rifle, machine-gun and artillery fire. At the centre of the 51st's front, ammunition ran out and a withdrawal took place from the new front, allowing the counter-attacking Germans to form a sharp salient defined by the Letterbotterbeek and the road leading north-west to Poelcappelle.

On the Letterbotterbeek flank a company of 1/7th Argylls, two platoons of 1/8th Argylls and a company of 1/9th Royal Scots held the line, and on the Poelcappelle road flank, the line was formed by 1/8th Argylls and the 1/4th Seaforth Highlanders. The attacking Germans were enfiladed and a counter-attack was mounted by the elements of the 51st that had withdrawn in the face of the Germans, had collected ammunition from the dead and wounded, and had been reorganised. The Germans were driven back and a line consolidated beyond the first objective of the day, the 51st having conceded about six hundred yards of territory taken in the morning.

The Germans 234th Division suffered heavily in its counter attacks on the 51st and 58th Division on its right: the history of the 234th admits that very heavy losses were suffered, some of the battalions losing 60%

of their officers and up to 50% of their strength.[48] The success of the attacks and failure of the counter-attacks were largely attributable to the artillery.

> 'Crown Prince Rupprecht . . . in his diary. . . quotes a Bavarian officer who was on the plateau on 20th , and who was also in the Verdun battles, that the weight of the barrage had surpassed all precedent.' [49]

In his memoirs Ludendorff stated that:

> 'the power of the attack lay in the artillery, and in the fact that ours did not do enough damage to the hostile infantry as they were assembling, and, above all, at the actual time of the assault.' [50]

154th Brigade was relieved by 152nd Brigade on the night of 21st/22nd September and held off German counter-attacks on the 23rd. The 51st was relieved by the 11th (Northern) Division on 26th/27th September.

The Official History put the 51st's casualties at 43 officers and 1141 other ranks, a total of 1184, from the five battalions involoved. The 39th Division had fewer casualties (976) in the Battle of Menin Road, having committed only one brigade to the initial assault. From right to left Second Army's casualties were: 19th 1,933; 39th 976; 41st 3,123; 1 Aus 2,352; 2 Aus 1,773 and Fifth Army's divisional casualties were: 9th 2,191; 55th 1,944; 58th 1,236; 51st 1,184; 20th 1,409. The 39th total makes no distinction between killed and wounded, all the others do. Comparing the 9th (Scottish) with the 51st shows:

> 9th Division: officers 21 killed, 56 wounded, 24 missing; men: 374 killed 1,594 wounded and 122 missing. The 51st: officers 12 killed 27 wounded 4 missing; men: 173 killed, 827 wounded and 141 missing.

With the exception of the missing the 51st's casualties are approximately half of those suffered by the 9th Division.[51] Both were Scottish, aggressive and successful on 20th September. Was the 51st lucky, or was this proof of Harper's sparing us of his men? Harper's desire to diminish casualties is recognised by one historian, who concluded that a result of his frugal deployment of men was that the 51st was the only division to concede ground won, although not every division achieved its objectives, and that the 51st disadvantaged its neighbours.[52] The only division not to achieve all its objectives was the 20th, on the 51st's immediate left, so that on this flank, the 51st was hindered rather than hindering. Bewsher wrote:

> 'the battle affords an admirable illustration of the economic use of troops. . . only five battalions were employed in the attack and subsequent counter-attacks; that these five battalions – though through want of ammunition they did not hold their entire gains – had established themselves for a while in their final objective and had accounted for every German garrisoning the area allotted to them for the attack. Moreover these battalions were not only facing their front, but also facing their left flank, as the Division on their left had not made equal progress in the attack.' [53]

He paid tribute to the standard of training and initiative of the men, their skill in fire and movement and platoon and section tactics. He noted that nine counter-attacking German battalions faced the 51st, and were stopped by it. He praised Harper for anticipating the direction of the German counter-attack and having placed his reserves in the appropriate positions to forestall the Germans, and claimed that the Germans were 'completely outmatched in generalship, leadership, tactical skill and skill at arms.'[54]

He is justified: it was a successful phase of the Battle of Third Ypres, but the objectives were strictly limited, compared to the over-ambitious expectations of the 31st July. The author of the history of 1/8th Argylls reflected:

> '. . . it was another of these costly engagements which does not appear to have effected any considerable gain, but it evidently had some wider significance at the time since the Field Marshal himself went to 18 Corps Headquarters and congratulated the General on 'the successful attacks of 51 and

58 Divisions' and 'their splendid victory in the battle of 20th September'.' [55]

In a battle report an officer commanding tanks with the 51st claimed 'the general tendency of the infantry is to get too close to the Tank. It was found that a suitable distance for infantry to be maintained behind tanks was about 200 yards.'[56] Something to be borne in mind in the context of the next battle.

The inevitable replacements were integrated into the depleted battalions and supporting arms. Many medical students had volunteered for combat roles and the war had taken its toll on doctors, and by 1917 battalion and field ambulance Medical Officers from British sources were in short supply. Before the 51st left the Salient it received its first batch of U.S. Army Medical Officers Reserve Corps (M.O.R.C.) doctors. Rorie, 1/2nd Highland Field Ambulance, claimed that 'a week up the line was usually sufficient to adjust their outlook. . . they were always fresh and stimulating. . . they gave us an outfit of terse and vigorous slang. . . and shewed us new methods of losing our spare cash at games of chance. . .'[57]

The Battle of the Menin Road ended the 51st's tour in the Salient. Harper received the following messages:

1. From Lieut.-General Sir I. Maxse, K.C.B., D.S.O., commanding XVIIIth Corps.

'Before the 51st (Highland) Division quits the XVIIIth Corps, I desire to express to its commander and to all ranks in the Division how highly I have appreciated their services through three months of strenuous fighting.

'What has struck me most is the thoroughness of the organisation within the Division, and the fact that all the usual war problems have been thought out beforehand, discussed in detail, and are embodied in simple doctrines well known to all ranks. The result is the Division fights with gallantry, and can be depended upon to carry out any reasonable task allocated to it in any battle. For this reason I venture to place it among the three best fighting divisions I have met in France during the past three years.

'Its record in this Corps comprises:

'(1) On 31st July 1917, a shattering assault on High Command Redoubt, the capture in their entirety of three separate systems of German defence lines, an advance of two miles in depth into hostile territory, and the consolidation and retention of the line of the river Steenbeek and all the objectives allocated to the Division.

'(2) On the 20th September 1917, an assault on a sector of the Langemarck-Gheluvelt line which had resisted capture for more than a month, an incursion into hostile territory, and the consolidation of important hills south-west of Poelcapelle and at Bavaroise House. The same afternoon these two hills were repeatedly attacked by five Prussian battalions, all of whom were defeated with sanguinary losses.

'In conclusion, I wish good luck to all ranks, and hope to serve again with them in this war.' [58]

Maxse had a high regard for the 51st. He had been anxious to know how well the second line 58th (2/1st London) Division had performed, and particularly the 2/8 Londons (Post Office Rifles). Its successes were transmitted to him by their immediate neighbours on the battle field and 'as evidence of the Post Office valour is entirely derived from the Highlanders on their immediate left I feel I can accept it as absolutely correct.'[59]

2. From General Sir H. de la P. Gough, K.C.B., K.C.B.O., commanding Fifth Army.

'In bidding farewell to the Highland Division, the Army Commander wishes to express his great admiration for and appreciation of their splendid record during the fighting of the last two months.

'Their fine advance, their gallant defence of ground, even against repeated enemy attacks, and the severe punishment they inflicted on the enemy during the last battle, will ever remain one of their proudest records, and has helped materially towards the enemy's final defeat. He heartily wishes them all success in the future. Scotland for ever.' [60]

The 51st was fortunate that it was in only two of the eight battles of Third Ypres. It left with its reputation enhanced. Bewsher stated that the Germans had been so impressed with the efficiency of the 51st that they published a list in which they judged it the most formidable division on the Western Front. [61]

The Territorial Divisions 1914-1918 states: 'About this time the enemy published the fact that at this time they considered the 51st the most formidable Division on the Western Front.' [62]

Rorie footnotes: 'The order of *Furchtbarkeit* ('much-to-be-feared-ness') was: 1. Fifty-first Division. 2. Twenty-ninth Division (reformed) 3. Guards Division.' [63]

Neil Munro wrote that: 'the Germans placed the Fifty-first first in formidableness on a list of hard-fighting British divisions.' [64]

Nicholson referred to it as 'The hardest fighting of the divisions.' and 'in 1917 they were reckoned by the Germans as our fiercest fighting division.' [65]

This alleged German endorsement of the 51st was much repeated after the war and sceptical historians have rightly noted that there is no written evidence of this document. Does that mean that such a document did not exist? It may have been a local assessment captured in a trench raid, and its contents rapidly passed by word of mouth. If it is asserted that it never existed, the only possibility might be that it was fabricated to enhance the 51st's reputation, as all the individuals who quoted the alleged German list had close associations with the 51st. Would a fabrication have emanated from officers whose code was basically honourable, or, given the 51st's self regard, was it necessary? The evidence is missing, but the repetition of the assessment, by Bewsher, Rorie and Munro, and others, suggests that such a list may have existed, even if it is yet to be found!

Ten days after leaving the Salient the 51st was in the front line again.

NOTES

1. J.C.Milne *The Orra Loon and other poems* (Findlay) 1946 p.8.

2. Haldane pp. 216-7.

3. Harper Letter 6.7.1917 to 'Dear Charles' TNA.

4. Paddy Griffith *Battlefield Tactics on the Western Front* The British Army's Art of Attack 1916-

1918 Yale University Press 1994 p.59.

5. Bewsher pp.192-3.

6. Peel and MacDonald pp.38-9.

7. Bewsher p.194.

8. Sutherland p.120.

9. War diary1/6th Gordons 7-8, 7. 1917

10. Haldane p.217.

11. Rennie recollections.

12. Harper Notes on Infantry Tactics and Training. Appendix, p.126.

13. OH v.2 1917 p.157.

14. Bewsher p.205.

15. War Diary 1/6th Gordons 31.7.1917

16. Peel and MacDonald p.41

17. Edmonds OH v.2 1917 p.159.

18. War diary 1/6 Gordons 31.7.1917

19. London Gazette 6.9.1917

20. London Gazette Supplement 14.9.1917

21. Wauchope p.166.

22. Bewsher p.212.

23. Wauchope pp.166-7 account by unnamed member of D company 1/6th Black Watch.

24. Peel and MacDonald p.43.

25. War diary 1/6th Gordons 1.8.1917.

26. 153 Brigade notes post 31/7-1/8 1917 TNA.

27. Haldane p.224.

28. War diary 1/6th Gordons 1 and 2.7.1917 .

29. 152nd Brigade Summary 31.7.-1.8.1917 TNA.

30. Bewsher p.215

31. 152nd Brigade MG Report 31.7-1.8.1917 TNA

32. 152nd Brigade Report Summary 31.7 -1.8.1917 TNA

33. 152nd Brigade's Report Summary 31.7-1.8.1917 TNA

34. 153rd Brigade's Report Summary 31.7-1.8. 1917 TNA

35. Bewsher p.214

36. Hubert Gough *The Fifth Army* p.203.

37. Gough p.205.

38. Edmonds OH v.2 1917 Page 266 and footnote 2

39. Bewsher pp. 217-218
40. Haig's diary 18.9.1917
41. Edmonds OH v.2 1917 p.270 footnote 1.
42. Bewsher p.221.
43. Bewsher p.222.
44. War diary 1/9th Royal Scots 20.9.1917
45. War diary 1/4th Seaforths 20.9.1917
46. Bewsher p.224.
47. Bewsher p.227
48. Edmonds OH v.2 1917 Page 276 ex *Hohe Hausnummern an der Westfront* pp 94-111.
49. Edmonds OH v.2 1917 Page 277 footnote.
50. Ludendorff ii p 488 quoted ex John Terraine, *The Road to Passchendaele*
51. OH v.2 1917 Note p.279.
52. Sheffield and Todman editors Command and Control on the Western Front Spellmount Ltd 2004 Chapter VI (John Lee) pp.138-139.
53. Bewsher p.230.
54. Bewsher p.231.
55. Malcolm p.45.
56. Report on action of 20th September 1917 by No.12 Company D Battalion, Tank Corps working in conjunction with the 51st Division, XVIII Corps TNA
57. Rorie p.149
58. Bewsher pp.231-2.
59. Baynes p.178.
60. Bewsher p.232.
61. Bewsher p.205
62. Stirling, J. *The Territorial Divisions*, Dent and Sons 1922 p.81
63. Rorie p.135, and footnote.
64. Introduction to Farrell's The 51st Division, War Sketches p.14.
65. Nicholson pp.60 and 48.

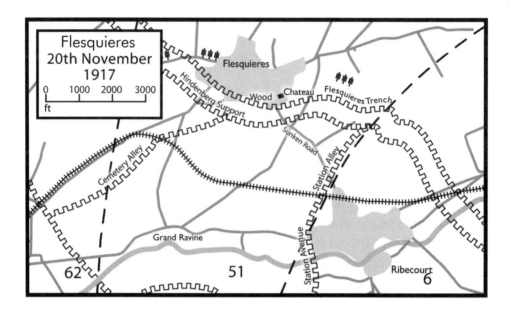

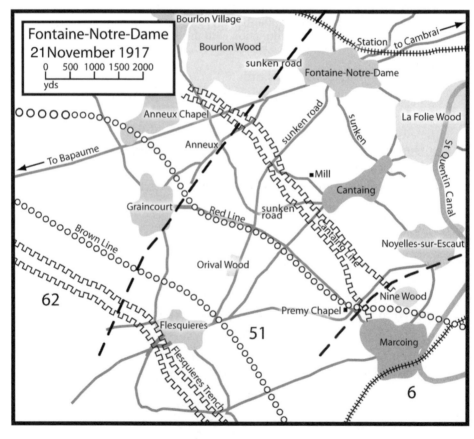

CHAPTER 7

CONTROVERSY
Cambrai

'His (Harper's) tactics were purely silly.' [1a]

'Harper was a criminal.' [1b]

While in the autumn of 1917 Third Ypres continued, the 51st had moved to Achiet-le-Petit, thence to a sector south-east of Arras, between Heninel and Wancourt. Plans were being made for the first massed tank attack in history. Tanks had been introduced on the Somme in September 1916, and were found to be mechanically unreliable – the urgencies of war meant that prolonged product testing was impossible. At Arras in 1917 the wet weather adversely affected the tanks' performance, and Third Ypres was the nadir of the tank, with mud, breakdowns and enemy fire eliminating most of the 200 tanks that were committed. Major J.F.C. Fuller, an enthusiastic proponent of tanks, served on the staff of Brigadier General Elles, who commanded them. Both had raged at the deployment of their tanks in unsuitable conditions, and worried that their failings in soft and broken terrain might jeopardise their continued existence.

After Third Ypres some dramatic success was necessary. The Hindenberg Line had been weakened by the withdrawal of German troops to Flanders. 'Of these weakened sectors the Cambrai front had been selected as the most suitable for the surprise operations in contemplation.' [2] Fuller and Elles wanted a lightning raid, to demoralise the Germans and prove the worth of tanks, but Byng, of Third Army, decided to capture and hold territory.

On a front of six miles, between the Canal de l'Escaut on the right and the uncompleted and dry Canal du Nord on the left, the Third Army was to crack the Hindenberg Line, take Flesquieres Ridge and Bourlon Wood, and push forward five cavalry divisions to cut off Cambrai. Thereafter an advance on Valenciennes was planned – 25 miles from the British start line. After three years of failure to attain over-ambitious objectives, it is incredible that such an optimismtic outcome could even have been contemplated. There were insufficient reserves for a prolonged battle, so it was to last only forty eight hours. A large number of tanks were to be secretly concentrated, and after a short, accurate barrage, advance on dry, firm, relatively unbroken ground.

Brigadier-General Tudor, c.r.a., 9th Division, Third Army, had evolved a means of laying a barrage from the map, without registering the guns with preliminary ranging shots, or the need for visual sighting of targets. These conventional processes announced to even the dimmest German soldier that something unpleasant was imminent. A timetabled lifting barrage would precede the tank advance: the ground would not be disturbed much, to the advantage of both tanks and infantry. The barbed wire would not be shelled: instead the tanks would flatten it and create paths for the infantry. As the Hindenberg Line trenches were wide and deep, tanks were provided with fascines, bundles of brushwood, compacted with chains, carried on top of the tanks, to be released into trenches, to form tank crossing points.

The 51st had minimal tank co-operation at Beaumont-Hamel, when the crew of a ditched tank fought as infantry. At Arras neither of the two tanks allocated to the Highland Division had arrived. At Roeux tank C7 had cleared houses in the village for the 1/7th Argylls and C22 had helped the 1/4th Gordons at the Chemical Works. The 1/6th Seaforths had enjoyed the support of tank 'Gordon' at the Battle of Pilkhem and the 1/8th Argylls had been reinforced and resupplied by a tank that had broken down on the Poelcappelle Road, the only one of the twelve available to the 51st to fulfill a useful function.

Brigadier-General Craufurd of 18th Brigade, 6th Division recorded that Harper was sceptical about the plan of attack – possibly as a result of the 51st's limited experience of tank support, when much of the promised help had foundered, broken down, or been knocked out. [3] Harper knew that tanks attracted enemy fire, and that infantry close to them would be at unnecessary risk. Once Harper had digested the plan he was anxious that his division's anticipated success would not be jeopardised and when Haig visited the 51st on 15th November he noted:

'The Division is now over 13,000 infantry strong and in great form. . . Harper pointed out that if the 62nd Div on his left did not get on, his advance might be held up. I indicated that it is possible for him to form a defensive flank on his left and press forward with his right as rapidly as possible and get behind the enemy by seizing Bourlon Wood etc.'

All seemed very pleased with the operation and confident of success if it is launched as a surprise.[4]

Fuller stipulated that the tanks were to advance in two waves, a hundred yards apart, leading the infantry, who were to follow in single file, or worms, with the leading sections of infantry close behind each tank but dropping back 25 to 50 yards as it approached the wire. The leading wave of tanks was to work in threes, with the first going through the wire turning left and firing on the enemy in the front line trench. The next would drop a fascine into the front line trench, cross over and turn left along the rear side of the front trench, and the third would go to the support trench, drop its fascine, cross it, turn left and fire on the occupants.

The infantry were to put bombers into the trenches to mop up the remaining defenders, supported by the tanks, put up barricades in the trenches, clear wire, consolidate, and form an advanced guard beyond the captured objective, before the next wave of the attack went forward. The Official History comments that this gave the infantry a mixed message as it permitted them to detach themselves from their tanks while they cleared the trenches. [5]

The 51st's introduction to the forthcoming battle was:

'a lecture by Brigadier-General Pelham Burn, to all officers of the 152nd Brigade, which was attended by many officers of the Tank Corps. . . The lecture was held at Dainville, on Guy Fawkes' Day in a Y.M.C.A. or Church Army hut. Great secrecy had to be preserved, and even the good man of the cloth in charge of the hut was led protesting from its precincts, while stout sentries were posted at each window when the general talked. We soon discovered why, in our training, the Colonel had developed a new passion for sending us in a stupid procession after empty half-limbers; they had represented tanks, and tanks were to figure largely in the scheme that was unfolded.' [6]

Lieutenant Birk, of the tanks' D Battalion, recalled:

'Liaison with the Highlanders consisted of simple tactical exercises by day and the most colossal binges by night. . . Liaison, at any rate with our Battalion of the Black Watch was very close, very intimate, very cordial, and both sides understood precisely what was required and expected.' [7]

The signals to be used between tanks and infantry were:

1. All clear-come on. Red and yellow flag waved through the roof of a tank.

2. Tank broken down – don't wait. A shovel through the roof of a tank.

3. Tank required by infantry. A steel helmet on a rifle held above the head.

These primitive means of communication were judged to have been successful in battle 'on several occasions'. [8]

'Several' suggests that in the fog of war these signals did not always work.

Harper's procedure differed from Fuller's: the tanks were in fours, and were to advance in two waves, the first to deal with the enemy's outpost line, crush wire, and proceed to the support line, followed by the second wave. On reaching their objectives the centre tank was to push through towards the support trench while the others had to deal with the occupants of the trench, they were to turn right, rather than left. Instead of following in the tracks of the tanks in single file, the men were to advance in open order in two ranks, as distinct from the Tank Corps' recommended 'worms', and were instructed not to be closer than 100 yards to the tanks, rather than 25 to 50 yards behind. 62nd Division, on the 51st's left, separately evolved tactics akin to those of the 51st.

Camouflaged tank assembly positions were in the woods behind Havrincourt, and their arrival was covered by the noise of patrolling aircraft and spasmodic gun fire: artillery positions were dug and concealed before the guns arrived. Narrow trenches were widened, and where troops had to pass over trenches footbridges were provided. Telephone cables could not be buried in the standard six feet trench without the enemy noticing, so armoured cable was laid on the surface, in ditches and in trenches to link with each divisional headquarters, from where it divided and led to brigades; telephone lines would follow the advance, beyond the second objective. Each brigade had a wireless tank, two power buzzers, pigeons, runners and visual signaling posts [9]

On 18th November 1/6th Gordons: 'marched (from Rocquigny) to the village of Metz and on arrival there at 8.5 p.m. was billeted in the ruins of the village. Billets were quite comfortable and were chiefly elephant shelters. The men had tea and turned in. No lights or fires were allowed.' On the 19th 'All the men with the exception of special parties to draw stores were kept under cover in billets. . . The Commanding Officer accompanied by the Company Commanders spent the forenoon reconnoitring the various assembly positions of the companies.' [10] Despite the security measures the Germans identified the 51st on 19th November and although some German commanders were worried by its presence, others thought that it had been sent south to recover from Third Ypres, and was in no state to attack.[11]

At 6.10 a.m. on 20th November, with their noise of their movement covered by low flying aircraft, the tanks moved forward, followed by their supporting infantry. Ten minutes later, at 6.20 am, the barrage fell on the Germans.

III Corps was on the right, and its right division, 12th (Eastern), by 8 a.m. had taken its first objective. The victors paused for 48 minutes, to allow the British barrage to lift and fall on its next group of targets. Then it took its second objectives, overcoming determined resistance, in which three of their six tanks were destroyed by close range artillery fire. On their left 20th (Light) Division reached all its objectives by 11.30 but eleven tanks in support of the right hand 61st Brigade were also lost due to guns close to the enemy line. [12] 6th Division on the left of III Corps reached all its objectives by 11a.m. With them in the leading tank, which ditched on the way to Ribécourt, was Brigadier-General Elles, commanding the Tank Corps, flying the Corps' new black red and green flag, symbolising mud, blood and the green fields beyond.

On IV Corps' front the 51st was on the right, preceded by 34 tanks of E Battalion. On the 51st's right 1/5th Seaforths pushed 800 yards beyond the first objective, to the railway line. A machine-gun nest in Station Road, west of Ribécourt was troublesome and Lance-Corporal R McBeath volunteered to deal with it. His V.C citation reads:

210171 L/Cpl. Robert McBeath, Sea. Highrs. (Kinlochbervie, Lairg, Sutherland)

'For most conspicuous bravery when with his company in attack and approaching the final objective, a nest of enemy machine-guns in the western outskirts of a village opened fire both on his own unit and on the unit to the right. The advance was checked and heavy casualties resulted.

L/Cpl. Robert McBeath

When a Lewis gun was called for to deal with these machine-guns, L/Corpl. McBeath volunteered for the duty, and immediately moved off alone with a Lewis gun and his revolver. He located one of the machine-guns in action, and worked his way towards it, shooting the gunner with his revolver at 20 yards range. Finding several of the hostile machine-guns in action, he, with the assistance of a tank, attacked them and drove the gunners to ground in a deep dugout.

L/Corpl. McBeath, regardless of all danger, rushed in after them, shot an enemy who opposed him on the steps, and drove the remainder of the garrison out of the dug-out, capturing three officers and 30 men.

There were in all five machine-guns mounted round the dug-out, and by putting them out of action he cleared the way for the advance of both units. The conduct of L/Corpl. McBeath throughout three days of severe fighting was beyond praise.' [13] [Born in Kinlochbervie, he was 19 years old in 1917, survived the war, emigrated to British Columbia with his wife, joined the Vancouver Police and was murdered by a gunman on 9th October 1922.]

To the left of Ribécourt it was easier:

'To show how unexpected was our attack we captured in the valley to the left of Ribécourt a Boche cooker, a kind of four-wheeled iron waggon with a fire and boilers, in which hot meals are cooked and brought up near the trenches. The first wave pounced upon the waggon with the horses yoked and the Boche dinner cooking away merrily, but the driver elected to run away, much to his own detriment, for he did not run far. The morning air had created a keen appetite among the members of this Company, and right heartily did they tackle that hot meal of beef and vegetables which the cooker contained. Some aver that the so-called beef was horse-flesh, but, horse-flesh or not, it was very acceptable on that cold winter morning, and the cooker was soon empty, and thereafter brought back by the two Boche horses, but with a British driver, to the 'Fifth's' transport lines.' [14]

On the left of 1/5th Seaforths, 1/8th Argylls had few problems and Private James Campbell, writing from hospital in Abbeville recalled:

'The tanks crossed our front line early in the morning and were all lined up in front. As soon as the barrage opened we went over the top and got in front of our wire and lay down until the tanks were well forward and then we got up and walked towards our objective. We had no opposition until we came to an advanced sap where there was the odd Fritz prepared to show a bit of fight but a few bombs soon quietened them down and any that were left soon shoved up their hands.' [15]

By 9.10 a.m. both battalions had reached the railway line.

On 1/8th Argylls' left, 153rd Brigade advanced, led by 1/6th Black Watch and 1/5th Gordons, following 28 tanks of E Battalion, and took the first objectives.

The second wave moved through the captured first objectives. On the extreme right of the division, 1/6th Gordons leap-frogged 1/5th Seaforths:

'7.50 am. At this hour the leading waves of the Battalion, 'B' Company on left, and 'D' Company on right, began to move forward to the attack, followed at an interval of ten minutes by the second waves, composed of 'C' and 'D' [sic 'A'] Companies. The advance from this point was carried out in section columns and the formations were admirably kept. The men were very keen. [There was a delay to avoid getting involved in the 5th Seaforths' battle.] On reaching the line of the railway the correct number of tanks [six] were seen pushing forward on the battalion front, and the first wave extended. The whole advance up to the SUNKEN ROAD was carried out in a very excellent manner, and without a single casualty. The tanks were going well and the first wave was following their advance at about two hundred yards distance in readiness to capture their objective. On the tanks appearing over the skyline in front of the HINDENBERG SUPPORT LINE, an enemy battery came into action at point blank range and succeeded in putting out of action every tank on the battalion front. Owing to the configuration of the ground and the irregular shape of the enemy's wire, it seemed to those in charge of the leading wave that the tanks had managed to pass over the wire before becoming casualties, and so they went on.

Too late they discovered the real situation and as they neared the belt of entanglements, they came under very heavy machine-gun fire from the direction of FLESQUIERES WOOD which was on the left flank. Thus the leading wave was held up and here the first casualties occurred. [16]

1/6th Gordons dug in and formed a defensive flank in Station Alley, facing Flesquieres. They were unable to make their way left along the Hindenberg Support Trench.

1/6th Seaforths were on 1/6th Gordons left. They had watched and waited as the first wave moved forward:

'It was 'nervy' work; and the sky gave an aggravating promise of rain. . . while . . . the smoke of the battle completely obliterated from our view the momentous happenings in front, each man of the Sixth set him down to enjoy a plate of hot porridge. The meal was finished in comfort . . Everyone was in high spirits, without being hysterical, as a move was made out of the trenches. . . A and C overtook the tanks just beyond the broad gauge railway that ran into Ribecourt. Thousands of prisoners of all shapes and sizes were met on the way to the cage. . . One gallant of the Fifth Seaforths caused much amusement when he appeared mounted on a captured horse [heavy draft]. The tanks glided along. . . but their numbers had been sadly depleted. Only seven were in action, and poor C Company had none to follow. These seven – Emperor II, Edinburgh, Endurance, Exquisite, Eurvalius, Egypt and Eileen were the names – were soon astride the trench on the left battalion front, and making short work of the garrison. The first strong line [of] A Company had little difficulty in entering. They lost but three men in the process.

It was otherwise with C Company. On their territory no tanks were present to lead the attack. The wire was untouched. . . The Germans fired straight and often. With the greatest daring, the officers and men pushed on, ultimately forcing their way through terrible wire and fire into the trench. . . There followed hard and bitter fighting.' [17]

1/6th Seaforths tried to link with 1/6th Gordons on their right, by moving on the surface along the Hindenberg Support trench, shooting and bombing, but were suppressed by fire from Flesquieres, and established a block in the trench between themselves and the Germans. The two 1/6th Seaforths' supporting companies passed through:

'. . . then a dreadful disaster befell the tanks and the troops witnessed a terrifying spectacle. It is enough to record that, as each tank reached the crest of the Flesquieres Ridge, they were caught and totally destroyed by the devastating fire of a field gun fired at point blank range and from but a stone's throw over the ridge. In most cases the machines caught fire, and there were terrible scenes. Many of the crews escaped to take their revenge alongside the infantry. One inspiring incident will remain long in the memories of those who were there. A youthful officer [whose name we afterwards discovered was Bion], when his tank was rendered useless, dismounting one of the Lewis guns, gaily clambered onto the top of his tank, and fired drum after drum of bullets into the village. His very boldness was his preservation. He remained in this exposed position until his gun became too hot to fire.'[18]

When Bion ran out of ammunition he scrambled from his tank and reported to 1/6th Seaforths' Captain George Edwards, who fell dead with his brains and blood bursting from the back of his head. The senior N.C.O. asked Bion to take command, and with the remains of a company he fought off a German counter-attack. The 51st recommended him for the Victoria Cross, but the 19 years old Second Lieutenant, when interviewed by a general about the event, responded diffidently that he was unsure if he had killed any of the enemy, and was awarded the D.S.O. instead. [19]

Without the tanks, direct assault was stopped by machine-gun fire from the trench and the wall surrounding the chateau, although Lieutenant Donald Grant and his orderly, initially followed by others who rapidly became casualties, charged together towards the objective, with the officer 'bayonetting his way along a communication trench with a precision and determination that little could have withstood. Grant, closely followed by his faithful orderly, cleared all before them. Presently they were seen to leave the trench, pressing on. They went forward only a few yards when both fell almost simultaneously, fatally wounded.' [20] In this wild advance of two Seaforths, anger, courage, desperation, frustration, loyalty and the red mist of war stripped aside all logic. Mixed with blood 1/6th Seaforths' morning porridge was already congealing on their line of advance.

By then the two companies had only one officer each, and the C.O., Lt.Colonel MacDonald arranged covering fire from the stranded tanks, and personally led attacks against the village. Flesquieres Trench was taken and held but 1/6th Seaforths could not enter the village.

On the left of 1/6th Seaforths 153rd Brigade attacked. 1/7th Gordons took 100 prisoners as they stormed the Hindenberg Support line, then fought their way into Flesquieres Trench. 1/7th Gordons tried to take

Flesquieres, without tank support, and at one point had a Lewis gun dominating the main street, but it had to withdraw, as had other 1/7th Gordons, when the Germans counter-attacked Flesquieres Trench, part of which was held by three 1/7th Gordon platoons.

On the 51st's left two of 1/7th Black Watch's tanks ditched crossing the front line and as the infantry approached the Hindenberg Support line heavy fire from Cemetery Trench held them up. With the aid of their remaining tanks they took the Hindenberg Support but as soon as the tanks crossed this trench they were destroyed. They did not take Flesquieres Trench until the late afternoon.

At 5 p.m. six tanks drove into Flesquieres village, forcing the Germans into their dug-outs and cellars. The attack was not well co-ordinated with the infantry, and when 1/6th Seaforths, from the north end and the woods, advanced, they were slowed by the enemy and when they arrived in Flesquieres, the tanks were withdrawing, and the Germans emerged from hiding and forced the 1/6th Seaforths out. By the end of the day the 51st had failed to reach its second objective, the Brown Line, over Flesquieres Ridge.

On the left of the 51st the 62nd (2nd West Riding) Division's 185th Brigade's right hand battalion's tanks were late, but it took the outpost line, and the tanks arrived to lead the next wave on to the second objective. The left battalion had difficulty in taking the outpost line, and tanks found movement through the remains of Havrincourt Forest slow, but the infantry took Havrincourt village. 187th Brigade's left battalion had to attack without tank suport, which arrived fifteen minutes late. They took the outpost line. The second wave had tank support and by 10.30 had reached its second objectives, but elements outran the tanks, followed the barrage and crossed the Canal du Nord. Some of 62nd Division reached Graincourt but had to halt their advance because of the delay at Flesquieres. This was the opposite situation from one optimistically posited by Harper to Haig, when he worried about 62nd Division falling behind the advancing 51st. 1st Brigade, Tank Corps, reported that the men of the 62nd Division were too tired to go on:

'On the 20th November, although Tanks were ready and

anxious to rush on to BOURLON VILLAGE and FONTAINE, which could have been taken without opposition, the 62nd Division were unable to go further owing to complete exhaustion.' [This misses the point that the 62nd Division had been ordered to await the advance of the 51st, but is significant in that it makes no criticism of the 51st.]

Note: If on any future operations it is intended to pierce the line to any considerable depth, it is essential that the troops, supporting the Tanks beyond a certain point, should be brought up as far as possible by means other than 'foot slogging'. [21]

On the extreme left the 36th (Ulster) Division took their objectives.

By dusk on 20th November there was a German salient, with a flat top at Flesquieres and the bases of its flanks at Noyelles and Graincourt. Attempts to organise co-operation with 6th Division on the right of the 51st and 62nd on its left, with a view to outflanking the Germans in the Flesquieres salient, did not succeed, due to slow communication, lack of knowledge about the exact whereabouts of friendly battalions and the shortening November day.

The British had pushed forward between three and four miles, taking most of their second objectives. Troops of the 29th Division had crossed the Canal d'Escaut, providing a bridgehead for the cavalry drive towards Cambrai. Casualties had been low, but the cavalry break-out had not taken place, nor had the tactically important Bourlon Ridge been taken, III Corps had no infantry reserve and IV Corps had only a reserve of three brigades. The 40th Division was eight miles away and there were five divisions of cavalry, but such cavalry as had been involved on the 20th had fallen foul of barbed wire and machine-guns.

On 21st November, on the right, III Corps prepared for a German counter-attack, with 29th Division defending east of the St. Quentin Canal, and 6th Division consolidating round Nine Wood and Noyelles. The key to the battle on the 21st was the capture of Bourlon Wood, dominating the road to Cambrai.

During the night of 20/21st November patrols of 1/7th Gordons and

1/7th Black Watch reached the Brown Line, the 20th's second objective, and at 2.45 a.m. reported this to their battalions, which moved forward and consolidated the Brown Line, as did 1/6th Gordons and 1/6th Seaforths on their right. 'Within twenty-fours hours of the attack having been launched the Brown Line was occupied in its entirety, largely due to the vigilance with which the 153rd Brigade had kept in touch with the enemy's movements by patrolling.' [22] Thus Bewsher sugared the pill of the 51st's late arrival on the Brown Line, taken the previous day by the divisions on its flanks!

At 7.05 a.m. the Highland Division's artillery shelled the Red Line, on the Premy Chapel to Graincourt Road, and at 7.30 a.m. 1/5th Seaforths, 1/8th Argylls, 1/6th Black Watch and 1/5th Gordons advanced through the Brown line, taking the Red Line, and 70 prisoners. By 9 a.m. the 51st was at last in line with the 62nd Division at Graincourt.

> Fontaine-Notre-Dame, on the outskirts of Cambrai, was the 51st's objective. Tank support was planned but B Battalion's tanks, in Grand Ravine, about two miles behind the infantry, did not receive their orders until 9.00 a.m., 30 minutes before zero, four hours after they had been sent from the II Tank Brigade's headquarters, six miles behind Grand Ravine. Brigadier-General Buchanan of 154th Brigade waited until 10.30 a.m. for the tanks, then started without them, 1/4th Gordons on the right and 1/7th Argylls on the left. The former's advance was witnessed by 1/6th Seaforths, consolidating the Red Line: 'The sights which we witnessed as we lay in our new position brought fresh hopes. There were enthralling scenes – the cavalry cantering into action in perfect formation (not, unhappily to be maintained for long); the 4th Gordon Highlanders, with pipes and drums, marching as a revue in column of route; the sight of a real live battery galloping into action and coming into action at our ears, and the constant covey of aeroplanes, low flying and intrepid.'[23]

Ahead of 1/4th Gordons was Cantaing, part of the rearmost defences of the Hindenberg Line: Cantaing's trenches were largely completed by October 1917 but the rest of the Cantaing Line, running north-west to Bourlon Wood, was 'spit-locked' – a spade's depth: but machine-gun positions and dug-outs had been established, and the Cantaing Line was well wired.

A German who had been in Cantaing reported:

> 'Everywhere on the enemy's side movement can be seen, cavalry are at Nine Wood, and the infantry are assembling on the road Marcoing – Graincourt. It seems impossible but we think we hear sounds of music in the middle of a great battle. The sounds become clearer and we realise they are made by bagpipes. In company columns, the Highlanders are advancing. The commanders are mounted and can easily be identified through field glasses. These beautiful targets remain unengaged. Can't our artillery observers see them? But nothing is being done on our side. The British advance stops and the numerous waves take cover. The British must indeed feel sure of victory. . . The Britsh deploy and advance their companies at about 700 metres. Our 52nd and 232nd Divisions open rapid fire. The company commander telephones to the Battalion: 'It is an absolute shooting match. We are shooting standing as fast as we can.' The British advance stops and the numerous waves take cover.' [24]

Private
Roderick Mclennan

1/4th Gordons engaged the Cantaing garrison until noon, when B battalion tanks, 1/4th Gordons, a squadron of the Bays (2nd Dragoon Guards) and men of 14th Durham Light Infantry [25] entered and cleared the village by 1.30 p.m. On the south west side of the village a company of 1/4th Gordons was held up on the Cantaing-Flesquieres road on the German side of the wire until they were supported at 3 p.m. by a tank.

A company of 1/4th Seaforths had been inserted between 1/4th Gordons and 1/7th Argylls, as they had been drawn apart towards Cantaing village and Anneux respectively. Lieutenant E. Alan Mackintosh's platoon was halted by fire from Cantaing Mill and took up a defensive position in a sunken road south of the mill. His death was witnessed by 18 years old Private Roderick Mclennan, 1/4th Seaforths: on the few occasions when he spoke of the war he usually told of Mackintosh's death. His grandson wrote:

'Roderick Mclennan was second man on a Lewis Gun Team. The Company were just beginning to prepare for a German counter attack during the Cambrai operations [as memory serves me this all happened near to or at a sunken road which was being fortified to receive the counter attack]. Lt. Mackintosh was alongside my grandfather and the soldier who was firing the Lewis gun preparing to spot targets as they appeared. My grandfather had just placed a full 'pan' (magazine of Lewis Gun ammunition) onto the gun in preparation for firing. The bullets were 'cracking' around them. Lt. Mackintosh who was alongside them and slightly forward of them lifted his head to get a better view of the oncoming Germans and was shot directly through the mouth into the head. He died instantly.

Lt. E.A. Mackintosh

'He was an officer who was well loved by his men and was spoken of fondly by my grandfather. He was a man who cared deeply for the soldiers under his command and sought the best for them on every occasion. . . the company moved forward later that day and I believe that the Germans were treated to a fair amount of cold steel [a rumour had circulated that no soldier wearing a kilt would be taken prisoner]. This was reciprocated in kind'[26]

On the left 1/7th Argylls:

'moved forward from Railway in Artillery formation but was held up by fire from ANNEUX at 10.10 a.m., right by Cantaing. C Coy was detailed to go and assist 62nd Div. with attack on ANNEUX which was captured at 11.20 a.m. Advance was then continued towards FONTAINE by companies on a two platoon frontage in two waves. . . Companies were held up by heavy rifle fire and M.G. fire from CANTAING line at 12 noon and Companies had to dig in there. 2 p.m. Tanks advanced and reached CANTAING line about 2.55 p.m. when line was captured and about 80 prisoners taken.' [27]

With the fall of Cantaing and the Cantaing Line, tanks, 1/4th Seaforths and 1/7th Argylls moved on Fontaine-Notre-Dame, forming a deep salient, overlooked on their left by Bourlon Wood. Harper issued orders for the advance to halt until Bourlon Wood had been taken by 62nd Division, but the orders did not reach the forward battalions. 1/7th Argylls:

> 'Tanks proceeded through Fontaine-Notre-Dame followed by 'A', 'B', part of 'D' Coy. One company of 4th Seaforths reached FONTAINE as they had been sent to fill a gap which had occurred on our right. Our companies consolidated defence of the village on N & W sides. Some prisoners were taken and many civilians were sent back. The night was quiet and the defence securely consolidated. [28]

On the 51st's left the 62nd Division was held up at Anneux Chapel by fire from Bourlon Wood. By dusk on 21st November, the men of the 51st in Fontaine-Notre-Dame were in a vulnerable salient, on the right side of which was a dangerous gap between 1/4th Seaforths and 1/4th Gordons and Queen's Bays in Cantaing. On the previous day the 51st had made least progress, on the 21st it penetrated further than any of its flanking divisions. By then the Germans had recovered and were rushing reinforcements to the front. 1/7th Argylls and 1/4th Seaforths were extremely exposed. This was neither their fault, nor Harper's.

On the 22nd 1/7th Argylls' 'B', 'D' and three platoons of 'A' Coy were relieved by 4th Seaforths during the morning and . . . before the fourth Platoon of 'A' Coy could be relieved the enemy delivered a very strong counter-attack about 10.30 A.M. on FONTAINE. [29]

The defending troops fired S.O.S. flares for artillery support, but these were not seen by the 51st's artillery, most of which had moved forward to the Premy Chapel-Graincourt road. 1/4th Seaforths' attributed the failure of the artillery to respond to thick mist. [30] An artillery liaison officer rode to the guns, which brought fire to bear on Germans attacking the north side of the village. This was the last useful artillery support that 1/4th Seaforths and 1/7th Argylls had in the subsequent battle. A dozen German aircraft circled the village and strafed the defending infantry throughout the morning. [31]

A ferocious infantry battle ensued as the Germans attacked along the entire perimeter of the village. They pushed the left back and moved up a sunken road into the village and by noon it was clear that the Germans were retaking it. 1/4th Seaforths were ordered to retreat to the sunken road occupied by 1/7th Argylls. On the Cambrai road, at the east end of the village 1/4th Seaforths' adjutant, Captain Peverell held until the last moment then ordered the remnants of his small party to retreat. He was described by a fellow officer as 'roaring with laughter, as though it were the greatest joke in the world.' [32] Peverell was taken prisoner and left in the open for fifteen hours. Having had his valuables taken from him by various German soldiers, and fearing from time to time that he might be killed, a German officer assured him that he would write to Cox's Bank in London to let them know that he had been taken prisoner. [33] A small party under Lt. Colonel Unthank, the C.O., conducted a fighting retreat to the sunken road leading to Cantaing.

Lietenant A. Macdonnell R.F.A. was involved in the episode:

'The day was so misty that the S.O.S. was put up and not seen, so the other gunner officer got on the C.O.'s horse, which we saddled up most feverishly, and galloped off under machine-gun fire to the batteries – most spectacular. I got a rifle and ammunition and dashed out into the main street, feeling horribly frightened for a moment, for as I reached the street a shell went through the 'R.F.A. mess.' In the street I found fifty odd men, at a loose end, with no officer. It occurred to me to give some orders, and to my surprise the men obeyed.

After that I began to recall O.T.C. days, and started establishing posts in the side streets, and took the rest in a wild dash up the road. . . to help the Adjutant (Captain Peverell), who was in a tight corner. We got there and had a most hectic time in a furious barrage, with the Hun machine-guns chipping bricks all around us. The barrage got too bad and was impossible, so we retired. . . we lined the road and

held him for about half an hour, when our ammunition began
to give out.

Our right flank was in the air and I went off to get help and
brought another twenty men to prolong our line, but
suddenly the centre caved in and the whole Boche line got up
and broke into the village.

We loosed off the remainder of our stuff at them, and then,
hotly pursued, we bunked off across the fields with hundreds
of shots at us! How we ran for about 1000 yards! But we had
not many casualties. We stopped and reorganized in a sunk
road, and after posting the men I went to try to secure
assistance. I ran like mad over the open, with a machine-gun
spurting shot round me. I got through and got help.
Eventually we were relieved, and I had a huge drink and went
to bed. Quite a brisk day's work. I was so pleased that I didn't
lose my head at all from the moment that the men did what I
told them.' [34]

Amongst 1/4th Seaforths' casualties was Roderick McLennan, who
had witnessed Lt. E.A. Mackintosh's death on the 21st. A German 'plane,
machine-gunning in support of the counter-attack, hit McLennan in the
upper arm:

'He struggled back with blood pouring from his wound
soaking his tunic and Mackenzie tartan kilt and apron. He was
saved by a private from the Royal Scots who left his trench and
carried him to safety. The soldier turned out to be his cousin
Kenny Scougall who had no idea whom he had rescued until
back at the dressing station. He was awarded the Military
Medal for this action. Unfortunately he succumbed to the 'flu
epidemic of 1918.' [35] [Kenny was the family name – he was
Private George Scougall*, 1/9th Royal Scots, who were on the
right of 1/7th Argylls.]

After the evacuation of Fontaine-Notre-Dame the remnants of
1/4th Seaforths joined 1/7th Argylls who reported:

'Our Companies held on to Consolidated positions and

checked the counter-attack. Some difficulty was experienced in getting forward supplies of S.A.A. [small arms ammunition] but the 154th T.M. [trench mortar] pack ponies under 2nd Lieut. R.M. Park rendered valuable assistance in taking forward S.A.A. under heavy fire.' [36]

Harper has been ciriticised for not reinforcing the village, accused of disregarding the lives of his men, and believing that it could be taken when Bourlon Wood was secure. [37] Whatever Harper's shortcomings, he did not throw away troops. Bewsher defended the decision not to reinforce:

'No number of troops could be expected successfully to hold Fontaine against counter-attack so long as the enemy held Bourlon Wood. . .

'The village was indeed the point of junction of two defensive flanks. Only two policies appeared possible: either an attack must be delivered against Bourlon Wood by the Division on the left [62nd Division – author's note], or Fontaine must be evacuated. To put more men into the village would have been to expose more men to certain defeat in the event of counter-attack. It would have been the equivalent of putting a large nut within the grip of crackers instead of a small one.' [38]

The 51st's line held firm for the rest of the day. Despite the fact that the 48 hours agreed as the duration of the battle had passed, Haig insisted that Bourlon Wood be taken, and Lieutenant-General Sir Charles Woollcombe, IV Corps, ordered Harper to retake Fontaine and was overheard by Major Furse of King Edward's Horse saying, 'if you don't take Fontaine, General Harper, God help you! Harper looked as if he did not like that.' [39]

During the night of 22nd/23rd November 1/7th Black Watch relieved 1/7th Argylls and 1/4th Seaforths, and on their left 62nd Division was relieved by 40th Division. The attack was originally planned for 6 a.m. but it was postponed until 10.30a.m. Participating from right to left, were the 51st, 40th, 36th, and 56th Divisions. Bourlon Wood was the objective, and could only be secured if Fontaine was retaken and Moeuvres on the left fell to the British.

There was little enthusiasm for the attack in the 51st. Harper discussed it with his brigadiers then 'standing at the door of the main entrance to the chateau (of Flesquieres) General Harper produced a coin and with a 'heads' 152, 'tails' 153, sealed the fate of the former, and incidentally, that of our Battalion (1/6th Seaforths). It was an historic incident.' [40] As the men stood in their assembly positions on the morning of the 23rd Brigadier Pelham-Burn attempted to cheer them up by telling them that they would be relieved that night.

Twelve tanks were allocated to the 152nd Brigade, and others came forward in the course of the day. There was friction between the tanks and the infantry.

'It was discovered that there was no responsible senior officer with the Tank Contingent [who were also ready for the fray] with whom the details of the attack might be discussed with the Brigadier, except one rather haughty Battalion Tank Commander, who was averse to taking orders from mere infantry. . . the tanks were miserably organised, or rather they were miserable by their want of organisation. Throughout the day on 23rd November they came into action in futile driblets. On no less than three separate occasions three different sections, each comprising eleven of the monsters, with no knowledge of the situation, and with no orders except to get on with the war, appeared outside our Brigade Headquarters. Their commanders neither knew to which Brigade they were to attach themselves, nor had they any pre-arranged plan whereby they might achieve their noble purpose.

In good time, however, all things for the early morning's attack were amicably arranged and staged, and promptly at 10.30 a.m. the Sixth Seaforths and Sixth Gordons moved off.'[41]

The tank and infantry attack had been preceded by half an hour's artillery barrage.

Ahead of the infantry, 13 B Battalion and 6 C Battalion tanks entered Fontaine, where they were attacked by machine-gun fire and hand grenades: only three of B Battalion's tanks returned to their base. 1/8th Argylls were to maintain the line between Cantaing and the advancing

1/6th Gordons on their left, and next to them were 1/6th Seaforths. The barrage moved ahead of the infantry at 200 yards every ten minutes. The infantry were exposed to frontal and flank fire. On the right Germans in La Folie Wood punished 1/6th Gordons, some of whom fought their way to the outskirts of Fontaine, before withdrawing 500 yards to the south of Fontaine, and digging in.

The 1/6th Seaforths were to take ground between Fontaine and Bourlon Wood, in co-operation with the 40th Division, but were held up by the enemy in Fontaine and Bourlon. Twelve H Battalion and 3 C Battalion tanks fought with them and they reached the north east corner of Bourlon Wood. Individual aggression was part of the formula: 'A sergeant put a gun out of action by heading an attack along a trench occupied by a party of about thirty Germans, of which he bayoneted three himself, thus cowing the others into surrendering.'[42]

Attempts to take Fontaine from the north east were futile: 'Tanks paraded the village street and fired into the semi-devastated buildings; no enemy was in view and the tanks pressed on. Yet any attempt to enter the village brought dozens of enemy rifles and guns to cellars, windows, attic and skylight.' [43]

Two companies each from 1/5th Seaforths and 1/8th Argylls were sent to reinforce 1/6th Seaforths by advancing on their left, but this coincided with a Germans counter-attack, which pushed back elements of the 40th Division, and exposed the left of 1/6th Seaforths, which had to withdraw to protect the flank. The 51st dug in on the line of its previous day's retreat and linked up with the 40th Division, which held a large portion of Bourlon Wood, and was in a salient. Haig recorded: 'Officers of G.H.Q. who accompanied General Davidson to the battle front today, think the 51st Division is tired and several other units are very short of sleep. Many men can hardly keep awake.' [44]

Major Furse, King Edward's Horse 'watched Harper standing by the roadside as his weary and unsuccessful troops marched back. An A.D.C. stood beside him with a huge pile of boxes of chocolate. Sadly Harper handed a box, as a present from himself, to each depleted company as it passed him – so like that kindly, human, but stubborn man.'[45]

On the night of the 23rd/24th November the 51st was relieved by the Guards Division, some of whom jeered the 51st for failing to take Fontaine-Notre-Dame, provoking fisticuffs, and some injuries. [46] The division rested at Baisieux. British attacks continued at Fontaine-Notre-Dame and Bourlon Wood. On the 24th, after two vigorous German counter-attacks in Bourlon Wood, a planned attack by 40th Division was postponed until the 25th because insufficient tanks were available. The postponement did not reach 40th Division and its men passed through Bourlon village, but attempts to reinforce them and clear Bourlon village on the failed, and the troops that had passed beyond it had to surrender.

On the 27th six Guards' battalions attacked Fontaine-Notre-Dame and the north-east edge of Bourlon Wood. They reached the village but were driven back to their start line. On their left the 62nd Division reached Bourlon village but had to retire. Seven days after what had been planned as a 48 hour offensive, the British attacks stopped and the line was consolidated.

The Battle of Cambrai still provokes controversy, and those with partiality for armour have described Harper as criminal, [47] indifferent to human life, [48] and silly. [49] Brigadier-General Baker-Carr, whose 1st Tank Brigade supported the 51st and 62nd Divisions, wrote in his Battle Report:

> 'The principle of co-operation between Tanks and Infantry as adopted in this battle was so satisfactory that it rather suggests the desirability of always training the same tank formations with the same infantry formations. . . The formations adopted by the infantry of the 2 divisions with which this Brigade was operating differed slightly, but in principle were the same. Both were highly successful.' [50] [Under 'Future Training' he noted that:] 'Owing to lack of suitable ground, training in firing from Tanks with 6-pdr., and Lewis Guns was extremely limited and undoubtedly many splendid opportunities of killing the enemy were lost through want of experience on the part of the Gunners. A great deal of attention should be devoted to this point during our future training and demonstrations given to show the difference between good and bad shooting.' [51]

This is hard on the tank crews, who were incarcerated in fume filled, unsprung metal boxes, deafened by engines and hits on their vehicles, unsighted by their protective visors, tiny apertures, and the smoke of war, but tempers some of the blame Baker-Carr later laid on the 51st's infantry for not eliminating individual German artillerymen. Baker-Carr recognised the difficulty of co-ordinating tank/infantry training because infantry divisions were not always available on time and suggested that 'some notes on Tank and Infantry operations should be written and distributed to Divisions, who would practise the formations, using G.S. Limbered wagons to represent the Tanks.'[52] This is what the 51st did before its officers were briefed on the Cambrai operation on 5th November 1917. In *Tanks in the Great War* (1920), Fuller made little negative criticism of the action on 20th November.

Oddly, later criticism of Harper emanated from Baker-Carr, followed by Liddell-Hart and Fuller. In his autobiography Baker-Carr asserted that Harper's 'method of 'co-operation' was that the tanks outdistanced the laggard infantry and were massacred by the action of a single man whom one well-directed bullet would have settled.'[53] This refers to a German anti-tank gunner who was alone reputed to have destroyed the tanks on the front of 1/6th Gordons, where they had driven over the ridge in single file, easy targets, in a formation not laid down by either by Fuller or Harper. [54] Had Baker-Carr forgotten that tanks were armed with Lewis guns, potentially more likely to eliminate an anti-tank gunner than a rifle fired by an infantryman who had just climbed an incline? And that he had originally reported that tank gunners were under-trained. [[51] above]

Perhaps his opinion changed as the tank led battle was not an unqualified success, for which he was not prepared to assume blame. Interservice competition for limited resources in the inter-war period, traditionalists' scepticism about tanks, and the promotion of tanks at all costs may have prompted his and Liddell Hart's vilification of Harper. That their subjective opinions have been so often repeated is regrettable. Harper was unable to defend his decisions, having died in a car crash in 1922.

Liddell Hart incorporated Baker-Carr's opinions in *The Real War* and asserted that the 'laggard infantry' referred to by Baker-Carr could not find gaps in the wire and were held up by machine-guns.[55] Fuller thought that Harper's tank/infantry tactics 'were purely silly.' [56] Each 51st soldier, following the tanks in open order, rather than 'worms', faced the enemy, rather than the back of the man in front of him, allowing him to observe a wider area and to respond more quickly to sight of the enemy. Not all the attacking battalions stuck to Harper's 100 yards directive. After citing three examples from war diaries of supporting battalions one author concluded that Harper's instructions were broad guidelines within which battalion commanders could and did vary. [57] An author specialising in the war from the German side stated that German accounts noted that the British infantry followed the tanks closely, and made no distinction between the 51st and other divisions' tank/infantry tactics. [58]

The real problem, acknowledged by objective authors since the 1960s[59] is that when the tanks crossed the summit at Flesquieres, they faced the German 54th Division's well trained 108th Field Artillery Regiment, which had regularly and systematically practised anti-tank gunnery and had destroyed French tanks in the Nivelle offensive. [60] As the 51st's success was built on training, so too was that of the German gunners. As if to excuse the delay at Flesquieres Haig seized upon the tale that:

> 'One officer, however, was able to collect a few men and with them worked a gun, and from his concealed position knocked out Tanks after Tank to the number of eight or nine. This officer was then killed. This incident shows the importance of Infantry operating with Tanks and at times acting as skirmishers to clear away hostile guns and reconnoitre.' [61]

This ignores the fact that infantry were following the tanks, and depended upon them to flatten the barbed wire to get at the artillery-men, who fired at the tanks at a range of 500 yards. [62]

Harper's presumption that the 62nd Division might retard his division indicates that he was optimistic about the plan of attack, and had no idea that well-drilled anti-tank gunners were ahead of the 51st. That was a failure of military intelligence, not of Harper's.

Tanks and infantry were not well co-ordinated in their efforts to take Flesquieres and Fontaine-Notre-Dame: this is attributable to bad communications, unpunctuality, breakdowns, fuel and ammunition shortages, German tactics, shortage of training time before the battle, and the absence of any joint infantry/tank training in urban warfare. The infantry appreciated this and 1/4th Gordons' battle report stated that: 'a method of street fighting with them (tanks) should be laid down.'[63]

Harper could have committed the 152nd Brigade to the attack on Flesquieres, but it is debatable if throwing more infantry at the village without co-ordinated tank support would have worked. Harper legitimately saved 152nd Brigade to take the Red Line. Deploying more men at Fontaine-Notre-Dame on 23rd November would have been unlikely to have altered the outcome of the battle.

Owing to the failure of some tanks to break the wire, the infantry could only summon the artillery to destroy it, but the artillery, firing from the map, to a precise timetable, predicated on a timeous advance of both tanks and infantry, and with bad communications, was unable to retarget batteries. Given that the gunners had been enmired in the minimal advances of trench warfare for three years this inability to cope with open warfare is unsurprising, but it was overcome in 1918, culminating in close and flexible artillery/infantry co-operation in the Hundred Days. Harper can be criticised for not adapting to the changing situation, or being close enough to the battle. On a visit on 22nd November Haig:

> '. . . left in motor car with Butler and went via Bapaume to Trescault. H.Qrs of 51st Division were in dugouts about 500 yards from the road. We walked there and saw General Harper, Commanding Division. His leading troops are now in F.N.Dame. I thought the Divisional HQrs. were rather far back! But the Division has done very well, notwithstanding the distance from its Commander.'

Harper was not alone in being 'rather far back'. 'I thought B (Braithwaite) should also have been closer up with his Division (62nd).'[64] They may have been far back, but their two divisions were forward of their neighbours.

Communications were not always broken by accident. Captain David Sutherland, signals officer of 1/5th Seaforths raged:

> '. . . the antediluvian fossil in charge of one sector of the cavalry front knew so little about modern warfare that on coming to occupy as his battle headquarters a dugout in the British front line, a dug-out which was also the cable-head of that front, he ordered the signal corporal and sapper in charge of the terminal board out of the dug-out, having seemingly never seen or heard of such innovations as buried or ground cables in his life before.' [65]

The cavalry had only made minor contributions, and were not commanded at its highest level with much flair, and tank-crushed entanglements deterred horses. Captain David Sutherland of 1/5th Seaforths was disillusioned with the cavalry, having seen them go forward on the 20th and 'come wending back next morning (21st) having accomplished nothing. . . some batteries of Royal Horse Artillery were still in their original positions behind the British front line when the Field Artillery were 3 or 4 miles into the German lines.'[66]

Had the battle ended on the Premy Chapel to Graincourt line, within the allotted 48 hours, and its gains consolidated, it would have been a success, as much ground had been gained at relatively low cost. That it was continued beyond the set time limit was a mistake, as experience had already taught that the Germans could mount increasingly weighty counter-attacks, the tanks were suffering attrition, and there were insufficient reserves to sustain a breakthrough, had it been achieved.

. . .

Between 28th November and 3rd December German counter-attacks drove the flanks of the British salient inwards. The 51st was about to celebrate St. Andrews Day, 30th November, when it was moved to the Léchelle area, south west of Bois d'Havrincourt and on 1st and 2nd it took over 56th (1st London) Division's front.

The 51st was on the vulnerable left of the salient, which the Germans probed constantly. On 4th December Haig, realising the salient's vulnerability, and with insufficient reserves, told Byng to withdraw his troops to a line roughly on the Hindenberg Support Line, thus forming the Flesquieres Salient. The 51st's 6000 yards front was between Demicourt and Boursies, in old trenches that the British had dug during the German retreat to the Hindenberg Line in 1917. These trenches were not part of a systematic plan of defence so Harper instituted an entrenching plan, which involved all the 51st:

> 'The depth for all trenches was laid down as six feet, their width at the top as eight feet, later increased to nine feet six inches. Each fire-bay was to be fifteen yards in length, with a twenty three feet traverse separating it from the next one . . . To ensure continuity of effort within the Division, General Harper in his memorandum laid down fixed principles on the system on which trenches were to be sited, and on the actual method of construction of trenches, dug-outs, entanglements, &c, and standardised their dimensions.'

> [Harper's memorandum ended:] 'a Division that digs well will attack well. . . officers and men must realise that good work stimulates interest, and consequently tends to keep up morale, and that a good trench system economises men and minimises losses.' [67]

A soldier of the 51st, visiting a neighbouring division remarked, 'It's easy seen these trenches belong to some other bodies.' [68] and Byng, after a visit recognised 'the extremely good work done by the Division in the strengthening of the defences of the line.' [69]

NOTES

1.a. Fuller Memoirs of an Unconventional Soldier Nicholson and Watson 1936 pp.198-199
   b. Lt.Col.[Rtd] Royal Tank Regiment to author, Cambrai. November 2007)
2. Haig's dispatch Bewsher p.235.
3. PRO, CAB 45/118 Craufurd to Edmonds OH editor 1945.
4. Haig's diary 15.11.1917.
5. Miles OH 1917 v3 footnote p.33.
6. Peel and MacDonald p.52.
7. Birk quoted Hussey British Army Review 117, p. 81 ex The Royal Armoured Corps Journal v.3 No.4 Oct 1949.

8. Report on Tank Operations by 1 Brigade TC 20-23.11.1917

9. Miles 1917 v.3 p.37.

10. War diary 1/6th Gordons 18.11.1917.

11. Dr.Alex Fasse per Jack Sheldon.

12. Miles1917 v.3 pp.52- 53.

13. London Gazette 11.1.1918.

14. Sutherland pp.138-139.

15. Pte James Campbell 1/8th A&SH letter to parents 25.11.17 from 3rd Australian General Hospital, Abbeville A&SH RHQ.

16. War diary 1/6th Gordons 20.11.1917.

17. Peel and MacDonald pp.33-4

18. Peel and MacDonald pp.54-55

19. Bion pp.165 and 172-173.

20. Peel and Macdonald p.55

21. Report on Tank Operations by 1st Brigade Tank Corps on Nov. 20th, 21st, 22nd, 23rd 1917 p.12.

22. Bewsher pp.249-50

23. Peel and Macdonald p.55

24. Royal Tank Corps Journal September 1936 source not stated. Stated as prisoner in Bryan Cooper *Ironclads of Cambrai*. MacMillan 1970 p.127.

25. Hammond p.213

26. Kenny McLennan – e-mail to the author – his grandfather's recollection. This conflicts with the account in Hammond pp. 218-219 in which Private Frank Brooke, 1/4th Seaforths said that Mackintosh was killed by a shot between the eyes as the attack went uphill towards a heavily defended village.(Fontaine-Notre –Dame?) This author has a copy of a newspaper map of the Cambrai area, from Mackintosh family sources, with two crosses marked, one at Orival Wood Cemetery, where Mackintosh is buried, and one on a sunken road uphill and south of Cantaing with cross on sunken road – where he was killed – looking downhill towards Cantaing Mill or the village. When the author e-mailed for permission to use this extract Kenny McLennan wrote: 'don't recall whether or not I mentioned it to you before – but the man's last words were to my grandfather and the Lewis Gunner was with to 'keep their heads down'. †

27. War diary 1/7th A&SH 21.11.1917.

28. War diary 1/7th A&SH 21/22.11.1917.

29. War diary 1/7th A&SH 21-22.11.1917.

30. Haldane p.246.

31. Bewsher p.254.

32. Haldane p.253 O'Donnell.

33. Haldane p.248

34. Haldane pp.249-253. Lieutenant A Macdonnell RFA

35. McLennan – grandfather's recollection

36. War diary 1/7th A&SH 21/22.11.1917.

37. Cooper p.139

38. Bewsher pp.253-255.

39. Furse. *Cavalry Memories of the Great War* (publisher unknown) quoted in

The First Tank Battle Robert Woolcombe (Barker) 1967 p.136.

40. Peel and MacDonald p.57.

41. Peel and MacDonald p.57.

42. Bewsher p.258.

43. Peel and Macdonald p.58.

44. Haig's diary 23.11.1917

45. Woolcombe p.157.

46. Hammond p.278.

47. Lt.Col.(rtd) R.T.R to author Cambrai 2007, when the author merely mentioned the 51st!

48. Cooper p.139.

49. Fuller *Memoirs of an Unconventional Soldier* (Nicholson and Watson) 1936 pp.198-199.

50. Report on Tank Operations by 1st Brigade Tank Corps on Nov 20th, 21st, 22nd,23rd 1917

W.O.95/98 Paras 19d, 21(A.1) and 22 – Hussey Footnote 46 p.91 British Army Review.

51. Op cit. p.11, Para 2. TNA

52. Op.cit. p.12, Para 6 (1).TNA

53. Christopher D'Arcy Baker-Carr *From Chauffeur to Brigadier* (Ernest Benn) 1930 pp.269-270.

54. Hussey BAR p.85.

55. Basil Henry Liddell-Hart *The Real War 1914-1918* (Faber and Faber) 1930 p.376.

56. Fuller pp.198-199.

57. Hammond IWM Review No. 10 p.96.

58. Jack Sheldon E-mail to author

59. E.K.G.Sixsmith *British Generalship in the Twentieth Century* (Arms and Armour) 1962 pp.121-122. Robert Woolcombe *The First Tank Battle* (Barker) 196 p.103. Richard Holmes *Tommy* (Harper-Collins) 2004 pp.429-430. Bryn Hammond IWM Review op cit) *Cambrai 1917: the Myth of the First Great Tank Battle* (Weidenfeld and Nicholson) 2008. p.162 John Hussey (BAR op cit.) Jack Sheldon *The German Army at Cambrai* (Pen and Sword) 2009 pp. 37-39.

60. Miles 1917 v.3 p.59 footnote 2.

61. Haig diary 22.11.1917.

62. Hussey BAR op cit p.85.

63. Report of action 1/4th Gordons 20-24/11/1917 Lt.Col. Rowbotham. Dated 26/11/1917

64. Haig diary 22.11.1917.

65. Sutherland p.142.

66. Sutherland p.142.

67. Bewsher pp.265-266.

68. Bewsher p.267.

69. Bewsher p.268.

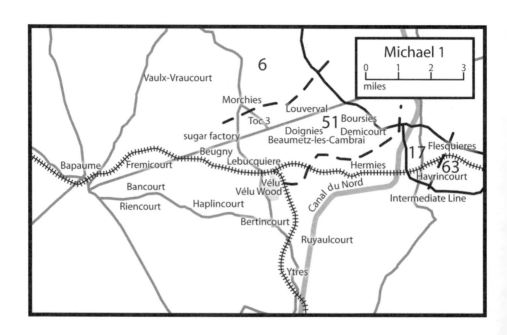

CHAPTER 8
RESILIENCE
Michael and *Georgette*

'These few hot days.' [1]

Optimism was rare at the dawn of 1918, for there was still deadlock on the Western Front. Although the United States of America had entered the war in April 1917, America was unprepared, and its troops were as inexperienced as Kitchener's Army in 1915 and 1916. The U.S. troops had to be partly equipped from British and French sources, and trained. General Pershing insisted that his troops would not be piecemeal reinforcements for the British and French, but would fight as the U.S. Army – an understandable stance, but one which personnel -starved Allied commanders found frustrating.

The 1917 revolutions had rendered Russia militarily useless and even before the war in the east ended with the Treaty of Brest-Litovsk in February 1918, the Germans had been redeploying their best divisions, including Guard and Prussian divisions, to the West, leaving behind *Landwehr* and cavalry divisions. With these and the Allies' significant manpower losses, the Germans planned a breakthrough.

After Third Ypres Prime Minister Lloyd George was reluctant to authorise reinforcements for the B.E.F, as he thought that Haig would squander them. To adapt to the lack of manpower it was decreed on 10th January 1918 that all infantry brigades should lose one of their four battalions, and that these should be transferred to other divisions. This affected the tactical deployment of brigades and divisions, and stretched human resources, as there was no reduction in the yardage of front to be held by divisions. There was also a morale deficit in removing long established battalions from their divisions. The 51st lost 1/8th Argylls, 1/5th Gordons and 1/9th Royal Scots, to 61st (South Midland) Division TF.

Hindenberg gambled everything on his planned 1918 offensive. At a War Cabinet in London in January 1918 Haig 'stated that I thought that the coming four months would be a critical period. Also that it seemed possible that the Enemy would attack both the French and ourselves, and hold reserves ready to exploit wherever he succeeded.'[2] His diary for that day also recorded his view that the British should maintain their attacking initiative in Flanders!

The 1918 British defensive system was composed of a lightly held Forward Zone (Blue Line) from which, under heavy attack, the defenders would fall back to the Battle Zone (Red Line), about 2500 yards behind the Forward Zone. The Battle Zone varied in depth, and depended on wired strong points and redoubts, sited to give the defenders advantageous fields of fire. To the rear of the Battle Zone was the incomplete Corps Line (Green Line).

Like Tudor, 9th (Scottish) Division's C.R.A., the Germans' artillery expert Bruchmüller had practised 'off the map' ranging against the Russians, and proposed to do the same with the British. 6,473 guns, would fire 1,160,000 shells, and 3,532 mortars would provide a barrage at shorter ranges.[3] High explosive shells would alternate with phosgene and tear gas, as the latter could penetrate British gas masks, irritate, and tempt the wearer to remove his mask, and succumb to phosgene. The British artillery positions would be targeted with four gas shells to every high explosive shell. There would be a five hour hurricane barrage on the British trenches and on key targets well behind the lines. The German guns were to be brought as close to the front as possible, without detection.

Storm troops, equipped with light automatic weapons, flame-throwers, rifles and grenades, were to penetrate as deeply as possible into the British defences, abandoning the convention of eliminating every strongpoint before continuing the advance: following troops would eliminate surviving British strong points.

Ludendorff's plan, code named Michael, was to break through near St. Quentin, north of the junction between the French and British, take Peronne, then force the British north by constantly threatening to outflank their right. 63 German divisions were available, 32 in the first wave, about 31 in the second wave, plus 11 holding divisions maintaining the German line. The British had 30 infantry divisions and 3 cavalry divisions, each of whose rifle strength was equal to that of an infantry brigade. Gough's Fifth Army garrisoned 42 miles with 11 divisions in the line and General Byng's Third Army, to the north, had 28 miles of front with 10 divisions in the line. This reflected the British calculation that the main German attack would fall further north.

On 1st January 1918 the Germans had distributed a secret report on the quality of the British Army. It concluded that despite heavy losses in 1917 the British Army was fully capable of fighting in 1918. It noted a blurring of the original distinctions between regular, territorial and Kitchener divisions, and asserted that battlefield experience meant that both older and newer divisions had become of equal value. It stated that German experience and prisoner of war interviews indicated that British divisions could be graded, normally on the basis of tradition, origins and leadership and that the majority of the best divisions were some regular divisions and the majority of divisions with Scottish, London, Canadian and Australian and New Zealand soldiers. They had established that these divisions were called upon for key operations and that, in the Germans' opinion, their performance was of great importance.

The Germans observed that once the British had broken through their leadership did not cope well with mobile warfare, and, at a lower level, that the tactical training offered to battalions was rigid, and unsuitable for open warfare. They queried the ability of individuals and leadership in unforeseen circumstances.

The document listed the British and Empire divisions: four columns beside each division show its number, its category (regular, T.F. Kitchener) the number of its appearances in 1916 and 1917 on the Somme, Arras, Flanders and Cambrai and a rating. Divisions' service in other theatres is also noted. Subsequent pages list all the divisions in numerical order, with the German Foreign Armies Department assessment:

Besonders gute Angriffsdivision [especially good assault division], *gute Angriffsdivision* † [good assault division], *gute Durchshnitt* [good average], *Durchshnitt* [average], *Mittelmaessig* [mediocre].

Rated as especially good assault divisions were: Guards; 7th [Regular]; 9th [Kitchener]; 29th [Regular]; 33rd [Kitchener]; 51st [Territorial] , 56th [Territorial]; 63rd [Naval]; 1st, 2nd, 3rd, and 4th Canadian; 1st and 2nd Australian and the New Zealand Division.

Good assault divisions: 1st, 2nd, 3rd [all Regular], 11th 14th, 15th [all Kitchener], 20th, 21st, 30th, 47th, 58th [all Territorial], 3rd and 4th Australian.

Good average divisions: 8th,14th, 16th ,18th ,19th, 23rd, 25th, 32nd, 41st, 46th, 55th.

Average divisions: 4th, 5th, 10th, 12th, 13th,17th, 22nd, 24th, 26th, 27th, 28th, 31st, 35th, 36th, 37th, 39th, 48th, 50th, 52nd, 53rd, 54th, 59th,60th, 74th, 75th, 5th Australian.

Mediocre divisions: 6th, 34th, 38th, 40th, 42nd, 49th, 57th, 61st, 62nd, 66th.

Divisions not included in the above were not assessed. [4]

It is notable that the three 'most to be feared' divisions of autumn 1917 are in the January 1918 assessment – does this lend retrospective credibility to the autumn 1917 list? The sender of the list commented, 'bearing in mind the performance of the Canadians and Australians in the second half of the war, to be bracketed alongside them by the Germans is something to be proud of.' [5]

As the Germans recognised, many of the especially good assault divisions represented distinct minorities within the B.E.F. It has been suggested that the Australians, New Zealanders and Canadians had something to prove, as their national identities emerged from their subordinate relationship to Great Britain.[6] The two Scottish divisions represented a small nation within a predominantly English army, and arguably they too had to excel for their national self respect, as had the South African Brigade of the 9th Division, which would give that division an extra edge; and there would have been informal rivalries between the 9th Division's 26th (Highland) and 27th (Lowland) brigades. The 63rd Division had to keep up the reputation of the senior service! The 33rd (well leavened with regulars) was nominally a London division as was the 56th, bearing the capital's reputation on their shoulders, and the Guards had a long standing reputation to maintain.

On 11th March the 51st Harper was given command of IV Corps, and replaced as G.O.C. by Major-General G.T.C. Carter-Campbell, c.b., d.s.o., from command of the 94th Brigade, 31st Division (New Army).

The 51st was in Harper's IV Corps of Byng's Third Army and at the northern edge of the Flesquieres salient. Part of the initial German assault was to pinch off the salient's flanks, leaving the divisions in its centre free from major assault. With this in mind an Intermediate Line had been created across the base of the salient, to which the garrison might withdraw.

Private Wrench of 1/4th Seaforths, attached to 154th Brigade's Headquarters noted on Wednesday 20th March: 'there's some breeze around here now with the rumour that the attack is coming in the morning. Which might only be another rumour after all. Tonight Charlie File is off on leave so I am detailed for General's orderly again. Here's hoping I'll have a good easy time as before.'[7]

This was a vain hope: the German barrage began at 5 a.m. on 21st March and lasted until 9.30 a.m., raking rear areas, batteries, trench mortars, command posts, telephone exchanges, billets and bivouacs, front line trenches and communication trenches, with high explosive and gas shells. Close behind the barrage, at 9.30 a.m., were the German infantry.

All accounts from this time can be qualified by the 1/7th Argylls' introduction to their reports of the ensuing days:

> 'it is very difficult to give an accurate account of the action of the Battalion because from the 21st onwards Companies, and, in many cases, platoons were split up fighting on their own, and also because, owing to the numerous cases of Company

and Battalion H.Q. having had to withdraw rapidly, practically all the messages received and sent have been lost and most of the leaders are casualties.'[8]

Fog blanketed the front, lying densely in valleys, and reducing visibility to as little as ten yards. The survivors of the German bombardment were often surprised or quickly outflanked by the German infantry. The thinly spread Fifth Army was evicted from its outpost zone and battle zone south of St. Quentin. Elsewhere it managed to control varying depths of its battle zone.

The Third Army's 47th (2nd London) Division met the Fifth Army's 9th (Scottish) Division, at the southern end of the Flesquieres Salient. The centre of the salient had been soused with mustard gas, which indicated, because it lingered, that the Germans were not planning to occupy it immediately. Its garrison divisions, the 63rd (Royal Naval) Division and the 17th (Northern) Division were subjected to token attacks. The same applied initially to 1/4th Gordons, next to the 17th Division and to the battalions on their left, 1/7th Argylls and 1/6th Gordons, who noted: 'Some gas shells. Heavy bombardment started on left at 4.30 a.m. No attack developed on Battalion front.' [9]

The German outflanking attack on the salient fell on 1/6th Black Watch on the extreme left of the 51st when:

> 'Shortly after 6.60 a.m. all communication was cut, both forward and back, and the ground mist and smoke and dust prevented successful visual signalling. Runners were unable to get forward, but succeeded in reaching Brigade Headquarters, which was under a heavy barrage, with considerable gas shelling.
>
> 'Observers at Battalion Headquarters were unable to see more than a few yards beyond our wire, until about 10 a.m., when the bombardment lifted off the Intermediate Line and Battalion Headquarters, and, the mist clearing, the enemy infantry was seen moving about our support line.' [10]

Not only mist and fog hampered vision; the spoil on the parados of the newly deepened line obstructed the view to flanks and rear. This hazard had been recognised but the attack came before the problem was remedied: thus the Germans and could attain grenade throwing range without being observed. [11] The front trenches were on forward slopes, and the exposed communication trenches which led back to Boursies and Louverval were heavily shelled. 1/6th and 1/7th Black Watch companies in these trenches ceased to exist and their remnants fell back to the right, on to 1/5th Seaforths, who had not sustained direct assault. All were then driven across to 1/6th Gordons as the Germans grenaded, shot and bayoneted their way up the 51st's trenches. The cascade reached 1/7th Argylls on the right at 10 a.m. when they moved two platoons to protect their vulnerable left flank. At 2.45 p.m. 'a party of 6th G.H., who had been badly attacked by *Flamenwerfer* and were in a state of panic. . . created a panic among the troops. . . until they were rallied by the Coy. Comm (Company Commander).' [12] On the same day 1/7th Argylls had to evacuate a trench near Demicourt: 'owing to one of our howitzers shelling DEMICOURT in the vicinity of the cemetery all afternoon.' [13]

Private Wrench wrote:

> 'They [the enemy] broke through the 6th Division on our left and with a flanking movement enveloped the 153rd and 152nd Brigades failing to break our front with a frontal attack. So they reached Doignies through Boursies and in between the bde. H.Q. and our front in an effort to cut off the 154 bde in the rear. The slaughter was terrific. Lieut. Leith* was killed here in the morning and God knows how many of us have yet escaped.' [14]

A captured German recalled that 'the few Scotsmen remaining alive were taken prisoners and sent to the rear, their cigarettes having been taken from them. We had by this time several casualties. In the evening we were in possession of Doignies, where we captured several guns. . . '[15]

At Morchies, (West of Louverval) Captain Behrends, R.G.A., has been visiting gun sites. When his car reached the sugar factory at the junction with the road to Cambrai he turned towards Cambrai and was halted by an anxious Highland officer who asked him what he was doing. Behrens replied that he was checking up on his batteries, and was told by the officer that the Germans were about 200 yards away. Behrens left his car and walked to Toc 3, his battery position, which was totally deserted. The Highland officer had orders to dig in and Behrens advised him to occupy Toc 3's deserted gun-pits and dug-outs, which were protected by wire. They made their farewells then Behrens' driver 'Thompson gave the starting handle a turn and the noise of the engine vibrated through the cold stillness with startling loudness. A burst of machine-gun fire which sounded less than a hundred yards away startled me out of my wits-it was so totally unexpected and hitherto everything had been so quiet. . .' [16]

As the Germans had planned, the rear areas were hit hard. Private Herbert Steele, 5 Platoon, B Company, 1/6th Seaforths, reserve battalion, 152nd Brigade:

21st March

'Our reveille. . . was not however the familiar bugle call but the equally familiar sound of heavy gunfire – unfamiliar certainly in that form for several months and at that distance behind the line for we were lying at Lebucquiere near Beaumetz-les-Cambrai. . . so at 4 o'clock we had our breakfast with the shells dropping over the huts and short of them. We were quickly told to dress and fall in while the fire increased. Nearer and nearer the shells dropped and when we left the camp [not by the road, which formed a distinct and frequent target for the enemy's fire] the shells were bursting less than 50 yards from our camp and soon several fell amongst the huts. . . we were almost at our destination, a reserve trench dug above Beaumetz, before our first casualty occurred. With another soldier I stayed behind until the S.B. [stretcher bearer]

Private Herbert Steele

arrived and glad I was to get on for it is better to keep moving than to lie in a shell hole – better I mean in the sense of being less trying.

When I rejoined my platoon several more casualties had

occurred. The trench was a regular death trap. Not a dug-out, not a shelter. Only a trench with firesteps, a 7ft. wide trench, a splendid and much patronised target.

There was, even then, too much selfishness amongst our fellows. Soon all our S.B.s [stretcher bearers] were engaged in carrying wounded while many able to walk had already gone away. Then C. Brooks* was wounded and his foot nearly blown off. He was about 70 yards down the trench and no-one would take him down. It was certainly not the place of riflemen to act as S.B. [which I may say in my opinion is a 'cushy' job in a quiet sector but awful at this stage of the operations] but how could we allow him to lie there and probably die, for he had a tourniquet on and it was a case of his losing his life or his leg. Others refused; I could have done so. But I was trained with him, came out with him and had always been in the same platoon with him. So I took him down. But I took a good rest at the dressing station.

'By this time our artillery, which at first had replied fairly well, had quietened. . . it may be they were silenced, it may be they were withdrawn, though I incline to the latter supposition. But all the time the German fire continued on our trench and our casualty list increased.' [17]

The 19th (Western) Division was sent to prop up the collapsing front and at 7p.m. 12 tanks and its 57th Brigade failed to retake Doignies and occupied a sunken road south-east of Beaumetz and 'from this time the 57th Brigade was involved in the fighting and was on the right of, and to some extent, mixed up with, the 51st Division.[18] At 4.20 p.m. the 57th Brigade was put under the command of the 51st.

To the left of the 51st the 6th (Regular) Division was driven to the rear of of its battle zone, as was 59th (2nd North Midland), 34th (New Army) and the right of 3rd (Regular), conforming to 34th Division. The Flesquieres salient was being outflanked and Haig permitted Byng to pull its garrison back to the Intermediate Line. Between 1.30 a.m. and 4.30 a.m. on the 22nd, the right of the 51st withdrew to the Hermies Line, which joined the Beaumetz-Morchies Line, to which many of the 51st had retreated. The night allowed the reorganisation of shattered units, the collection of stragglers and resupply.

Captain David Sutherland of 1/5th Seaforths reflected:

'If every Division on this front had been as well dug-in and
wired-in as ours, the enemy would never have broken the line,
but when one Division puts forward every effort to make
things secure, while the next on the right or left is allowed to
take things in easy fashion, or devotes its work parties to the
less essential, it is evident that the chain will snap at its
weakest link, and so it was in March, the weak links then
being those Divisions which had not worked systematically all
the spring at defensive works.' [19]

Friday 22nd March

On the 22nd Fifth Army's left had been pushed in. The 47th, 63rd and
17th Divisions, reinforced by 2nd Division, in the flattened Flesquieres
salient, held off attacks, but as the day wore on the right of the salient
was exposed by Fifth Army's withdrawal.

On the 51st's front on Friday 22nd a bombardment from 6 a.m. to 10
a.m was closely followed by the German infantry. Major Campbell, 1/6th
Black Watch: 'While the artillery pounded us, the infantry was steadily
trying to work up to our wire and line, but the defence held, in spite of
many casualties.' [20] On 1/7th Black Watch's front 'the enemy 'dribbled'
down to a position on our left flank.' [21]

Private Wrench, 1/4th Seaforths:

'. . . absolute Hell here. Cold-blooded murder and mass
slaughter. The Germans in their mass formations get it from
our Lewis and machine-guns while they give it to us
unmercifully with their artillery. There seems to be few of our
guns left in action now, all I hear being the siege battery a few
hundred yards down the road. They won't be able to remove
them anyway so will save their last shells to spike the guns
before retiring.' [22]

Everywhere the Germans were threatening to outflank the British,
who responded by protecting their flanks, then withdrawing as the new
flanks were further threatened by outflanking or encirclement – a

domino effect exacerbated by the difficulty of covering the front with diminishing numbers and the extension of the front as the enemy bulged salients into British territory. 6th Division, on the 51st's immediate left, lost ground at Vaulx Wood mid-morning but held until mid-afternoon, when ammunition ran short and the Germans reached Vaulx-Vaudricourt, north of the 51st, and outflanking it.

Major Campbell, 1/6th Black Watch:

> 'Parties of the enemy were also pushing up the valley towards Bapaume and we were almost surrounded. One party leading the enemy rush consisted of an officer and about eight men, was well up the sunken road when Colonel McClintock, of the 7th Battalion The Black Watch, and I got out of the dug-out and climbed up on to the bank to try to stop the rush.
>
> Colonel McClintock had a rifle and shot the leader, but his men came on. We then saw parties working round our rear, and immediately decided to try and hold the Cambrai road as left flank, to protect the 152nd Brigade on the south side of the road. Earlier in the afternoon a party of Loyal North Lancashires had been sent forward to reinforce the Beaumetz-Morchies Line, and, with a mixed force, very few non-commissioned officers, and almost no officers, we had difficulty in getting the line formed. We extended towards Beugny in an endeavour to hold the enemy who had passed us, but unfortunately when we moved towards the vital spot the line we had formed broke and fell back. About 25 men of our brigade were left. . . and we settled down to fight two parties of the enemy who tried to surround us. One officer followed by a dozen men, turned down the Bapaume Road and indicated by signs his desire that we should surrender. He waved his revolver in one hand, and his cool impertinence so puzzled me – I was standing up to try to see enemy movements – that I ordered 'Cease fire!' lest he be one of ours. Realising my mistake, I flattened down with celerity and we at once fired on the party. I missed that officer but got one of his men. . . we decided to fall back on Beugny village. . . we took up shell hole positions outside the village, found some ammunition, and waited for the Boche. . .
>
> 'After a council of war. . . we got in touch with the 6th

Battalion Seaforth Highlanders, who still held the Beaumetz-Morchies Line south of the Cambrai Road.' [23]

Private Herbert Steele, 1/6th Seaforths:

'On Friday night I accompanied an officer of the 25th Division [the 25th Division was in reserve and on its way forward] to find Battalion Headquarters. This however we could not do and I returned alone to my Company. After several hours of inactivity in which our only job was to watch and fire several shots to let the enemy know we were still in position and on the alert, we found the position becoming untenable owing to the success of the enemy's attack on our left towards Beugny. Indeed it was the continual failure of the troops on the left which was the cause of our retirements.

'Thus late on Friday night after the enemy had forced back the left so as to render it possible to fire on our rear, and when the position became more and more costly to us, we retreated down the light railway to positions below Beaumetz. To effect this our platoon was spread over a large front to deceive the foe while other Companies effected their retiral. We then followed successfully.

'At this point several went astray for when I say we carried out our retirement successfully I mean the enemy remained in ignorance at least as far as I am personally aware. When we had taken up our new position I found that my section commander was missing, whether captured or killed I at present do not know. I therefore found myself in command of my section, dug in on the left of a sunken road leading into Beaumetz.' [24]

Bewsher asserted: 'The Jocks were at the top of their form, were inflicting great losses on the enemy, and were complete masters of the situation . . . all ranks had, in fact, the greatest confidence in their ability to defeat the enemy's attempts so long as the line north and south of them held firm and secured their flanks.' [25]

On that day Captain Sutherland of 1/5th Seaforths remembered that 'a little parachute, seemingly fired from a rifle, fell in our lines and was found to bear attached to it the following message: 'Good old 51st! Still sticking it. Cheerio!' Such was the message we got from some Boche with more chivalry than most of his compatriots.' [26]

It is a measure of the 51st's skill at self-advertisement that 'Good old fifty-first' inspired a song composed by David Rory (probably David Rorie, R.A.M.C. A. writer of pre-war songs and author of *A Medico's Luck in the War*), and Eric Stanley of the 'Balmorals'.

The German success in pushing back the left of the 51st and the entire 6th Division was duplicated all the way north on Third Army's front, so that the troops of IV and V Corps were in danger of being outflanked from both south and north.

However well parts of the 51st held their ground on the 22nd, Captain Behrend R.G.A. was looking up the Cambrai road towards Fremicourt:

'Along the road a slow stream of traffic was moving towards Bapamue and beyond, first waves of a tide which rolled westwards for days and days. Here and there a battery in column of route, walking wounded in twos and threes, an odd lorry or two, a staff car carrying with undignified speed the dignified sign of Corps Headquarters, a column of horse transport, and a biggish batch of German prisoners captured by 51st Division. The procession reminded me of a film; it was with something approaching a shock that I realised everything was in retreat.' [27]

Saturday 23rd March

On Saturday 23rd, Fifth Army fell back between four to six miles. Although its centre was fairly intact a three thousand yards gap had developed between the Fifth Army and the Third Army.

In the small hours of the 23rd orders were issued that V Corps was to withdraw to avoid being trapped in the diminishing Flesquieres salient. The 51st, on the right of IV Corps, was to fall back to Bancourt, about 7500 yards to the west of its existing positions, return two borrowed brigades to the 19th and 25th Divisions, and regroup. It was a wearing day in face of intense German pressure from north of the Cambrai-Bapaume Road. The attack began on the left, held by troops of the 25th

Division and by the 51st's machine-guns on the left. At 7 a.m. the Germans attacked and were held by 1/5th and 1/6th Seaforths, 10th Worcesters and elements of two R.E. field companies. The Germans attained Lebucquière, 2000 yards behind the men of the 51st who were holding the remnants of the Beaumetz-Morchies line east of Beaumetz. Major-General Carter-Campbell ordered the brigade to withdraw through Vélu Wood, south west of Beaumetz, and go to Bancourt.

The 1/4th Seaforths recounted:

'Enemy in overwhelming numbers all around us. Machine-guns enfiladed our trench and inflicted many casualties. Enemy brought up light batteries of field guns . . . which fired point blank at our trench. About 3 p.m. enemy entered our trench. He was held up for a time but made progress owing to bombs of which we had not a sufficient supply. More of the enemy threatened to enter the trench from all sides. It was decided to withdraw to the supporting troops on railway behind. On arrival it was found that all troops had evacuated positions. The WARWICKS were forming a line facing VELU WOOD.' [28]

Private Herbert Steele, 1/6th Seaforths, Saturday 23rd:

'The enemy advanced again and the left gave. This caused the whole line to be imperiled and a general retiral was certain. [It is noteworthy that on every occasion we were told that the positions must be held at all costs, yet we were given no support.] Soon the order came to retire through Vélu wood to the Corps line, for the Germans were well up on our left and were in a sunken road at right angles to our line and not 50 yards from our post, thus endangering greatly our line of retirement. It was then a case of 'sauve qui peut', and we fell back, but with great loss, stopping where occasion occurred to fire on the enemy who advanced with great rapidity and force.

'Even then we did not forget our hunger. We were lucky enough to come across a deserted canteen in Vélu Wood and here we, who were lucky enough to pass the hut, obtained biscuits.

'We fell back through the wood and here we saw the first signs of artillery support since Friday. There were one or two guns galloping back and later we came across them sending occasional shells into the wood we had passed.

'. . . we came across the first signs of support or any systematic attempt at forming a defence line. This was the 2nd Division and through them we fell, a small handful of men of what had been once one of the best Divisions in France. Before the attack the Germans had said they were going to capture the whole Highland Division or wipe it out. While it remained intact it could never do the former and I must say they had nearly succeeded in the latter. For when we arrived back at Grevillers where our transport lay I found that there was 40 left of my Company. And when we went into action next, which was the next night, of the whole of my Brigade there was left only sufficient to make up a very weak Battalion, perhaps 500 men or less.

'We arrived at Grevillers then and had a great reception. Our Colonel turned out the band to play the march past 'for my brave men' and at once we had soup, tea etc. given to us.' [29]

154th Brigade in the remnants of the Beaumetz-Morchies Line had been under attack from 6 a.m. by close range artillery fire: right to left, were 1/7th Argylls, 1/4th Seaforths, 8th Gloucesters and 10th Royal Warwicks, part of 57th Brigade, 19th Division, which had been attached to the Highland Division on the 21st. The men were intermingled:

'. . . the German attack was a good one, for machine-guns on the flanks swept the Highlanders' parapet and the infantry came on doggedly. It was a nerve-racking ordeal. Men lay dead and dying in the trench; others were falling every minute. Two of the Gloucesters and some Seaforths were in one bay, making their fire tell with deadly effect on the enemy; first one of the Seaforths fell, next moment one of the Gloucesters was hit through the windpipe. He collapsed and was choked by his own blood. His comrade stopped for a moment to look at him, but seeing he could not help, quietly took up his rifle and went on with his task. These Gloucesters were gallant men.' [30]

The History of 19th Division, from which these Gloucesters came, states that:

> 'the 51st Division began to withdraw, which left the flanks of the 10th Warwicks and 8th Gloucesters in the air. They held their ground with grim determination until 11 a.m. and then began to withdraw, the 10th Warwicks to north of the railway between Velu and Velu Wood and facing Velu Wood.'

It states that the only 51st troops in the area were a machine-gun officer and his men. [31] (Major Harcourt of the C Company 51st Machine Gun Corps.)

The same history complains that at 3 a.m. that day: 'Headquarters, 154th Brigade, disappeared 'into the blue' with the expressed intention of getting back to Fremicourt; but from that time no further communication whatever was received from the Brigadier of that brigade.' [32] There is a reminder of this on the following page.

Private Wrench's diary touches on the problems of that move:

> 'Left with the General and staff at 4 a.m. via Velu and Haplincourt, a long round about road and most of the way we were shelled like hell. We got down (to Fremicourt) just before daybreak and are now heaped here together with the div. H.Q. and the other brigades as well as the artillery and R.E.s in perfect chaos. The shelling is terrible.' [33]

The two 19th Division battalions were pushed back and formed a left flank facing the northern edge of Velu Wood: at 2.50 p.m. they withdrew to Bancourt. On the right of the 51st the 17th Division withdrew. 1/7th Argylls noted:

> 'this left the right and the left flanks of the position in the air. However the remnants of my three companies and of the 4th Seaforths fought on until 3.30 when they were almost completely surrounded and had to withdraw with heavy losses. . . the intention was to withdraw and line up with the 17th Division, but on arrival it was found that the 17th Division had not stayed. . . consequently these three

companies took up a position astride the BERTINCOURT-YTRES road with the 63rd Division. . . They were afterwards directed to rejoin their Division by an officer of the 63rd Division.' [34]

1/4th Seaforths' resistance persisted in the headquarters trench until the adjutant and about twenty men had to escape, their retreat covered by four men who had been surrounded and expended the last of their machine-gun ammunition before being overcome. [35] The withdrawal of the remnants of the Beaumetz-Morchies Line defence was covered by Major Harcourt, C Company, 51st Battalion, Machine-Gun Corps, whose men protected the narrowing escape corridor with 'five guns and some Lewis guns in position between Velu Wood and the railway, and with them held up the enemy advance for five hours.'[36]

In his report on the March battles Brigadier-General Buchanan wrote of 1/4th Seaforths and 1/7th Argylls:

'The value of the foregoing defence cannot, I consider, be exaggerated. Apart from inflicting a heavy loss on the enemy, it partly assisted the 152nd Brigade to withdraw, and very greatly assisted the 17th Division on the right in this respect. The defence is also a valuable example of holding out for over five hours with both flanks gone and the enemy having penetrated over 2500 yards directly in rear.' [37]

1/7th Black Watch was at Bancourt all day. There were not many of them.

'The night of the 22nd/23rd passed quietly and the Battalion consisting of Lt.Colonel S.R.McClintock D.S.O., Capt. J. Reid M.C. and 30 other ranks took up a position in the old GERMAN TRENCHES in front of BANCOURT in support of the 19th DIVISION. The day passed quietly and hot rations were brought up during the evening. The night passed without incident. Enemy aeroplanes dropped pamphlets for his own troops stating the extent of the advance.' [38]

On the 23rd, Captain Behrend, R.G.A., heard pipes and drums and ran outside:

221

'It was magnificent and too moving for words. No music, not even the trumpets of the French cavalry which I heard screaming their wild song of triumph after the armistice, has stirred me as deeply as the sobbing, skirling pipes of the 51st Division playing their survivors back to the battle, and I shivered with pride as I stood there, watching these grim Highlanders swing by – every man in step, every man bronzed and resolute. Could these be the same weary, dirty men who came limping past us yesterday in ragged twos and threes, asking pitifully how much further to Achiet-le-Grand? Who could behold such a spectacle and say that pomp and circumstance of War is no more?' [39]

The 51st had found reinforcements from men returning from leave and from courses, and from stragglers. The 51st had ceded ground, was battered, severely depleted, but still fighting,

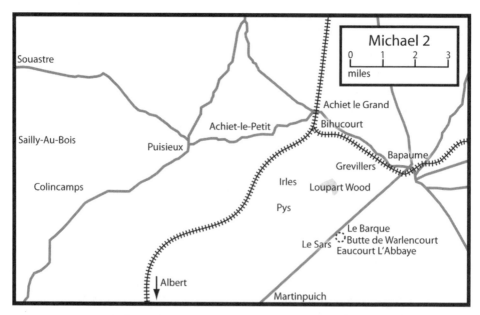

Sunday 24th March

In the Fifth Army gaps widened between retreating divisions, the worst being between the Fifth and Third Armies, where the flanking divisions of both had to fall back to protect their armies.

On the right of Third Army V Corps was under heavy pressure as the

enemy tried to cut off divisions left too long in the Flesquieres Salient. The 47th Division was on the exposed right, on the edge of a four mile gap and the enemy threatened its flank all day. The overall withdrawal continued to the old Somme battlefield, where V Corps settled for the night around Martinpuich, Bazentin-le-Grand, Bazentin-le-Petit and High Wood. Its front was porous, and it had no contact with the Fifth Army on its right or the IV Corps on its left.

In IV Corps the Germans moved at 5 a.m. on the left on the 25th (New Army) Division, and on the right at 10 a.m on the 19th Division. The 19th Division front was heavily shelled throughout the morning, but there was no infantry attack, but when V Corps started to fall back the 41st and 19th Divisions of IV Corps began a fighting withdrawal. 1/7th Black Watch recorded that the morning of the 24th was quiet, in support of 19th Division , but that its units began to retire through their lines in the afternoon.[40] 1/8th Royal Scots (Pioneers) were east of Bancourt to the Cambrai Road, and had been consolidating all morning and were more precise about the 19th Division's retiral: they noted that there was a bombardment at 2.30 as the 19th Division troops passed through them and the 152nd Brigade, which was in front of Riencourt. 1/8th Royal Scots wavered:

> 'At 4.30 word was received that the Highlanders on the right (remnants of the 153rd Inf Bde) were retiring and that the right platoon of C Coy under 2nd Lt.W. Steel had forned a defensive flank. The whole battalion then retired a short way but Col Gemmill* went forward and led it back into the line. However, the right flank was now in the air so the Battalion retired by platoons from the right. [40]

At 4.30 p.m. men of V Corps passed through 152nd Brigade, which was forced to fall back through 154th Brigade, which was in support. The general confusion of withdrawal may have been added to as rumours abounded of Germans dressed as British officers ordering retirements, and spreading panic. This is discounted by the official history which attributes its origin to officers unfamiliar to soldiers giving them orders.[42] At 7.00 p.m. the right flank of 1/7th Black Watch was broken and with the rest of the 51st it retired through the 19th Division, which was east of Bapaume, and then formed a line from the Bapaume-Albert Road near the Butte de Warlencourt to the north-east corner of Loupart Wood. Along the entire front the British were leapfrogging to the rear, by divisions, battalions, companies, platoons and sections.

Private Wrench was near Riencourt when:

> 'The general went off in a hurry somewhere and called on me to follow and then a shell burst about 200 yards away. It seemed quite safe but a bit got me on the right arm near the shoulder. I got quite excited with the surprise of it more than anything else but a vision of getting quit of all for a time sent me happily back across the field with the signal officer shouting to me to 'Get the Hell out of this'. '

He found a deserted Casualty Clearing Station then walked on through congested roads until he found another at Grevillers, which had become, by the army's withdrawal, an advanced dressing station.

> 'Field guns are blazing away at the Germans out in front of this group of marquees while German shells are also bursting around and puncturing the tent. I was the last man to receive attention here and get into a seat on top of the last bus to leave. My arm wasn't bandaged again but a label tied to my buttonhole, then we moved off to C.C.S. no. 29 at Dernancourt near Albert where we were all innoculated against infection from wounds. A tin of hot cocoa was provided minus any sugar and a chunk of dry bread so thus catered for, after hanging around for hours, we were herded into the usual railway trucks with hundreds of other 'walking wounded' cases and started off to God knows where. It is perishing cold in these trucks with a freezing draught blowing up between the floor boards so sleep is out of the question.' [43]

As Private Wrench was leaving the battle, Private Steele, 1/6th Seaforths, was preparing for it:

Sunday 24

'A day of preparations which we hoped was precautionary for was it not said that there were Yankees coming and French.

Alas, in spite of our hopes, none arrived and again we dressed and marched off with rations for two days, the last rations some were to receive from the British Army for months, and some for ever. . . there was apparently no plan and for hours we wandered about, beginning to dig in here and there, then beginning afresh and finally taking up our position in shell holes. There we spent the remainder of the night. [44]

Like many other divisions the 51st thought itself isolated and 'throughout the night of 24-25th March no touch with British troops could be obtained on either flank, though it was known that the 19th Division was on the line from Le Barque to the east of Grevillers.' [45]

Monday 25th March

On the morning of Monday 25th March the 51st line from right to left, from the Butte de Warlencourt to north-east of Loupart Wood was composed of 1/7th Argylls, 1/4th Gordons, 1/4th Seaforths, 1/6th Gordons, 1/6th Seaforths, 6/7th Black Watch, 1/8th Royal Scots with 1/7th Gordons and 1/5th Seaforths in reserve. The official history recognised that: 'The troops of the IV Corps (Lieut. General Sir G.M. Harper) having all been in action since the 21st, were exhausted and low in numbers, but still full of fight.' [46] Its problem was that it was faced by fifteen German divisions, of which six were concentrated on the right of IV Corps.

At 4 a.m. 1/7th Argylls realised:

'. . . instead of the 2nd Division being on our right they had withdrawn to ALBERT leaving our right again in the air. No infantry action developed until 11 a.m. when the enemy occupied LABARQUE and began massing in the low ground. . . the enemy were easily held as far as our front was concerned and if our right flank had been protected this position could have been maintained indefinitely, but although the enemy only made half-hearted attacks on our front he could be seen streaming in masses along the high ground towards EAUCOURT L'ABBAYE and moving northwards from there towards LE SARS.'

At 1 p.m. 1/7th Argylls were ordered to hold their line but at 1.15 p.m:

'As no sign of any reinforcing division appeared and whatever British troops there had been on our right had long before been seen streaming back towards PYS, and the enemy were obviously attempting to reach PYS before us and so cut us off, I decided to withdraw according to written orders received the night before and confirmed verbally by the Brigade Major, to SERRE.' [47]

Private Steele, 1/6th Seaforths:

Monday 25th

'There was, we understood, a Division in front but this was wrong, for between us and the enemy who began to advance soon after seven or eight o'clock was only the Pioneer Battalion of our own Division... our line was, however, isolated, there being troops neither to the right or left of us. Before us were one or two machine-guns and several of our pioneers.' [48]

'From 10 a.m. troops of the 19th Division could be seen withdrawing and in the afternoon they were retiring through 1/7th Black Watch. [49]

'Soon we saw him (the enemy) in the distance and the increasing rifle fire told us he was in contact with those in front and the machine-guns. At this point we left our shell holes to take up positions in front. From the first it was apparent that we could never hold him and soon those in front fell back. [50]

By 2.15 p.m. the whole of the 51st fell back to prevent it being outflanked at both its extremes and amongst others, 'the adjutant and two other officers of the 6th Seaforths fighting with a party of men to the end, all being killed or captured.' [51] Private Steele, 1/6th Seaforths, was captured, whether it was with these officers is unknown:

'The enemy could be seen coming in dense masses, wave upon wave. Their formation was a series of waves, three, four, five or more, connected by files... it was his machine-guns which rendered his attack so overwhelming, more than his great superiority in numbers.

'We were forced back then, into a trench in our rear which was in the face of a slope. By this time there was very little order and I for my part can safely say with truth that I did nor see more than six officers from the time the battle began until I was taken. . . in the end we were forced back over the crest [and down from] and began to mount the slope behind.'

They were told to resume a position on the rear of the first crest, and did so.

'We could only continue to fire until it was useless to resist longer, especially as the foe were round almost in our rear on the right and left I was captured at the same time as W.F. with whom I had joined up, and with whom I had been since my enlistment. Immediately we were told to empty our pockets at rifle muzzle and we did not hesitate or argue.' [52]

The remnants of 1/6th Black Watch withdrew and 'reforming on the ridge N.E. of IRLES to meet the threatened enemy advance from the left, enemy shelled us and the shaken troops (mixed) moved back:- H.Q. mostly stood first in the Support Line.' [53]

Major Campbell, 1/6th Black Watch:

'On the ridge were Brigadier-General Beckwith, of the 153rd Brigade, and other officers of mixed units, who placed a line of troops in a shallow trench to await the enemy advance. About a hundred yards in rear of this line was a deep communication trench, and it was decided to get part of that force back there to form a support. Several Divisions and many battalions were mixed up and I feared trouble. The Boche had appeared on the ridge, and already we were under a heavy and accurate machine-gun fire. On top of this they gave us several rounds of 'whiz-bangs' from four field guns brought up behind the advanced infantry, at point blank range, and like one man the line moved back. Major Keir and Captain Reid of the 7th Battalion The Black Watch and Lieutenant Hewat* and myself did our utmost to hold the men, but failed, the men by this time being utterly worn out, and the enemy, seeing the target offered, gave them heavy shelling from these four guns.

'The Headquarters of the 6th and 7th Battalions The Black Watch were then in the awkward position of being alone in front, and when the men had taken cover, we crossed the open, one at a time, getting to the next trench without casualty. There we found about 250 men, mostly of the Highland Division, very undecided, and we called on them to stand fast and remember the Division they belonged to. I have always been proud of our men, but that moment showed how they could answer the call of an officer. As we were alone, and in a bad position, I allowed the men to move back, and behind Achiet-le-Petit, Major Newson, Second-in-Command of the 7th Battalion Gordon Highlanders, had collected a number of men before we reached that point. Major Keir and I, with two or three other officers, made a dejected party as we followed the retiring troops. We were not at that moment under fire, and could only follow in the hope that further back someone would collect the men. Major Newson, who was senior present, reported to 62nd Division, and we were given a line of slits and shell-holes to hold. I had then about 200 men of the Highland Division under my command.' [54]

It is apparent that the officers lost some control of their men although there is no reported defiance, but a recognition by the officers that the men had done all that they could, in confused and adverse circumstances. Their experience was that of most of the men in Third and Fifth Armies. Recall that 1/7th Black Watch had a strength of two officers and 30 men on the 23rd of March, and that units often existed only in name, and that men from different battalions and divisions were mixed up, lacking the stability provided by known and trusted officers.

1/7th Argylls withdrew successfully to Irles where 'we received orders to maintain our position there. By this time the troops were absolutely exhausted owing to lack of sleep, cold and fatigue. However, they faced about and manned positions in front of PYS till 4 p.m. when the whole Division withdrew.' [55] 1/7th Black Watch 'now became part of a Composite Divisional force and finally retired to a position in rear of the 62nd Division and there held slits till midnight when they were relieved and moved back to rejoin the remainder of the Division.'[56]

The 51st had been in action four four days and nights and by the

25th Bewsher admitted. . .

> 'vitality was at its lowest ebb. The remnant of the Division was thus left facing the enemy, its three brigade headquarters just in rear of the fighting line still in the same order of battle in which they had begun the engagement, but their fighting efficiency was gone. With no British troops on their right nearer than Albert, there was no other alternative left but to break off the engagement and withdraw. Orders were issued to the Division to concentrate at Colincamps.

> 'The withdrawal of all that was left of the Highland Division along the road from Puisieux to Colincamps was a melancholy spectacle: a long line of men and horses tired and exhausted almost beyond the limits of human endurance, dragging themselves along, many with undressed wounds. The men fell back in groups, not as formed bodies, but not in a disorderly rout. Every man retained his arms and equipment, and in spirit would have taken up any line ordered and continued the struggle; but in their acute stage of exhaustion further effective resistance was out of the question, and so was not asked of them.' [57]

The Official History confirms Bewsher's assessment by asserting that the 51st might have been routed in the early stages of its retirement on the 25th if the enemy had not been exhausted.[58] This conclusion may have emerged from the view of the G.O.C. 57th Infantry Brigade, 19th Division that:

> '51 Division simply ceased to operate as a unit from 23 March, and on 25 March made no attempt to stand but conducted a dour, deliberate and selfish retreat. Every day 51 Division retreated and left its neighbours 'in the air', [59] Jeffreys, G.O.C. 19th Division stated that on 25th March at a meeting of IV Corps' divisional commanders, Carter-Campbell said that his men were tired, demoralized and could no longer be relied upon to stand and fight.' [60]

All along the British front tired troops were being outflanked and most divisions were in a state of confusion with sections, platoons, companies and battalions intermingled with one another, and with other divisions. Why should the 51st have been singled out alone by the official historian as being in danger of being routed? Would this not have equally applied to any tired division still in contact with the enemy? Is this evidence of prejudice? Maybe this survived the draft of the Official History because Major-General Carter Campbell died on 21st December 1921 and was not available to query the Official History's editor. The 51st was not inactive on 25th March. There is enough evidence of resistance in the war diaries to indicate that this opinion was unsubstantiated. 'Dour and deliberate' suggests no panic and visible disorganisation, whilst still resisting. 'Selfish' could apply to every unit dropping back to guard its flanks, and unable to communicate its intention to its neighbours. On the 25th men of the 19th Division had retired through 1/7th Black Watch. ([49] above) Leapfrogging in retreat was endemic. That Carter-Campbell refused to put the 51st back into the line would have been based on the need to save men around whom the division would be rebuilt.

On the 25th/26th the 51st was at Sailly, and on the evening of the 26th at Souastre, in support, but not directly engaged in battle, although some men of the 51st captured Germans who had panicked at a counter-attack by twelve 'Whippet' tanks of the 3rd Tank Battalion. [61]

The C.O.of 1/7th Argylls explained why his battalion did not offer more effective resistance:

> '. . . It must be borne in mind that men of this Battalion had done, some of them 16 days and all of them 10 days in the line, and owing to the impending attack and the fact that a number of patrol and working parties had to be found they had very little sleep or rest. Consequently they were 'tired' at the start.
>
> 'The Artillery support throughout the whole fighting was negligible as far as this Battalion was concerned. The enemy on the contrary had batteries in action at point blank range within half an hour after his infantry had become engaged.
>
> 'We were harassed by low flying aircraft, and until the 25th

our planes were conspicuous by their absence, but from this date onwards they did magnificent work.

'No anti-aircraft fire of ours was seen in action during the whole battle. It is generally agreed in my Battalion that the enemy can throw his stick bombs further than we can throw our Mills' grenades.

'The use of *Flamenwerfer* had a very great moral effect, although the casualties inflicted by it were small.

'The work of the Battalion Transport in bringing up rations and ammunition was magnificent.

'The arrangements made to evacuate wounded were scandalous, and 90 per cent of my wounded had to be abandoned to the enemy. A detailed report of this has been forwarded to the A.D.M.S. by my M.O.

'It is suggested that in future, once the line has been broken, the field artillery should be allotted to an Infantry Brigade to work with them entirely.

'In every case the enemy massing to attack could be plainly seen by the infantry, and if only they had been able to call on any guns in the close vicinity massing could have been broken up before any attack developed.' [62]

Brigadier-General H. Pelham Burn, 152nd Brigade, was vitriolic in his criticism of Corps and Army:

'The following points were emphasized by the battle. A few of these may be described as lessons learnt, but the majority have long been known to those in the front line.

1. The absolute necessity of having all trench lines, front, support and reserve, and Army and Corps lines organised and constructed on an <u>Army</u> basis. Till we have this we can never hope to beat back a German attack. At present some Divisions work when in the line on one system, some on another, some do little work on trenches, dugouts or wire. . . Often the work that is done by one Division is undone by another. The waste of labour and material, everywhere evident, is colossal.

'The whole fault lies in the fact that there is <u>no system</u> in our

Army. We have no policy or plan for the siting or construction of trenches, we have not even got a standardized trench. . . dugouts are built, or are not built, according to the ideas of the temporary commander of the Divisional and sometimes the Brigade sector . . . the lack of efficiency, the indiscipline, misery and sickness brought about through having badly constructed trenches, is indescribable.

As regards the Corps Lines, I should like to call attention to the fact that the IV Corps line, or the BEAUMETZ-MORCHIES line as it was called, was dug by this Brigade during a period of rest from the front line. It was dug on my own initiative and, at first contrary to the wishes of the Corps, although they finally acquiesced in its construction. My Brigade dug 3,660 yards in 2 days, the firestepping being completed afterwards. It was in this line that the Highland Division made its main stand, a stand which admittedly saved the situation and saved the guns. Had a double line of this description been dug throughout III and V Army fronts the Germans would not now be nearing AMIENS.

2. C.T.s (communication trenches) to be so sited that they are switches first and C.T.s afterwards. They must be firestepped and well wired. . . All main lines of trenches must be laid out so that flanking fire in either direction can be brought to bear from selected parts of them at frequent intervals in their length. They should also give facilities for firing to the rear from special points.

Then he criticised training shortcomings.

'3. The necessity for the provision of rifle ranges behind the lines cannot be over-estimated. Through lack of practice on the range it is still undoubtedly the fact that our men have not yet got entire confidence in their rifles.

'The necessity for ranges for Lewis Guns is even greater. The large majority of Lewis gunners go into action having never fired their weapons on ranges longer than 30 yards.

'4. Brigadiers and Battalion Commanders, in open or semi-open warfare, should lose no opportunity of getting into touch with Batteries, and especially heavy batteries, with a view to informing them of the situation and getting them on to the best targets. It must be realised that batteries will usually be without any communication to the rear.

'5. The value of well-trained runners cannot be over-estimated. In all battles they are, and still remain, the one absolutely reliable means of communication from Brigade H.Q. forward. Runners must be expert map readers.

'6. In open warfare officers' chargers must be kept close at hand. In the retirement from Bapaume in no case did I see a regimental officer on horseback, with the result that the officers were as worn out as the men.

'7. A Brigade mobile reserve of Lewis Gun Drums, S.A.A., and long range rifle grenades is recommended, this reserve to be in close touch with Brigade Headquarters.' [63]

The 6th and 51st Divisions had sustained the weight of the German offensive on the left of the Flesquieres' salient. The casualty statistics from the 21st March to the 5th of April puts the losses of the 6th Division first (5161), the 51st second (4865) [64] and the casualties in other IV Corps divisions diminish roughly proportionately to the lesser number of days in which they were engaged. The 6th Division had been replaced by the 41st Division on the 22/23rd, whereas the 51st had to remain in contact with the Germans for a further three days, exposing it to greater fatigue and increased casualties.

The 51st's 'failure' on 21st March, linked to that of the 16th (Irish) and 36th (Ulster) divisions has been attributed to them being a 'Celtic' division, allegedly lacking the temperament for defence. [65] There is no detailed evidence provided for this assertion, and falls in the face of the 51st's defence of Roeux, of the Poelcappelle Spur at Third Ypres, or of the Beaumetz-Morchies line. This view of Highlanders may be a relic of Robert Graves' report of an officers' discussion at the 'Bull Ring' at Harfleur in early 1916, which concluded that Highlanders and the Irish could usually take their objectives, but often lost them to counter-attacks. [66]

On 1st April the 51st moved to the area around Bethune. Officers settled down to write to the relatives of their dead and missing, a wearing task, often characterised by formulaic phrases such as 'died instantly', 'a popular soldier' and 'will be much missed'. Relatives at home knew of the German offensive, experienced the non-delivery of normally predictable mail, and anxiously awaited official notification of their man's fate. Private Thomas Lindsay, 1/7th Black Watch was missing, and on 2nd April his officer wrote:

Private Thomas Lindsay

My Dear Mrs. Lindsay,

I am sorry to be the sender of bad news but sincerely trust that it will turn out less black as would at first appear.

Your son, No.229797 Pte. Lindsay T. is posted as missing as from 21st March the first day of the German attack on his front.

Everything became very disorganised that day and definite information in any sequence is very hard to obtain but your son when last seen was still fighting bravely. There is therefore reason to hope that he may be a prisoner or turn up in one of our hospitals but the thing is so big that reports will necessarily be slow in coming forward.

Your son was extremely useful to one on account of his talent for drawing and he carried out some very valuable work for me in the Sniping Section. Enclosed is a copy of one of his works in our own last Sector which I thought you might like to have. He did other work of this nature for me in other sectors and all proved very useful.

I know the anxiety you must feel and sympathise with you in it, but I hope that Lindsay may turn up safely.
Yours sincerely,
F I Gerrard Lieut [67]

Lieutenant Gerrard had the good fortune to have been sent to the Divisional Rest Camp at Doullens with nine men, on 20th March, and returned, probably sooner than he anticipated, with nine men, on the 26th of March, and was given command of the remnants of B Company, 1/7th Black Watch. On the 31st he was made intelligence officer for the battalion, which consisted of four small platoons. On 2nd April the battalion was reorganising and on the rifle range and Gerrard focused on the difficult business of writing to relatives. [68]

It is likely that Gerrard's letter from Burbure, west of Bethune, was delivered after the following, also dated 2nd April. On Army Form B. 104-81A, from the Infantry Record Office in Perth, 2nd April 1918:

> Madam,
>
> I regret to inform you that a report has been received from the War Office to the effect that (No.) 292767 (Rank) Pte (Name) Thos. Lindsay (Regiment) Royal Highlanders has been wounded, and was admitted to No.1 Canadian General Hospital, Etaples on the 24th day of March 1918. The nature of the wound is Gunshot Thigh, and Left Arm. (Severe)
>
> I am to express to you the sympathy and regret of the Army Council.
>
> Any further information received in this office as to his condition will be at once notified to you.
>
> Yours faithfully, J J illegible [69]

Mrs. Lindsay must have met this information with a confusion of emotions: relief that her son was alive, anxiety as to the nature of his wounds.

Representing typical Scottish letter writers was twenty years old Private James Burnett*. He had joined 1/6th Royal Scots in September 1914, guarded the River Forth in 1914 and 1915, then served with the Western Frontier Force in the desert campaign against the Senussi. In France in 1916 his depleted battalion had amalgamated with 1/5th Royal Scots, to form 5/6th Royal Scots, 14th Brigade, 32nd Division, and he had received a wound which got him home in January 1917. Fit again, he was transferred to 12th Royal Scots, 27th Brigade, 9th Scottish Division, and was wounded on 20th September 1917. On his recovery he was sent to the 51st's pioneer battalion, 1/8th Royal Scots, in early March 1918. His last letter before the March offensive was dated 11th March. Thereafter he was involved in the withdrawal, in which his

Private James Burnett

battalion fought as infantry. On 24th March he wrote, within the restrictions of a Field Post Card:

> I am quite well.
> I received your letter of 14.3.18
> Letter follows at first opportunity. [70]

Then another, dated 28th March, saying the same. By then the battalion was at resting at Canteleux, en route next day to Frévent. Released from the constraints of field post cards, but well aware of the censor, he wrote on the 28th:

'Dear Father and Mother,

Just a few lines to let you know I am alive and well. I am sorry to have kept you so long without a letter but owing to certain circumstances it has been impossible to write letters so I trust this will find everybody at home in the best of health. Please send me a sum of money out of the £4 about 10/- as I hope to be able to get a small present for the bairns' birthday in a few days... I remain,
Your loving son,
James [71]

There was no chance to buy presents. Next day the battalion marched to Frevent, where, 'whilst waiting for the train the King passed through the town and personally congratulated the Btn. and Division on the fight they had put up.' Their train left at 8 p.m. and arrived at 2.30 a.m. at Lillers from where they marched to Bas Rieux. They settled there until the 8th, reorganising, assimilating replacements and resting after their endeavours in 'Michael'. [72] There was an expectation that the division would rest for some time, and that they were in a quiet area. James Burnett's letter of 6th April reflects his pride in a job well done:

'. . . now the worst is over it is alright to be congratulated by the king and all the rest of the staff as we have been since these few hot days.' [73]

For the first seven days of April the 51st recovered from the March offensive near Bethune. 1/7th Black Watch carried out smartening drill, reorganised itself into four companies from its two temporary composite companies, and fired on the rifle and Lewis gun ranges. On four days it received drafts of unrecorded size of Argylls, Seaforths, Gordons and the 3rd Black Watch. [74] This randomness did not make officers' lives easier or encourage *esprit de corps*. As the infantry had priority over pioneers, 1/8th Royal Scots had to lend eight officers to the 1/7th Gordons. Over the week 1/8th Royal Scots concentrated on gas drill, bombing, shooting and integrating five separate drafts of 25, 73, 50, 83 and 50 men. [75] To make up for their losses of medical officers in Michael the 51st was 'joined by an excellent and efficient reinforcement of ten Australian medical graduates, who were deservedly popular with all ranks throughout their stay in the 51st Division.' [76]

On 7th April the 51st was ordered north to join the XI Corps, and took up reserve positions in the Robeq, Ham-en-Artois, Busnes and Gonnheim area, known to the 51st in 1915.

The official history recognised the difficulties faced by divisions that had endured the March Offensive. Drafts brought the depleted battalions up to 500 or 600 men, but few officers or N.C.O.s came to replace the casualties. There were equipment, transport and personal weapon and artillery gun shortages, all being dealt with on the hoof. In some cases brigadiers saw their resurrected brigades for the first time as they approached the forthcoming battle. [77]

Although *Michael* had failed, Ludendorff persisted with *Georgette*, targeted in the quiet area from La Bassée to the frontier of Belgium. It was flat, intersected by canals, ditches, dykes, fences and small farms. The water table, two to three feet below the surface made breastworks necessary. The area was sodden every winter and spring, and normally dried out in May, but in 1918 it dried out in February and March.

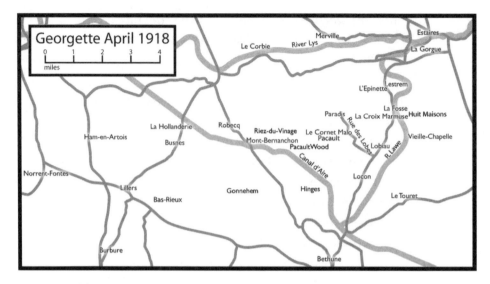

Georgette April 1918

Ludendorff knew that the two Portuguese Corps in the area were weak. They had arrived in France in February 1917 and been in the line since May; many of its officers were unmotivated and the winter of 1917/1918 bore hard on men from a milder climate. By April casualties had diminished their numbers by a quarter and it was decided to relieve their 1st Division on 4th April and their 2nd Division on 9th April.

Brigadier-General Crozier, 119th Brigade, 40th (Bantam) Division took a stroll to his right when his brigade moved into the line on the night of 7th-8th April, and was alarmed by what he saw:

> 'I go down the Portuguese front with a colonel. We walk seven
> hundred yards and scarcely see a sentry. We examine rifles
> and ammunition lying about. All are rusty and useless. The
> bombs are the same. 'Where are the men?' I ask my compan-
> ion. A snore gives me my answer. Practically all the front line
> sleeps heavily and bootless in cubby-holes covered with
> waterproof sheets, while their equipment hangs carelessly
> about. 'What a pretty mess,' I say, 'and on our flank'.'[78]

The 51st was the reserve of XI Corps, in support of the full strength 55th Division, which had recuperated for two months after Cambrai, and the Portuguese 2nd Division. To the left was XV Corps composed of the 34th, 40th and 50th divisions, all recovering from the March offensive. The Germans deployed eight divisions in their first wave and six in their second. One had been in the line since January 1918 and the others had been resting and training: none had been in the March offensive. [79]

The Portuguese had three brigades in the line when the German barrage hit them at 7.45 a.m. on 9th April, followed by four fresh German divisions. Most of the Portuguese broke or surrendered. Some fled on bicycles stolen from the Corps Cyclists, sent to reinforce the collapsing front. A minority fought on alone, or alongside British troops.

Although fiercely challenged, the 55th Division held firm, forming a hinge on which the divisions to the north swung back. The 51st's 154th Brigade was sent to reinforce the 55th Division, and remained with it until the morning of the 10th. 1/4th Seaforths became inextricably involved in the 55th Division's battle and remained with it until 13th April. They received drafts of 2 officers and 390 other ranks, and on the 10th, 1 officer and 118 other ranks, all of whom had to be assimilated as the battle developed. [80]

On the left of the 154th Brigade the 152nd Brigade moved forward: 1/5th Seaforths breakfasted, boarded buses and at 11.15 a.m. arrived near Fosse. Captain David Sutherland M.C., 1/5th Seaforths, was later officially reprimanded for accidentally breaking the leg of an escaping Portuguese officer whom he was trying to drag from a cart. [81]

For 1/5th Seaforths 'the shelling at this time was extremely heavy, but it was observed that practically no shells actually hit the road, the majority landing in the fields on either side, therefore companies were ordered to keep to the road as long as possible, thus, as it proved, avoiding the shelling and also avoiding the numerous dykes which would have had to be waded if the troops advanced across the open.' [82]

> 'The winter wheat was already 3 or 4 inches high, the fruit trees were all in full blossom, the garden seeds were bursting from the ground, some of the trees were half in leaf, when the battalion moved up to Fosse.' [83]

A Company of 1/5th Seaforths fought alongside troopers of 1st King Edward's Horse and the 11th Cyclists until they were enfiladed and bombed into retreating 300 yards, where they fought on until their flanks were further threatened, forcing them back to Fosse.

To the north the 153rd Brigade had moved up to the River Lawe and by the end of the 9th the 51st was positioned west of it, with three small bridgeheads east of it. The Official History is generous in its recognition of what the tired divisions accomplished:

> 'The 34th, 40th, 50th and 51st, had been rushed to their positions in a state of exhaustion, without their artillery, from a ten days battle in which they had lost seventy to eighty percent of their infantry. . . The 51st and 50th Divisions. . . accomplished almost a miracle in holding back victorious troops after being launched 'into the blue' to stop their advance in the Portuguese area.' [84]

With the 55th Division, at 9 a.m. on the 10th, 1/4th Seaforths reported that the enemy had been dribbling forward and had been trying to turn their flanks, but had been repelled, but by 1 p.m. the situation changed and 'the 1/5th K.O.R. Lancs. were subjected to an intense bombardment in LE TOURET and later when the enemy attacked they were forced to retire. . . the enemy taking advantage of this retirement tried again on two occasions at 4.30 p.m. and 5.15 p.m. to work round our right flank but was again held in check.' [85] They held the line throughout the night of the 10th.

At Vieille Chapelle 1/6th Gordons, under Captain J.R. Christie, and elements of 1st King Edward's Horse held out all through the 10th, although by nightfall all links between Vieille Chapelle and 1/6th Gordons' headquarters had been cut. The main bridge from Vieille Chapelle to the west was blown up, but other bridges could not be blown as German gunfire dominated them.

To their north 1/5th Seaforths, some 1/7th Gordons and King Edward's Horse, fell back from Huit Maisons, then held Fosse Post all day, despite heavy shelling and mortaring, but about 8 p.m. the enemy drove them to the west of the river, where their right flank kept in touch with 1/6th Gordons and King Edward's Horse at Vieille Chapelle.

The commanding officer of 1/5th Seaforths wrote in his battle report:

'I wish to express my appreciation of the work done by King Edward's Horse under Lt. Col. LIONEL JAMES. . . (who) personally directed operations with utter disregard for his own safety. Lieutenant ADDISON* and Lieut. RICH of KING EDWARD'S HORSE did most gallant work, both in defending FOSSE POST, and later, the defended locality which was formed in vicinity of Battalion headquarters. [86]

North of the 51st attempts to blow up the bridges near Lestrem failed and the Germans crossed the river. The 153rd Brigade retired and formed a line on the Lestrem-Fosse road but the Germans broke it and worked north, until stopped by 1/7th Black Watch at Lestrem, and south, until halted by 1/7th Gordons.

Early on the 11th the enemy launched heavy attacks, and broke the front between L'Epinette and Croix Marmuse, and it fell back to the Zelobes-Paradis road. The headquarters of the 152nd and 153rd Brigades were established close together between le Cornet Malo and Riez du Vinage. Brigadier-General Beckwith (153rd Brigade) finally succumbed to the gas he had inhaled in the March offensive and was replaced by Lt.Col. Dyson R.F.A. The German attack prevailed:

'Heavy fighting continued but the position was held until about 11 a.m. Units were much mixed and disorganized, few officers or N.C.O.s being left to maintain control. By continual pressure the line was forced back. . . intense machine-gun duels took place on this line, and heavy shelling of the position, and the line broke. . . Men were rallied and a mixed force of 4th, 5th and 6th SEAFORTH HIGHLANDERS, and 6th GORDON HIGHLANDERS, were organised on a line which held until 6 a.m. on 12th.' [87]

At Vieille Chapelle 1/6th Gordons and King Edward's Horse were holding out against heavy odds: in the morning they were completely cut off on their left and left rear and decided to break out:

'Then the troops at the right withdrew, and the enemy was seen streaming across a footbridge some 800 yards to the South. On this as on every other target the Lewis guns were turned. . . it was resolved to cut their way through the

241

enveloping cordon. Every attempt only brought them nearer the enemy, who poured fire on them from all sides. Assembling at a farm they determined on a final effort. So intense was the fire that scarcely a man could discharge his rifle without being hit. One enemy machine-gun at close range was especially harassing. Six men in succession manned a loophole in the endeavour to silence it. One by one they fell.' [88] Company commander Captain Christie was twice wounded trying to find an escape route. In the end the 20 survivors of the 100 who had gone into action at Vieille Chapelle surrendered. The commanding officer of King Edward's Horse reported: 'It is impossible to speak temperately of Captain J.B.Christie, 6th Gordon Highlanders, and his officers, and of Lieutenants Stein, Pinckney* and Laurtenson of King Edward's Horse.' [89]

Readjustments to the line took place late on the 11th and into the 12th. The 3rd (Regular) Division arrived on the right to support the 55th Division and the 154th Brigade, and the 61st Division moved in on the left to back up the 50th Division and the 51st. Four companies of the 61st Battalion M.G.C. covered an emerging gap on the left near the Lawe and were followed by 2/6th Warwicks and 1/5th Duke of Cornwall's Light Infantry, who were pioneers. The interventioin of these troops is credited in the Official History with saving the 51st from complete disaster. [90]

They covered the gap between 152nd and 153rd Brigades, and the 200 remaining men of 152nd Brigade were able to pass through them to reorganise. 153rd Brigade had no officers left and four Australian artillery officers volunteered and led four platoons on the 11th and 12th. When the troops returned to the battle to fill a gap between the 2/6th Warwicks and the 1/5th Duke of Cornwall's Light Infantry they were played back by the divisional pipers. [91]

While the 51st was holding firm on its right, adjacent to the 55th Division, its left was being driven backwards. Its northern neighbour, the 50th Division was holding on its left and being driven back on its right, and the Germans pressed through the ensuing gap.

Early on the 12th disaster struck, reported by 1/8th Royal Scots:

'About 2 a.m. the enemy delivered a heavy attack and broke
through on the left. B Coy were engaged all day in (deter)
mined fighting. . . ultimately this Coy. retired behind the
canal. A and C Coys fought on in the dark till practically
surrounded. The enemy were in their rear and captured Bn.
H.Q. from which all escaped except Major Todd and Adj. A.D.
Jones who were lost sight of and believed captured. 'A' Coy less
one platoon retired with other troops across the canal in front
of MONT BERNENCHON, the remaining platoon retired
south with elements of 152nd Inf.Bde. 'C' Coy on retiral from
the PARADIS position established touch with some R.Es. and
formed a line through PACAUT WOOD, where they held up a
strong attack about 5 p.m. . . finally at dusk in company with
other troops in the vicinity retired across the Canal. Orders
were shortly after received to march to BUSNES, where the
Division was assembling.' [92]

In the centre 1/5th Seaforths lost contact with 152nd Brigade's
Headquarters, near Cornet Malo, across the road from 153rd Brigade's
headquarters where:

'About 5.10 a.m. enemy rifle shots were heard outside Brigade
Headquarters. This was investigated and it was found that the
enemy had broken through (the) front and were advancing
due West through Cornet Malo and were only 200 yards E. of
Brigade Headquarters. The 152nd
Brigade were consulted and it was
decided to move at once
. . . by this time the enemy had
practically surrounded both brigade
Headquarters and opened machine gun
and rifle fire on any troops in the vicinity
of the houses. Brigade Headquarters
(153rd) personnel got clear of the
buildings, the enemy being actually in
them before the last man got away.' [93]
The Germans captured most of the staff
of 152nd Brigade, including Brigadier-
General Dick-Cunyngham.

Brigadier-General Dick-Cunyngham

Fred A. Farrell

1/5th Seaforths were watched from 8 a.m. by:

'. . . some observation balloons, one being especially close to
our positions, which positions were continuously shelled for 2
hours, during which time the enemy worked round our LEFT
flank with machine-guns and snipers. Our LEFT flank was
entirely in the air, and the line withdrew. . . Stragglers were
collected, including WARWICKS and men of other Divisions,
and placed in position to fill a gap between our left and the 1st
GORDONS [from 3rd Division, reinforcing the right]. This
position was held throughout the day, and at about 8 p.m.
orders were received for elements of 152nd Brigade to be
withdrawn. . . for reorganisation. . . and about midnight
orders were received for the Brigade to move to BUSNES,
where troops were billeted for the night.' [94]

Towards the left of the 51st 1/6th Black Watch reported:

'At 5.20 a.m. the enemy were seen dropping flares on our right
flank into the village of PACAUT. . . Enemy on our left in large
numbers shelled our lines and rear very heavily, and seemed
to have guns well forward. Machine-guns were enfilading us,
and we were forced to withdraw, which was carried out very
successfully by small parties at a time. All stragglers and
remainder of Regiment were collected at HOLLANDERIE
FARM, where the night was spent. All men belonging to my
Battalion were organised into Sections and issued with
ammunition, ready to move at a moment's notice.' [95]

At 7.30 a.m. on the far left in the area of Merville, Paradis and Le
Corbie the Duke of Cornwall's Light Infantry (61st Division) fell back
through 1/7th Black Watch, and there was enemy pressure on their right
flank; then German machine-guns opened fire at short range on the left
flank and:

'a few men, through lack of Section Commanders, now started
to fall back and the rot starting the whole fled with the
exception of three posts on the Right. These posts before
leaving caused some casualties among the enemy. . . the
retiral passed through the 61st Division and stragglers were
collected. . . and took up position. . . there were five officer
posts of about seven men each. . . the 61st Division Line now

fell back and our posts were ordered to proceed to the BRICKFIELDS at Le Corbie.' [96]

The battalion came under the control of General Elles of the Tank Corps, but had to retire again to avoid being completely surrounded. The 5th Division then retook the Brickfields and the battalion withdrew to Busnes. As a foil to the day's diet of bad news the day's the war diarist concluded, 'The weather all day had been perfect.' [97]

By the end of the 12th of April the 51st's principal part in the battle had passed, and stragglers, reinforcements and the surviving organised troops were reformed and 'FLEMING's FORCE, consisting of reinforcements of 153rd and 154th Brigades, was formed.' [98] This consisted of transport men, bandsmen, clerks, gas specialists, Canadian railway engineers, two machine-gun companies and some infantry. On the 13th the remains of 152nd and 153rd Brigades and 1/8th Royal Scots were formed into two composite battalions. Fleming's Force remained in the line until the 14th, when it was relieved by 154th Brigade, but by that time the 4th Division had recovered some of the lost battlefield, and 154th Brigade was in support for the next ten days.

For an already exhausted division, lacking familiar leaders and short handed, the 51st performed as well as could be reasonably expected.

Major General Carter-Campbell

Fred A. Farrell

On the 9th 152nd Brigade had been sent forward to relieve King Edward's Horse and later the 154th Brigade was put under the command of the 55th Division. Only the 153rd Brigade remained with Major General Carter-Campbell in Corps reserve and it was sent by the Corps Commander, Haking, to reinforce the junction between the XI and XV Corps. The division would probably have performed better had all of it been in Carter-Campbell's control all the time. [99]

There were occasional critical bad moments, as leaderless young men fell back in disarray, but it would appear that the presence of an officer or N.C.O. could bring them back under control and lead them back into battle.

At an administrative level the 51st suffered major disadvantages. The Divisional Commander had only been appointed on 11th March, just prior to the German offensive, and had to conduct a retiral, then command a depleted division faced with a further offensive. Brigadier-General Beckwith of the 153rd Brigade, ailing from gassing, was replaced on 11th April. Brigadier-General Pelham Burn of the 152nd Brigade had been replaced just before the battle by Brigadier-General Dick-Cunynghame, who was captured with his staff on the 12th. In static trench warfare, these men would have had time to master their new tasks and to set their stamp on their staffs and battalions. The loss of two brigade commanders in the course of the battle was serious, and meant that their successors on-the-job training was carried out in a context of near defeat.

Bewsher thought 'the part played by the Highland Division was a memorable one. The Division, after all the troops on its left had given, formed a defensive flank and brought the German advance to a complete standstill, in spite of many violent attacks.' [100] He qualified this by stating that it was the fact that its right flank, secured by the 55th Division, with the assistance of the 1/4th Seaforths that made this possible. He makes no reference to the 51st's reported rescue from destruction by the 61st Division on the 12th of April ([90] above) but it is clear from the small numbers of men mustered at the end of the battle that the 51st's human resources had been severely depleted and that it was nearing the end of its tether, akin to its situation on 25th March.

After the Battle of the Lys the 51st was stationed around Norrent-Fontes, 18 km N.W. of Bethune. Command of 152nd Brigade passed to Brigadier-General Thorpe, from 16th to 28th April, when he was replaced by Colonel Laing D.S.O., M.C., a Seaforth. Lt. Colonel Green, the commanding officer of 1/9th Royal Scots, which had left the 51st in February, took command of 153rd Brigade. French Prime Minister Clemenceau visited the 51st at Norrent-Fontes, recalled by Rorie of 1/2nd Highland Field Ambulance:

> 'Warned of the hour of his arrival, a guard of honour was duly posted; the General and his staff were lined up in front of the building [HQ] to receive the great man, as a great man should be received. The hour struck: a loud rumbling on the pavé as of approaching cars was heard: the guard presented arms: we came to attention – and into our surprised vision came the Thresh Disinfector on its motor lorry, driven by our old friend the nonchalant civilian in khaki, gazing at the proceedings with his usual air of dispassionate interest. Those not within range of the G.O.C.'s eye grinned happily: the others affected a stern yet sublime calm. Before the G.O.C. had quite finished a few remarks he evidently thought appropriate to the occasion, the 'Tiger' and his entourage, in three limousines, swung into view. . . ' [101]

Haig's diary for 3rd May makes it clear how quickly losses were replaced:

> 'Campbell said his Division and (except the Gordons and Seaforths) his Battalions were over strength. The Division has fought magnificently from the beginning of the Battle on the 21st March. I thought Campbell looked tired.' [102] [No wonder!]

On 3rd May the 51st moved to the familiar territory of Mont St.Eloi, Neuville St. Vaast, Ecroives, Bray and Maroeuil. A sector from Bailleul to Willerval was taken over from the Canadians on 6th and 7th May. The 52nd (Lowland) Division, which had arrived in Marseilles on 17th April from Egypt, was on the 51st's right, and the 15th (Scottish) Division was on its left.

The front line was in old reserve trenches. The outpost system which had failed in March was still favoured and the plan was to construct defensive localities with an all-round capability and have these planned so that when the enemy penetrated, he would be subjected to enfilade fire, as well as by fire from trenches facing him.

Bewsher stated that as the Division 'was now primarily composed of boys, who were unable to carry out the daily task equal to that of the old trained soldier, the work contemplated was more than enough to keep the Division fully occupied for several months. . . 'the traditions established in the Division for hard work were being well maintained by the new drafts.'[103] The drafts were replacing the 19 officers killed, 71 wounded, 47 missing and 197 other ranks killed, 1419 wounded, and 1213 missing – the 2966 men lost in 'Georgette'. [104]

With a division composed of young conscripts and weary veterans patrolling in No Man's Land was characterised by an unwillingness to engage the enemy and by 'live and let live', but the price was German ascendancy, which ended towards the end of May, when the 51st began to reassert itself. 1/6th Gordons noted:

> 'A raid made by seven sections of the 6th Battalion and six sections of the 6th Seaforth Highlanders on the 9th of July, was remarkable for the extraordinary dress of the men. The kilt was discarded. Faces, hands and legs were blackened. A few men wore shorts, a few wore service-dress jackets, but a number went over wearing only a shirt, with equipment above. The parties assembled in a sharp thunderstorm with vivid lightning and heavy rain. They reached their objective-Kent Road – after encountering many difficulties with the wire, but no enemy could be found, and the raiders returned with only one man slightly wounded. . . ' [105]

A British gas attack was launched on the 51st's front on 10th June, although the 51st took no part in it. The front and support lines in the gassing zone were evacuated and forty wagons of gas cylinders were brought up on a trench railway which ran behind the support line. When the wind was favourable the cylinders were electrically opened. This was the 'gas beam' technique of delivery and the Royal Flying Corps reported discolouration of the land up to 5000 yards behind the German lines, and 1/6th Gordons observed that 'everything was perfectly quiet and still except for the ceaseless movement of stretcher bearers coming forward to succour any who had escaped death from the fumes.' [106]

By 11th July the Canadians had relieved the 51st and it moved to the area round Monchy-Breton, Chelers and Dieval, north-west of Arras.

NOTES

1. Private James Burnett, 1/8th Royal Scots. Letter home. 6.4.1918

2. Haig diary 7.1.1918.

3. Middlebrook p.52.

4. HStAS [i.e. Hauptstaatsarchiv Stuttgart] M33/2 †B, 536. Abteilung Fremde Heere Nr. 4610 (Dr.Alex Fasse per Jack Sheldon, e-mail correspondence with author) and Judith Bolsinger, Haupstaatsarchiv, Stuttgart.

5. Jack Sheldon e-mail to author.

6. Neillands p.347.

7. Wrench 20.3.1918. His general was Brigadier-General K. Gray-Buchanan 154th Infantry Brigade from September 1917.

8. War diary 1/7th A&SH 30.3.1918.

9. War diary 1/6th Gordons 21.3.1918.

10. Wauchope pp. 177 and ff. account of Major W.P.Campbell, 1/6th Black Watch.

11. Bewsher p.295.

12. War diary 1/7th A&SH 21.3.1918.

13. Account of part played by 1/7th A&SH 30.3.1918.

14. Wrench 21.3.1918.

15. Arthur Behrend *As From Kemmel Hill An Adjutant in France and Flanders 1917 & 1918* (Eyre and Spottiswoode) 1963 p.167 appendix 3 Sgt Major of 46th Infantry German Army.

16. Behrend pp.70-1

17. Private Herbert Steele, 1/6th Seaforths, personal recollection, per Dorothy Mein.

18. Everard Wyrall *History of the 19th Division* (Arnold) 1932 p.139.

19. Sutherland p.150.

20. Wauchope p.180 Major Campbell 1/6th Black Watch.

21. War diary 1/7th Black Watch 22.3.1918.

22. Wrench 22.3.1918.

23. Wauchope p.182 Major Campbell 1/6th Black Watch.

24. Herbert Steele

25. Bewsher p.282

26. Sutherland p.157.

27. Behrend p.77.

28. War diary 1/4th Seaforths 23.3.1918.

29. Steele recollections.

30. Haldane pp.272-273.

31. Wyrall pp.148-149.
32. Wyrall p.147.
33. Wrench 23.3.1918.
34. War diary 1/7th A&SH 23.3.1918.
35. Haldane p.274.
36. Bewsher p.287/Farrell Plate 21.
37. General Remarks on recent Operations, Brigadier-General Buchanan, 154th Brigade – quoted Haldane pp.274-275.
38. War diary 1/7th Black Watch 24.3.1918.
39. Behrend p.82.
40. War diary 1/7th Black Watch 24.3.1918
41. War diary 1/8th Royal Scots 24.3.1918.
42. Edmonds 1918 v.1 p.401 footnote 2.
43. Wrench 24.3.1918.
44. Steele recollections.
45. Bewsher 24/5 March p.291.
46. Edmonds 1918 v 1 Page 482.
47. War diary 1/7th A&SH 25.3.1918.
48. Steele recollections.
49. Bewsher p.29/War diary 1/7th Black Watch 25.3.1918
50. Steele recollections.
51. Bewsher p.291.
52. Steele recollections.
53. War diary 1/6th Black Watch 25.3.1918.
54. Wauchope p.186 Major Campbell.
55. War diary 1/7th A&SH 25.3.1918.
56. War diary 1/7th Black Watch 25.3.1918.
57. Bewsher p.292.
58. Edmonds 1918 v.1, Page 487.
59. Major General Astley GOC 57 Inf Bde 19 Div to Edmonds 23/8/29 Cab45/187PRO)
(59 and 60) ex *The Killing Ground Travers* p.240 and footnotes 61 and 62.
60. Major Gen G Jeffreys GOC 19 Division to Edmonds no date CAB 45/186 PRO.
61. Edmonds v.1 1918 p.526.
62. Jas. Durie Lieut.Col. Commanding 7th A & S. H. 30.3.1918.
63. H.Pelham- Brn Brigadier-General Commanding 152nd Infantry Brigade. 7.4.1918.
64. Edmonds 1918 v.2 p.492.
65. Middlebrook p.326.
66. Robert Graves *Goodbye to All That* (Jonathon Cape) 1929/(Penguin) 1960 p.152.
67. The Estate of Thomas Lindsay.
68. War diary 1/7th Black Watch 20,26,31.3.1918 and 2.4.1918.

69. The Estate of Thomas Lindsay.

70. Pte.James Burnett letters.

71. Burnett letters.

72. War diary 1/8th Royal Scots 26.3.1918-8.4.1918.

73. Burnett Saturday 6.4.1918.

74. War diary 1/7th Black Watch 1-7.4.1918.

75. War diary 1/8th Royal Scots 3-7.4.1918.

76. Rorie p.203

77. Edmonds 1918 v 2 p.160 footnote.

78. Crozier *A Brass Hat in No Man's Land* (Cape)1930 p.205.

79. Edmonds 1918 v.2 p.165.

80. War diary 1/4th Seaforths 9.4.1918.

81. Per grandson David Sutherland's account.

82. War diary 1/5th Seaforths 9.4.1918 .

83. Sutherland p.159.

84. Edmonds 1918 v.2 p.189.

85. War diary 1/4th Seaforths 10.4.1918.

86. Battle report 1/5th Seaforths 15.4.1918.

87. War diary 1/5th Seaforths 11.4.1918.

88. MacKenzie p.156.

89. Lt.Col. James K.E.H. battle report Bewsher p.307.

90. Edmonds 1918 v 2 p.224.

91. Edmonds 1918 v.3 p.225 footnote.

92. War diary 1/8th Royal Scots 12.4.1918.

93. War diary 153rd Brigade 12.4.1918.

94. War diary 1/5th Seaforths 12.4.1918.

95. War diary 1/6th Black Watch 13.4.1918.

96. War diary 1/7th Black Watch 12.4.1918.

97. War diary 1/7th Black Watch 12.4.1918.

98. War diary 153rd Brigade 12.4.1918.

99. Edmonds 1918 v.2 p169.

100. Bewsher Page 320.

101. Rorie p.212. (Each division had one lorry mounted steam disinfector that could delouse fifty bundles of clothes in fifteen minutes at 60 degrees Fahrenheit)

102. Haig's diary 3.5.1918.

103. Bewsher p.322-323

104. Edmonds 1918 v 2 Page 493

105. Mackenzie pp.160-161.

165. MacKenzie p.161.

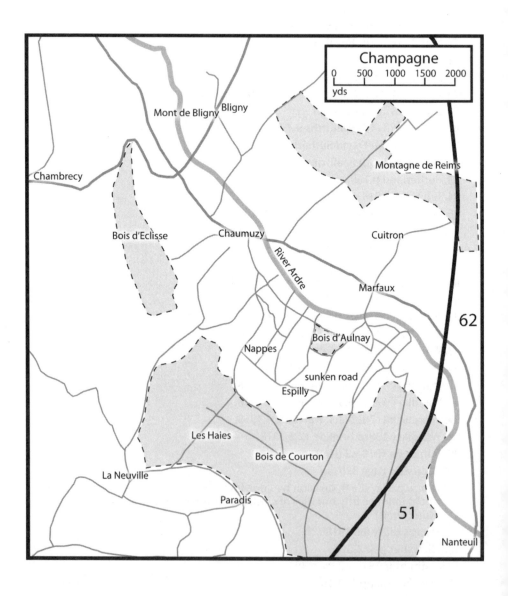

CHAPTER 9

ALLIANCE
Ardre

'Vivent les Ecossais!' [1]

Maintaining pressure on the Allies, on 26th May the Germans launched the *Blücher-Yorck* offensive on the French front, on the Chemin des Dames, between Soissons and Reims. By July they had taken Soissons and crossed the Marne at Chateau-Thierry. Foch, commanding the French and Allied armies, anticipated a further German offensive in July and requested British help. The last German offensive was launched on 15th July and had some success west of Reims, but was held by the French, Americans and Italian 2nd Corps on 17th July. At that time Lieutenant-General Godley's XXII Corps, composed of 15th (Scottish), 34th (New Army), 51st and 62nd (2nd West Riding) divisions were in transit to the French front: the 51st and 62nd were posted south west of Reims, and 15th and 34th were near Soissons. On the 18th the French launched a successful counter- attack and drove the Germans back.

On the night of 18th/19th July the 51st moved to Hautvillers, Champillon, Romery, and Bellevue on the southern edge of the Forét de la Montagne. For troops from the ravaged slopes of Vimy Ridge the journey had been an eye opener: Second Lieutenant John Oliver, 1/8th Royal Scots:

> 'The interval since I last wrote has been mainly filled with wearing holes in our socks and smoothing down the nails in our boots. It has been march, march, march with intervals since Tuesday night. (16th July) Our first train journey was a long and warm one. The weather all along has been very trying, and during the railway part of our trek we were sweltering. I have seen quite a lot of France since we started

our move, and the part we are now in is indeed worthy of the name La Belle France. We have seen a tremendous lot that is interesting, and the country everywhere is beautiful in the extreme. One thing pleasant about the train journey was that it took us straight in front of the palace of the old king of France and the journey through the woods around it was a perfect delight. Right up to our detraining point we passed through glorious fertile country. It was the start of a sort of triumphal progress. At every village the people were lining the hedges by the side of the railway, fluttering handkerchiefs at us, cheering and generally making themselves agreeable. . . we got to the town. . . and set off through the town (Romilly). The people were rudely awakened by the pipes and by the singing of the men. Everybody was friendly again, and an occasional cry of '*Tres bon*' or '*Tres jolie*' or '*Vivent les Ecossais*' helped put new life in our feet.' [2]

In the village of Moussy, south of Epernay, full of troops from all the Allied armies, two Scottish soldiers who:

'. . . taking advantage of the place going like a fair, donned the costumes of peasants and sold (to the cosmopolitan crowd of thirsty troops) the contents of a large and varied wine cellar that they had been fortunate enough to discover. Regardless of brand or of vintage, and to secure a ready sale with quick returns, each bottle was disposed of at the modest sum of two francs a head! Nay more! To regularize the affair and promote confidence amongst their customers, an obliging confederate did sentry-go with fixed bayonet in front of the establishment. . . rumour has it that the gallant and provident financiers cleared a well earned profit of 2,000 francs.' [3]

The divisional boundary was the River Ardre, with 62nd on its right, and 51st on its left. Its valley was full of arable farms with fields of two feet high corn, which provided cover for the enemy, and was dominated to its east by the Montagne de Reims, which rose to between two and three hundred feet and was well wooded, with thick undergrowth, and ideal for defence. Braithwaithe of 62nd Division had '. . . seen nothing thicker since I fought thirty five years ago in the Burmese Jungle.' [4] Its lower slopes were devoid of cover for attacking troops. To the west the

Bois des Eclisses overlooked the valley, with gentler slopes and small woods. Sunken roads ran across the line of advance, and there were small, intact, villages. The Germans had tried to outflank Reims' defences from the west and south west, by taking the Forét de la Montagne. The 51st and 62nd were co-operate with 2nd Italian Corps and the French.

The French wanted to exploit a German withdrawal to the west and an attack was planned for 20th July. Godley believed that the Germans were only holding an outpost line so XXII Corps' objectives were optimistically allocated. [5] The first objective, the Blue Line, the old French front line, was about four miles from the start line and the last, the Brown Line, was six miles ahead. As an additional spur to effort the 1/6th Black Watch's orders stated:

> 'all ranks will be warned that the attack wil be made before the eyes of the French Army and it is expected that they will maintain the prestige of the British Army.' and that: 'all Battalions of the 153rd Infantry Brigade will be in position by midnight of 19th/20th July. To arrive promptly and at the right place GUIDES will meet the Battalion. . . they will take Companies to a place where they will be handed over to other FRENCH guides who will explain, and put Companies in position. The following Guides will be supplied by the FRENCH: 1 Sergeant per Battalion. 1 Man per Company.' [6]

Like many plans, it did not work:

> 'Only one FRENCH guide available for the 6th and 7th BLACK WATCH, with the result that he was put to lead the 6th BLACK WATCH, who in their turn had to lead the 7th BLACK WATCH. The traffic on the road was tremendous and there seemed to be no control . . . lorries were upset causing considerable congestion and confusion. . . in some cases [I] had to take the Battalions through in file between guns and wagons of all descriptions.' [7]

The 1/8th West Yorkshires, 62nd Division, were in a similar predicament:

> 'It was not long before we were on a hard road, disentangling

ourselves from Italians, French, another unit of our Division, motor lorries, French transport, ammunition wagons, limbers and mules; countless mules carrying rations, mules carrying water, mules carrying ammunition and more [spare] mules. . . we plunged into the horrors of these forest depths and, in the early hours of the morning these dark woods, with their muddy paths and foul stenches of gas and decaying bodies of horses, began to tell on the spirits of the men.' [8]

From right to left were 2nd French, 62nd, 51st and 14th French divisions. Although scheduled to be in position by midnight on the 19th/20th the battalions arrived at 4 a.m. The creeping barrage, fired by French artillery, began at 8 a.m. but it fell too far ahead of the troops, leaving many enemy machine-gun posts intact, and following it closely amongst trees was hazardous, as the French shells burst prematurely on touching the trees. [9] On the right 2nd French Colonial Division made no progress and 62nd Division ended the day about half a mile ahead of its start line.

1/4th Seaforths led 154th Brigade on the 51st's right, up exposed slopes. They took the outpost line but passing over the summit beyond it they were held up by fire from Marfaux on their right and Bois d'Aulnay ahead of them. Some 1/4th Seaforths lost direction, no touch was made with 1/6th Black Watch on their left, and the attack faltered. 1/4th Gordons were sent to fill the gap between the two brigades and at 1 p.m. 1/7th Argylls reinforced the battle, but by the end of the day no further progress could be made, and many casualties had been suffered.

Sergeant John Meikle

Nineteen years old Sergeant John Meikle* M.M., 200854, 1/4th Seaforths, won the V.C. near Marfaux:

'For most conspicuous bravery and initiative when his company, having been held up by machine-gun fire, he rushed single-handed a machine-gun nest. He emptied his revolver into the crews of the two guns and put the remainder out of action with a heavy stick. Then, standing up, he waved his comrades on. Very shortly afterward another hostile machine-gun checked progress, and threatened also the success of the company on the right. Most of his platoon having become casualties, Serjt. Meikle seized the rifle and bayonet of a fallen comrade and again rushed forward against the gun crew, but was killed almost on the gun position. His bravery allowed two other men who followed him to put this gun out of action. The gallant non-commissioned officer's valour, devotion to duty, and utter disregard for his personal safety was an inspiring example to all.' [10]

Before the war Meikle had been a railway clerk at Nitshill, near Glasgow. He had enlisted on 8th February 1915, at the age of 16.

The battalions of 153rd Brigade were having as little success as their colleagues on the right. 1/6th Black Watch 'were able to push on after dealing with Machine-Guns. Progress was very difficult owing to the density of the woods and difficulty of keeping direction. Many enemy prisoners taken. Barrage put down on Battalion Headquarters. Very little artillery fire on troops in wood.' [11] They advanced just 600 yards.

Following 1/6th Black Watch, 1/7th Black Watch and 1/7th Gordons advanced ahead of schedule to avoid an enemy barrage, found a gap in it, and then drifted to the south-west of the sector. On the right 1/6th Black Watch lost the barrage and was held up by fire from Espilly. In the forest on the left, with vision limited to about fifty yards, with deep undergrowth, and staunch enemy opposition, the troops lost cohesion and fought in detached parties. French Senegalese and elements of 1/6th and 1/7th Black Watch, and 1/7th Gordons, hazarded the open ground between the Bois de Courton and the Bois des Eclisses but were exposed on both flanks and withdrew to a line about 200 yards north west of the La Neuville-Les Haies Road. Pressure pushed the line back to that road and in the night, further German attacks sent it back another 1000 yards into Bois de Courton. On their left the French 9th Division, one of France's finest, failed to take Paradis. Shortly after midnight of the 20th/ 21st the 51st and 62nd divisions were told to take the high ground on either side of the Ardre.

On the 21st the French Colonial Corps on the right of 62nd Division took no part in the battle. The leading troops of 62nd Division did not reach their start line until 10.20 a.m., just ten minutes before zero. Guides had left them 600 yards short of it and they had to double to catch the barrage, and were stopped by machine-gun fire. By the day's end the 62nd Division had made no progress.

1/6th Black Watch had gone into action on the 19th with only their iron rations and one full waterbottle each. In the small hours of the 21st their Commanding Officer was arranging food and water for his men when he was ordered to form a defensive flank on the left of 152nd Brigade, which was going to resume the attack at 8 a.m. His battalion was being relieved by 1/6th Seaforths when the order came through so he decided to leave his men in the wood:

> 'I met the Companies as they came from their positions. I
> issued out the water to the men who were exhausted through
> thirst and appealed to all ranks not to eat their rations but to
> follow me. I must say I have never seen or heard of a more
> gallant response and I led the Battalion, carrying their rations
> with empty water tins through the wood to the left flank of the
> 152nd BRIGADE. The Brigade was evidently held up by
> Machine Gun fire and in my opinion never even got to their
> proper 'Jumping Off' position.' [12]

As the 152nd Brigade struggled forward, the men of 1/6th Black Watch, 100-200 yards behind them, had time to rest and eat. [13]

The objectives were the north-west edge of the Bois de Coutron, the southern slopes of the Bois des Eclisses and then its northern slopes. The barrage began at 8 a.m. but 1/6th Gordons, who led, found that the planned start line was about 700 yards behind the enemy's front, because during the night the Germans had followed the retiring Highlanders, and had machine guns between the barrage and the start line. 1/6th Gordons fought into the open for 200 yards, outside the north-west edge of the Bois de Courton, then were forced back and consolidated just 200 yards ahead of their start line. After a confused day it was established that the 152nd Brigade had made no significant progress. Bewsher mentions that 'eighty one prisoners and a number of machine-guns and trench mortars were captured' but makes no reference to the cost in casualties for this small total. [14] On the left the French failed to take

Paradis, which exposed the left of the 51st.

On the 22nd twenty five French light tanks were offered, but the ground was too soft to use them. 62nd Division attacked in two columns, at 12.15 p.m., gaining between five hundred and seven hundred yards.

On the 51st's front the French and 1/7th Black Watch were to attack Paradis, but before they moved forward 1/6th Black Watch was to clear the Bois de Coutron as far as the edge north of Paradis. 1/6th Black Watch's objective was a line that they had occupied at 8 a.m. on 20 July, and their Commanding Officer was aware that it 'meant attempting a task which the 152nd Brigade had failed in two days and one night.' [15] The attempts of 1/6th Black Watch from 4 p.m. onwards to reach their objective by rushes and infiltration failed, and 1/7th Black Watch was unable to carry out its task. For 1/6th Black Watch 'no appreciable progress. . . was made in view of the heavy casualties sustained.' [16] On the left, at 5 p.m. the French attack on Paradis faded in the face of machine-gun fire. It beggars belief that there were three zero hours for the attacks by the 62nd, the 51st and the French 9th Division – shades of High Wood.

On the 23rd at 6.30 a.m. the 186th brigade, 62nd Division, reinforced by a dismounted men of the 2nd ANZAC Cyclist Battalion, supported by a French, Italian and British barrage, took Cuitron and Marfaux in fifty minutes, and their second objective, a ridge five hundred yards behind the road linking these villages, by 8 a.m.

On the same day 152nd Brigade was to take the line from Bois d'Aulnay to Espilly. The 1/5th Seaforths were on the right, 1/6th Seaforths in the centre and 1/6th Gordons on the left. On their left elements of 1/4th Gordons and and 1/7th Argylls were to approach Espilly from the west, through the Bois de Courton, and neutralise its western defences. The attack was to be supported by the artillery of the 51st and the French. The barrage began at 6.10 a.m. and the French barrage hit 1/8th Royal Scots, 1/6th Gordons, 1/6th Seaforths and 1/7th Argylls whose history says:

'the barrage neither helped nor hindered. Generally the shells exploded in the trees, and because of the density of the wood it was amost impossible to keep a line of men advancing steadily in one direction.' [17]

Convention then did not include details of 'friendly fire' or 'blue on blue' incidents.

Second Lieutenant Oliver, 1/8th Royal Scots, on the extreme left of the attack, in Bois de Coutron:

'On Wednesday (23rd) we advanced. I did not see much of it as I got a chunk of shrapnel in my leg before I had gone fifty yards. I had to lie where I fell, and as we were advancing through a dense wood, the stretcher bearers were not able to find everyone at once. While I was lying I got several more slight wounds from another shell, which landed near me. After some hours one of our stretcher bearers came along. He went and got four men, who carried me, turn about, on their back. There was too much undergrowth for a stretcher to be possible. We got to a road at last, and I was carried by stretcher to an aid post, where four German prisoners took me over and carried me back to where a motor ambulance was waiting. The next item of the programme was the C.C.S., where once more my wound was dressed.'

He was then taken by train to a hospital where a doctor inspected his wound:

'He said it was pretty bad, they might have some difficulty saving it. An hour after I had seen him I was in the operating theatre, and when I woke up I found my left leg still to be there, with a few tubes in it, but very decidedly there. This morning the doctor thought it was very much better.'[18]

On the right 1/5th Seaforths followed the barrage onto the Bois d'Aulnay. Next to them 1/6th Seaforths were slowed by machine-gun fire from their left, but eventually moved forward. 1/6th Gordons, 1/4th Gordons and 1/7th Argylls failed to make any impression on Espilly. 1/5th and 1/6th Seaforths took the northern edge of the Bois d'Aulnay but efforts by some 1/6th Seaforths and 1/6th Gordons to move on Espilly stopped in the sunken road between Bois d'Aulnay and Espilly. The downhill slope from the sunken road to Espilly was covered by fire from the northern edge of Bois de Courton. 1/7th Argylls advanced 400 yards through the forest and 'one platoon of 8th Royal Scots attached actually reached NW edge of wood in first attempt as they were not affected by barrage.' [19]

By the end of the day the 51st held a line from Bois d'Aulnay, below Espilly and into the Bois de Courton. This was the most successful day to date, with an advance of around 1200 yards.

In the next three days there was little patrol activity. 1/5th Seaforths established posts sixty yards ahead of the Bois d'Aulnay and 1/4th Seaforths advanced their line by 100 yards on the 25th, then by another 50 on the 26th. [20]

An attack was planned for the 27th of July, by which time the enemy was in a diminishing salient and preparing to withdraw from a strategically exposed position. The first objective was a line from the Ardre, north-west of the Bois d'Aulnay, passing north-west of Les Haies and going into the Bois de Courton. The second was from the Ardre, north-west of the village of Nappes, curving south west to the left of the first objective.

Two brigades of the 51st and 187th Brigade, 62nd Division, were to carry out the plan. The order from right to left was the 152nd, 187th and 153rd. Bewsher states that co-operation between the two divisions was such that 'these dispositions caused no lack of cohesion in the attack.'[21]

The attack began on the left at 6 a.m. with a short barrage, then 14th French Division and 153rd Brigade advanced, to be followed by 187th Brigade at 6.56 a.m. and 152nd Brigade at 7.45 a.m. There was German artillery fire, but their infantry had withdrawn. The first objective fell at 8.45 a.m., the second at 10 a.m., and the troops there could see Germans retreating from Chaumuzy. By 3 p.m. they were in Chaumuzy and an hour later it was ascertained that the Germans were retreating to the Bligny-Chambrecy road. Late at night it was confirmed that it was clear, and the 51st occupied the old French front line on the western side of the Bois des Eclisses, seven days after Godley had hoped to attain it.

By the 28th the German resistance had hardened. 62nd Division attacked at 4.30 a.m. and ran into severe machine-gun and artillery fire, but persisted. On their right the 77th French Division attacked later and it linked up with them at 4 p.m. they took Bligny, in which the 62nd had been fighting since the morning. On its right their 185th Brigade took the Montagne but was unable to drive the Germans off it completely.

The 51st, after some delay, launched an attack in co-operation with the 14th French division on its left. At noon the French failed to take Chambrecy, and at 3 p.m. they failed to take Ville-en-Tardenois, west of Chambrecy. The C.O. of 1/6th Black Watch wrote:

'I found orders awaiting me to move at 1.30 p.m. and attack North of CHAMBRECY, the intelligence being that the village of CHAMBRECY was occupied by the FRENCH. I immediately moved my battalion. . . to the WEST of the Bois des ECLISSE, and deployed for attack, throwing out patrols. This was about 2 p.m., my orders being that the 7th GORDON HIGHLANDERS would be with me on my right, but at this point I found that the 7th GORDON HIGHLANDERS were not ready to co-operate. I then got a verbal message that I was to beware of the barrage falling in front of me. To solve this state of things, I saw no other alternative than to personally proceed to the 7th GORDONS Battalion Headquarters, which was some distance in rear of the wood, and come to a clear understanding with the Commanding Officer, which I did. I found that he had received orders not to quit his Battalion Headquarters, but he very kindly gave me an Officer with full orders to settle the time of attack with his Companies. I then returned to my Headquarters and arranged with the Officers of the 7th GORDONS that they should attack with me at 4.30 p.m. By this time I saw that the French attack had started on the opposite side of the Valley and that they had been caught by a heavy enemy barrage which necessitated their retirement for a short distance, though no panic seemed in any way to be caused.

'At 4.30 p.m. I saw my Battalion launched to the attack along with the 7th GORDONS, and then withdrew to about 150 yards into the wood, where I had established communication with the Brigade Headquarters. Almost after the Battalion had covered 600 to 800 yards, a German barrage came down on them, though up to then things had been absolutely quiet, and Machine Gun fire opened on them from both sides of the Valley. I saw we were in a trap, but to come back would have been fatal, and to push on seemed to be the only possibility; this, the Battalion did, in most gallant style; though there were many casualties, it fought its way through the Valley in face of Artillery and Machine Gun fire right up and through the Valley and into and through the village of CHAMBRECY. Messages then began to come in showing 'A' Company to be on the N.W. side of the village of CHAMBRECY, and the remnants of C. D. and B. Companies on the N.E. side of CHAMBRECY, 'A' being detached to the left and apparently in a critical position, with one Officer remaining the other Companies equally depleted in Officers and Other Ranks. Night was then well on and the situation looked most critical as there was a possibility of all Companies being captured or annihilated in the event of any counter-attack on the part of the Germans. This was fully reported and orders were received that the 4th GORDONS would relieve the Battalion on a defined line, and withdrawing from the village of CHAMBRECY, I decided on a suitable line across the valley well indicated by a hedge to which the Battalion had advanced. To this hedge the remnants of the Battalion were withdrawn by Companies and the line correctly handed over to the 4th GORDONS, who I cannot speak too highly of for the way in which they adapted themselves to the situation, and took over the line under most difficult and obscure circumstances.' [22]

1/7th Gordons linked on the right with the 62nd Division on Montagne de Bligny. By the end of the day 62nd and 51st Divisions had advanced about a mile, and the French divisions on their flanks were forward with them. 154th Brigade took over the line, with 1/4th Seaforths on the right, 1/4th Gordons in place of 1/6th Black Watch (extract above) and 1/7th Argylls in the Bois des Eclisses.

On the 29th, 62nd Division pushed back the enemy on Montagne de Bligny, and 1/7th Argylls took over the line, consolidated and patrolled towards Chambrecy, which drew intense machine-gun fire. On the 30th the Germans shelled the Montagne de Bligny and at 8 p.m. launched a vain attack on 1/7th Argylls. On the night of the 30/31st the French relieved the 62nd Division and on the evening of the 31st they relieved the 51st.

Bewsher records that the 51st left behind 38 officers and 418 other ranks from a total of 173 officer and 3690 other rank casualties. (Bewsher page 352) Neil Munro in his introduction to Fred A Farrell's book of sketches put the numbers at 175 and 3390: the Official History puts the figure at 115 officers and 2950 other ranks: President Poincare in 1919 put the figure at 2000. All for an advance of four and a half miles. [23] The battle cost 62nd Division 118 officers and 3865 men.

Order of the Day Number 63 of the French Army, dated 30th July 1918, from General Berthelot of the Fifth French Army, to the officers and men of the XXII Corps concluded:

> 'Highlanders under the orders of General Carter-Campbell, commanding the 51st Division; Yorkshire lads under the orders of General Braithwaite, commanding the 62nd Division; Australian and New Zealand mounted troops, all officers of the XXIInd Army Corps so ably commanded by Sir A. Godley, you have added a glorious page to your history.
>
> 'Marfaux, Chaumuzy, Montagne de Bligny – all of those famous names will be written in letters of gold in the annals of your regiments. Your French comrades will always remember with emotion your splendid gallantry and your perfect camaraderie in the fight.' [24]

1/8th West Yorkshires (Leeds Rifles) and 1/6th Black Watch were awarded the Legion of Honour for their efforts in the Tardenois:

> 'The general officer commanding the Fifth (French) Army hereby specially mentions in orders the 6th Battalion Royal Highlanders. This battalion d'elite, under the brilliant command of Lieutenant-Colonel Francis Rowland Tarleton, has given splendid proof of its dash and fury in the course of several hard fought battles between the 20th and 30th July 1918. After seven days of furious fighting, in spite of exhaustion and heavy losses caused by intense enemy

machine-gun fire, it successfully stormed a wood splendidly
fortified and stubbornly defended by the enemy.'
[Guillaumaut, General Officer Commanding, Fifth (French)
Army] [25]

The 51st did not fight alongside the Italian Army, but when they met
the Italians 'they had never seen kilts before, and the sight caused a great
sensation. This was one of the rare occasions when the rations failed to
come up, and the 4th Seaforths drew them from the Italians, the
introduction to spaghetti causing a sensation on our side. The Italian
rations are said to have been very good and plentiful.' [26]

Representative elements of the 51st and 62nd Divisions formally
marched past General Berthelot, Fifth French Army, before returning to
the British front. 'The Jocks entraining on their departure from the
French zone were a memorable sight. They had exploited the resources
of the country with great industry, and every man appeared to have a
tin of bully beef in one hand and a bottle of champagne in the other.' [27]
Small compensation for their travails and losses. 1/7th Argylls' history
soberly reflected:

> 'A little ground was gained, but at a cost out of all proportion
> to the tactical advantage.' [28]

NOTES

1. Letters of Second Lieutenant John W.Oliver, 1/8th Royal Scots April to July
   1918.
2. Oliver
3. Rorie p.216.
4. Everard Wyrall *A History of the 62nd (W.R.) Division,* (John Lane) 1924 p.178
   footnote.
5. Bewsher p.330.
6. 1/6th Watch Instructions for the attack 19.7.1918 Appendix F.
7. 1/6th Black Watch Narrative of Operations from July 19th, 1918 to 31st July
   1918.
8. Private diary officer 8th West Yorkshire Regiment – History of 62nd Div
   pp.180-181.
9. Edmonds OH 1918 v3 p.246 footnote.

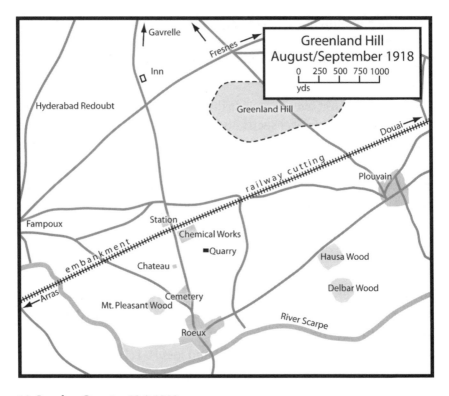

10. London Gazette, 13.9.1918
11. 1/6th Black Narrative of Operations from 19.7.1918 to 31.7.1918.
12. 1/6th Black Watch narrative 28.7.1918.
13. War Diary 1/6th Black Watch 21.7.1918.
14. Bewsher pp.338-341.
15. 153rd Brigade narrative. TNA
16. 1/6th Black Watch narrative.
17. Morrison p.44.
18. Second Lieutenant Oliver, letters 25/26.7.1918.
19. War diary 1/7th Argylls 23.7.1918.
20. Bewsher p.346.
21. Bewsher p.347.
22. 1/6th Black Watch narrative 28.7.18.
23. Bewsher p.352/Neil Munro/Farrell Page 28, Edmonds 1918 v 3 p288
    Poincaré quoted Munro/Farrell p.29.
24. Bewsher pp.353-354.
25. Bewsher p.355.
26. Haldane pp.291-292.
27. Bewsher p.355.
28. Morrison p.44.

CHAPTER 10
VICTORY
Greenland Hill and The Selle

'Second to none in the Allied armies.' [1]

After the enemy's failures in July 1918, Marshall Foch planned to break the German Army. He wanted Haig to attack south of the Lys but Haig preferred to put Amiens out of German artillery range. The main thrust would be by the Canadian Corps which had been spared the ravages of *Michael* and *Georgette,* having been in reserve or line holding from April to July. Its brigades still had four battalions and their divisions had 20,000 men, compared to the British average of 15,000. Canadians served in their own corps and had a consistent chain of command, unlike British divisional commanders who constantly had to assimilate new corps commanders' idiosyncracies.

To achieve surprise: 'the Staff allowed the rumour to circulate that the Corps was going into Belgium to attack.' This was fostered by 'our representatives up north 'accidentally' allowing an odd few prisoners to escape and talk at the top of their voices as soon as they reached their own lines.' [2] The Canadians north of Mont Kemmel had two infantry battalions, casualty clearing stations and a wireless section which broadcast messages which convinced the Germans that the Canadian Corps was moving into the Ypres sector. [3] The Canadian Corps secretly arrived just before zero. On their left was the ANZAC Corps, another élite formation, which also maintained four battalion divisions.

On 8th August, from right to left, the French, Canadians, ANZACS and British, backed by a thousand extra guns, and over four hundred tanks, fought over five miles through the Germans, on an eight mile front. Ludendorf called the 8th 'the Black Day of the German Army in the history of the war.' On the 9th the French widened the attack on the right and gained a further three miles. On the 10th, the German resistance stiffened, tank numbers were much reduced, the infantry were tired, and on the 11th the Battle of Amiens ended.

From 4th to 14th August the 51st was recuperating north-west of Arras, at Caucourt, Chateau de la Haie, Berles, Aubigny and Acq. Between 14th and 18th August it moved into the line between Fampoux, the River Scarpe and Bailleul (Sir Berthoult), as part of XVII Corps. 170th Brigade of 57th (2nd West Lancashire) Division was attached to the 51st and operated on the south bank of the River Scarpe. On 18th August 1/5th Seaforths were back in the vicinity of:

> '. . . the Chemical Works and Roeux. Here we found that, in the interval, our 1917 work had been largely undone, for the enemy had recaptured these two strongholds, and were also in possession of the greater part of Fampoux. The 51st, annoyed that its sacrifices had thus been in vain, volunteered for the difficult task of recapturing this area, an offer which was at once accepted, and with the Canadians on the south side of the Scarpe, they took up the task with right good will.'[4]

It is unlikely that the men shared this view, but Sutherland's War Diary of the Fifth Seaforth Highlanders was based on newspaper articles published during the war, and had to reflect enthusiasm and optimism.

It was thought that the Germans might transfer troops from the 51st's front to reinforce the battle further south and patrols found the German outpost line thinly held. On 18th of August the 170th Brigade took the enemy's front line, then penetrated another 700 yards. The 51st had less success.

On the night of the 19th/20th the 170th Brigade advanced 500 yards, but by the end of the day they had been shelled, driven off a counter-attack and been shelled again, and had withdrawn to their start line.

At 4.30 a.m. on the 20th 1/5th Seaforths attacked a sunken road north of Fampoux, reached it, were driven out, retook it at 8.30 a.m. and withstood a counter-attack in the late afternoon. 1/7th Gordons on their left failed to take the enemy's front line. On then 21st the 1/6th Gordons successfully took the area between the Fampoux-Fresnes and Fampoux-Gavrelle roads.

At 4.30 a.m. on the 24th 1/7th Black Watch took a trench west of the Fampoux-Gavrelle Road and a support trench, east of the road. Five gaps had been cut in the wire by the artillery and the objectives were taken by 11 a.m., although a few Germans held out until the next morning in the formidable Hyderabad Redoubt.

On the 25th 1/7th Black Watch gained more ground and by the end of the day the 51st had advanced its front to a line running south to north from the east side of Fampoux to within 600 yards of Gavrelle. The 51st's front was now ahead of that of the Canadians, and poised to guard their flank as they advanced south of the Scarpe.

On the 26th the Canadians advanced three miles. When Carter-Campbell heard at 8 a.m. that Canadians had taken Monchy-le-Preux he ordered an advance on Greenland Hill and by late afternoon 1/6th Gordons had taken Roeux Station and the Chemical Works: on their left elements of 153rd Brigade took a trench parallel to and four hundred yards east of the Gavrelle road. At 7 p.m. 153rd Brigade attacked and took a line running south-north from the railway on the west side of Greenland Hill, although 1/7th Gordons had trouble with German machine-guns in the railway cutting.

On the 27th 1/7th Gordons, with 1/6th Black Watch on their left, attacked Greenland Hill. As 1/7th Gordons neared its summit they were driven back by Germans debouching from the railway cutting. By 'about 11.30 a.m. without much opposition' 1/6th Black Watch had reached their objectives but suffered continuous sniping. Patrols were pushed out, and patrols were also sent to gain communication with the right and left flanks. These patrols found 1/7th Gordons on the right, but could not contact 1/4th Seaforths on the left. The enemy was probing both flanks and 'throughout the night there was constant shelling... and again it was with greatest difficulty that water and rations could be taken up.' [5] In the mistaken belief that 1/7th Gordons and 1/6th Black Watch had taken Greenland Hill 1/6th Seaforths were ordered to advance from their line east of Roeux and the Chemical Works and take a line of trenches west of Plouvain. After almost 1000 yards they were stopped by enemy machine-gun fire from Hausa and Delbar Woods, and from a chalk pit near the woods. On the left of the 51st 154th Brigade pushed 500 yards east of Gavrelle and linked up with the 1/6th Black Watch on its right and the 8th Division on its left.

On the 28th 1/6th Black Watch reported:

> '. . . all day there was heavy shelling by large guns, and it was noticed that the enemy had now brought up Field Guns, and there was a certain amount of Gas Shelling on the Right Flank. Throughout the day there were frequent Bombing attacks by the enemy to which we retaliated, our supply of bombs being supplemented by German bombs, of which there was a large quantity. About 400 bombs were detonated [i.e. fused] and prepared for use.
>
> 'During the night the bombing became more intense, and the enemy seemed to be developing round our flanks. . . twice artillery fire was called for which had most beneficial results, and a request was sent to the Officer Commanding, 2nd East LANCS asking him to bring pressure to bear on the enemy attacking our Left Flank. [The 8th Division, of which 2nd East Lancashires were part, had relieved the 154th Brigade on the left the previous evening.] This was done in the form of a Counter-attack by a Company of the 2nd EAST LANCS.' [6]

On 29th August 1/4th Gordons on the right and 1/7th Argylls on the left attacked Greenland Hill at 6.30 a.m., behind a barrage by the 51st and 16th (Irish) Divisions. It had been anticipated that the Germans would realise that the marshes within the concave curve of the Scarpe south of Plouvain could entrap them if their resistance on Greenland Hill and Hausa and Delbar Woods collapsed: the 51st's advance persuaded them to abandon the latter two positions, with little opposition, and avoid the trap. By 10 a.m. Greenland Hill was in the 51st's hands and on the right 152nd Brigade moved forward and was on the east side of Delbar and Hausa Woods by 1.30 p.m. Thereafter 1/6th Seaforths moved forward and took a trench 1500 yards west of Plouvain.

On 30th August, anticipating a German counter-attack, the defences of Greenland Hill were completed by the Royal Engineers and 1/8th Royal Scots. The 51st remained in the line until 14th September.

Fred A. Farrell

1/4th Gordons take Greenland Hill

Arthur Currie of the Canadian Corps wrote to the 51st on 30th August:

'Now that the gallant 51st Division is passing from my
command, may I be permitted to say that I shall always
remember with the greatest pride that for six stirring days you
formed part of the Canadian Corps. I remember very well
when the Division first came to France in May 1915, and that
we took part together in the fighting at Festubert and
Givenchy. Again we were associated in the memorable battle
of Arras in April 1917, and now again we have kicked off side
by side in an advance the results of which I have every reason
to believe will be far-reaching. That your Division was able
after the continuous fighting in which it has been engaged
this year to take and keep the strong position of Greenland
Hill, testifies in the strongest possible manner to the fact that
the fighting qualities of the 51st are second to none in the
Allied armies.

On behalf of the Canadian Divisions I thank you most
sincerely for the splendid help and support you have given to
the main advance south of the river. I wish you all the best of
luck always, and have every confidence that the splendid

reputation that the Division now enjoys will ever be maintained.' [7]

In the Second Battle of the Scarpe the 51st's had secured the left flank of the advance at the cost of 1145 casualties, of whom 4 officers and 182 other ranks were killed or missing. [8]

The 51st left the line on 14th September then returned to it from 24th September until 4th October. Bewsher reflected:

'. . . that the men of the 51st had come to consider that they were doing more than their fair share of battle fighting. They had, indeed, been engaged in nine major operations in the period of seventeen months from April 1917 to August 1918.'

He then pointed out that the men coveted the longer rest periods given to:

'the more fortunate Corps and Divisions, which occasionally were given five or six weeks' rest in which to regain their form after an operation.'

The effect of repeated engagements on the survivors must have been immense. Bewsher's asserted that the men:

'comforted themselves by the thought that they were so continuously employed in the forefront of battle because the Higher Command had learnt to rely on them to carry to a successful issue any task that was set them.' [9]

It is difficult to believe that anyone can be 'comforted' by the knowledge that they were deployed more often than others, whatever their efficiency.

From 5th and 8th October the 51st moved to the Quéant-Inchy area, west of Cambrai. In the middle of this move, on 6th October, the 1/6th and 1/7th Gordons amalgamated to form 6/7th Gordons. 1/7th Gordons' place in 153rd Brigade was taken by the 1/6th Argylls, returning from the 5th Division, to which they had been transferred in 1916.

The 1/6th Argylls appreciated their Highland homecoming:

'Battalion welcomed [en route] on rejoining 51st (H) Div. by 1/
7th A.& S.H., 1/4th GORDON HDRS., 1/4th SEAFORTHS, 1/
6th and 1/7th BNS. ROYAL HIGHLANDERS & played into new
camp by Pipe Bands of the two last named Battns.' [10]

On the 10th the 51st was transferred to the Canadian Corps: 152nd
Brigade was at Bourlon village, 153rd north-east of Bourlon and 154th
in Fontaine-Notre-Dame. The 51st was to relieve the 2nd Canadian
Division and began the move on the morning of the 11th. At 4 p.m. on
the 11th it was returned to XXII Corps and ordered to pursue the
retreating enemy next day.

On the 12th the attacking brigades relieved the 4th and 6th Canadian
Infantry Brigades and approached the start lines, 1000 yards east of Iwuy:
the 49th Division was on the right; from right to left were 1/5th Seaforths,
6/7th Gordons and 1/4th Seaforths. The objective was a line from and
including Avesnes-le-Sec, the line of the Lieu St. Amand road to Maison
Blanche Farm, then west to the railway at Hordain. The Canadian 2nd
Division on the left was to clear the Germans from the area between the
railway and the Canal d'Escaut. Although reports came in that the enemy
was retreating before the 49th Division, the 51st stuck to its original zero
hour – noon.

The contrast between peace and war, as witnessed by 6/7th Gordons,
was stark:

'Morning revealed a beautiful picture. Eastward stretched a
gently rolling, rich, agricultural land, bearing everywhere the
proof of industrious tillage, showing no signs of the ravages of
war. The country was open, scarcely a hedge obstructing the
view. Dotted over the peaceful landscape were trim farms and
neat copses. To the north, nestling in a hollow, lay the village
of Lieu St. Amand, its tall church-spire rising gracefully from
the tiled roofs that glowed red in the bright autumn sunshine.
At ten the distant howitzers boomed; the nearer field-guns
spat venomously. The peaceful landscape vanished; farm and
village became a ruin of falling masonry shrouded in brown-
grey dust. The active infantry slipped cautiously forward,

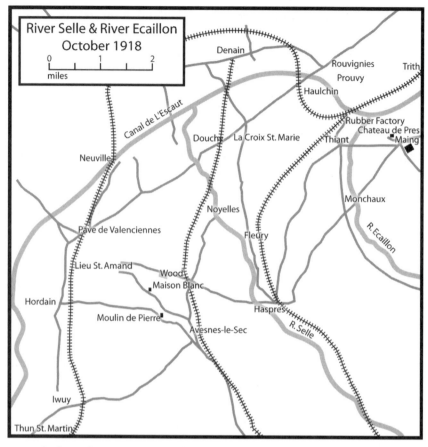

feeling their way round farm and belt of wood, and by mid-day the Gordons, meeting little opposition, had established themselves on the road leading from Lieu St. Amand to Avesnes-le-Sec, with Headquarters in a windmill, Moulin de Pierre, some 200 yards in rear.' [11]

Passing through the first wave, 1/7th Argylls' objectives were Lieu St Amand and the Valenciennes-Cambrai road near Pave de Valenciennes. Machine-guns in Lieu St. Amand killed 8 and wounded 80 Argylls as they crested the rise above it, but the rest:

'got to within 200 yards of the village, but were forced to take what cover they could. . . in full view of the enemy.' [12]

Supporting guns destroyed some machine-guns, but others were so well hidden that it was impossible to locate them. The artillery withdrew when German heavy guns targeted them. 1/7th Argylls persisted and one platoon crawled 200 yards along the furrows of a field to within reach of the village, then were halted by machine-gun fire from the railway on their left. The attack was called off, but one platoon did not receive the order, advanced on the village with heavy losses, and hung on to some buildings until darkness covered their escape.

The 13th October's objective was a line drawn east to west from a railway running 1000 yards north of Haspres, running east of Fleury and Noyelles and to the railway north and west of Lieu St. Amand (Pavé de Valenciennes/Gare Bouchain), On the right 1/5th Seaforths attained a line 1000 yards north east of Avesnes Le Sec, but 2500 yards short of their objective on the eastern edge of Noyelles. They dug in on the railway north of Avesnes Le Sec but had to give up the position. The 1/5th Seaforths, like their colleagues on their right and left, had gone as far as they could. Captain David Sutherland describes a retiral, then individual initiative and courage, as if to draw some consolation from a relatively unsuccessful attack:

> 'At 2 p.m. a slight retiral took place, and here again the casualties were severe. During this retiral, 2nd Lieut. T. S. Hennessy with about 20 men remained out in front, and successfully withstood all enemy counter-attacks. He thus gave time for the remainder of the battalion to withdraw, and to be reorganized in its new position. He held stubbornly on until dusk when he safely withdrew his men. For this gallant work he was awarded the M.C.

L/Sergt. Hector MacKenzie, who had won the D.C.M. in Mesopotamia, was awarded a bar for gallant and invaluable service on the I3th. When the left of the line began to waver under heavy machine-gun fire, he ran across from the right of the line, a distance of over 200 yards, under very heavy fire, rallied and encouraged the men and formed a defensive flank.

Stretcher-bearer James MacKenzie, on the same date, went out on five separate occasions and brought in wounded under very heavy fire, working continuously for ten hours, although he himself was wounded and gassed. On another occasion he heard a wounded man's cries, and had just got to him when a shell burst near and buried him. In spite of his own injuries, he lifted the wounded man, and carried him in until he died in his arms.

L/Corpl. Donald Omand, owing to heavy officer and N.C.O. casualties was left in charge of a platoon, and set such a splendid example, by moving freely among them under heavy fire, that he kept them advancing, and got them to establish posts, and even after being wounded he refused to go to the Aid Post, remaining on duty till badly gassed the following day.' [13]

On 1/5th Seaforths' left 6/7th Gordons were equally unsuccessful:

> 'In the centre of our front was a considerable wood, some 600 yards long and 300 yards broad in centre. It was flanked on the north and west by small copses, while in rear, to the east, ran a railway line*, always easy of defence. The enemy did not fail to turn these natural advantages to the best use. After a heavy artillery bombardment the Battalion again advanced. Small groups pressed forward to seize the wood and the railway, but everywhere were met by the deadly fire of concealed machine-guns. The enemy swept the approaches with a prodigal expenditure of high explosives and gas shells. Undismayed, the resolute infantry pushed forward from front and flank. A number of men forced a way to the outskirts of the wood, but losses were so heavy that they had not the weight to drive the attack home. Leader after leader fell. Lt. Col. Thom, observing and directing the attack from the top of the windmill, fell wounded, and, by noon the weakened remnants trickled back to their assaulting positions.' [14]
> [A branch of the metre gauge Societe de Chemins de Fer de Cambrésis ran from Caudry to Denain, via Avenses Le Sec, Noyelles and Douchy-Les-Mines – closed in 1960. Traces visible on Googlemap and Multimap.]

The battalion had over 300 casualties, German machine-guns killed three machine-gun officers and destroyed six machine-guns, and neutralised the supporting trench mortars. [15] The 6/7th Gordons' Medical Officer, Captain Burton Maltby (U.S. Army's Medical Officers

Reserve Corps) could only protect his wounded at his aid post behind Moulin de Pierre by using it as a shield and laying the wounded out in a line parallel to the incoming machine-gun fire. He cleared space for the living by pushing the dead into the line of fire. [16]

1/4th Seaforths, on their left, attained Maison Blanche farm, west of the wood that troubled 6/7th Gordons, then ended back on their start line due to the failure of 1/7th Argylls, at Lieu St. Amand, who followed a barrage at 9 a.m. and:

> 'headed for the village in attack formation. Enemy put down an intense artillery and MG barrage but line went on steadily to within 100 yds of village where they were held up again after suffering many casualties. Enemy artillery were firing at point blank range and again owing to exposed positions orders were given to withdraw which movement could not be done until dusk and men lay out all day in heavy machine-gun fire. Flanking units were also held up. Party of 30 Germans came out from village after dusk and were fired on by our men causing casualties.'[17]

1/7th Argylls lost two officers and 16 men killed and 96 wounded. Neither 49th Division or the Canadian 2nd Division made any progress on either flank of the 51st.

From the 14th to the 18th the line was held, reliefs took place, and the infrastructure behind the advance was repaired. An attack was planned for 20th October, but on the 19th the enemy began an overall retiral. When the Germans shelled Lieu St. Amand it was clear that they had left, and at 2.30 p.m. 1/6th Argylls' patrols entered the village.

The 51st was ordered to form bridgeheads at Fleury, Noyelles and Douchy, all on the River Selle. The advance began at 3 p.m. 1/4th Gordons, on the right, whilst protecting their right flank from the enemy in Haspres, entered Fleury and occupied the west bank of the River Selle. On their left 1/7th Argylls established a bridgehead on the east side of the river at Noyelles. They made contact with 1/6th Argylls, pursuing the Germans. Lt. J.McPhie, B Company 1/6th Argylls:

'. . . continue to follow him [the enemy] up until he stopped us again at Douchy. Went over with No.8 Platoon presumably to attack but found Boche had gone. Dug in for the time being. Moved off again after dark and followed him to the Canal de L'Escaut where we again dug in.' [18]

On 1/6th Argylls' left 1/7th Black Watch's war diary similarly reflects a day of relatively easy progress:

'The day was misty and at 1600 hours, daylight patrols were pushed out . . No opposition was encountered and 'B' and 'C' Companies advanced in Battle formations. LIEU ST. AMAND was entered at 1730 hrs. Battalion H.Q. then moved forward. . . then moved on to PAVE de VALENCIENNES, arriving there about 2100hrs. Operation orders were then issued to carry on the advance. . .' [19]

At night, on the right, 1/4th Gordons piled straw, branches and beams into the narrow Selle, crossed it south of Fleury and occupied Fleury at 6.45 a.m.on the 20th. At Noyelles 404th Field Company R.E. bridged the Selle and 1/4th Seaforths and 1/7th Argylls crossed at 5.30 a.m. and began to advance. The Germans defended a line from Haspres, through la Croix St. Marie to Denain, and 1/4th Seaforths had to dig in, and 1/7th Argylls' patrols ran into strong resistance.

On the left 1/6th Argylls reached the rubber factory across the Canal d'Escaut from Prouvy and captured Haulchin. Moving forward on their left 1/7th Black Watch noted:

'at about 0030 hrs the advance was continued. The weather was now very wet. 'A' Coy. reported a large number of civilians in New Ville [sic]; which was entered without opposition. . . The Battalion on our right (6th Argylls), and our right company were held up by machine-guns EAST of DOUCHY. DOUCHY was entered without opposition and was full of civilians.

'The civilians were evacuated from DOUCHY during the forenoon – at 1045 hours a barrage was put down and the advance continued. Casualties were very slight. In the afternoon the advance continued; and the final objective

Fred A. Farrell

404th Field Company Royal Engineers bridge building

reached. . . Battalion H.Q. moved up to CROIX de Ste. MARIE.
Two platoons of 'C' Coy. Moved forward to try to intercept
some of the enemy who were retiring from ROUVIGNY [*sic*:
Rouvignies] They were, however, unable to cross the CANAL
de L'ESCAUT, and rejoined at 0330 hours (on the 21st).' [20]

On the 21st 1/4th Seaforths, on the right, were looking down on
Monchaux and the River Ecaillon and in line with the 4th Division on
their right. No progress could be made on the exposed downward slope
to the Ecaillon as it was covered by German positions in sunken roads.

On the left 1/7th Argylls had overcome minor resistance in Thiant
and by 9 a.m. were in position west of the Ecaillon, facing a determined
enemy on the other bank. Contact was made with the Canadians at
Prouvy at 10 a.m.

The 21st until the 23rd were spent preparing to cross the River
Ecaillon. The River Selle bridges had been destroyed and to allow lorries
and artillery forward sappers rebuilt the bridge at Douchy using R.E.
bridge components, and at Noyelles, repaired a damaged German bridge
and built a trestle bridge outside the village. The infantry were ordered
to exploit any opportunity to cross the Selle: at Thiant on the 21st 1/7th

Argylls managed to push a small party across the Ecaillon, which was forced back, and on the 22nd 1/4th Seaforths took a sunken road west of Monchaux.

The attack on the 24th was carried out by 153rd Brigade, with 1/6th Black Watch on the right and 1/7th Black Watch on the left. The first objective was to cross the Ecaillon, the second the western outskirts of Maing, the third was Maing and the high ground south east of it, and the railway running south to north between Maing and Famars was the last objective. In some places the Ecaillon was 20 feet wide, from 4 to 6 feet deep, with steep, muddy embankments from 3 to 6 feet high and all covered by enemy fire. Footbridges made from duckboarding and empty petrol tins or cork floats were made.

At 4 a.m., under an artillery and machine-gun barrage, three companies attacked, each with eight bridges, carried by two or four men. The right company of 1/6th Black Watch suffered heavy fire from Monchaux. Initially only one platoon, commanded by Second-Lieutenant McCaig-Walker, reached the river bank, where the rear of their bridge stuck on a fence and the front fell in the water, far from the opposite bank. Covered by a Lewis gun McCaig-Walker decided to swim and jumped into the water, followed by the rest of his platoon who swam or waded across. Two other platoons used this crossing. McCaig-Walker's men cleared two machine-guns from houses on the left of the crossing, then turned right and eliminated 13 machine-gun nests in the village of Monchaux. [21] McCaig-Walker was awarded the D.S.O. and this action has been cited as a classic example of the initiative and versatility shown by platoon commamders in the Hundred Days. [22]

The left hand company of 1/6th Black Watch made unopposed crossings and on their left a 1/7th Black Watch company had varied fortunes, but succeeded in overcoming the enemy on the opposite bank. The western edge of Maing was the next objective for both battalions.

On the right 1/6th Black Watch was held up by fire from sunken roads and from the south-east corner of Maing. 1/7th Black Watch was held up west of the village by machine-guns in the Château des Pres, which they Lewis gunned then stormed. With close artillery, machine-gun and

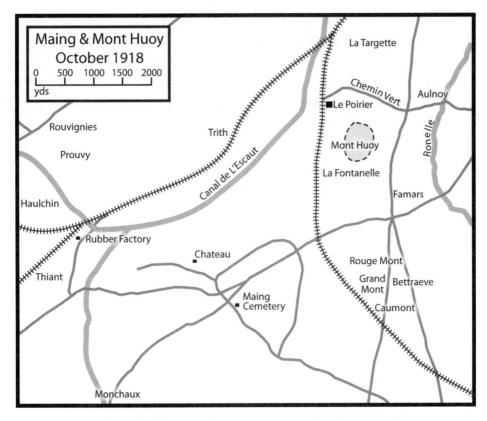

Maing & Mont Huoy
October 1918

0   500   1000 1500 2000
yds

La Targette

Chemin Vert   Aulnoy

■Le Poirier

Rouvignies   Trith

Mont Huoy   Ronelle

Prouvy

La Fontanelle

Canal de L'Escaut

Haulchin   Famars

■ Rubber Factory

■ Chateau   Rouge Mont

Thiant   Grand   Bettraeve
                                      Mont

                    Maing   Caumont
                  ■ Cemetery

Monchaux

trench mortar support, most of Maing had been captured by 3 p.m., along its eastern edge to the cemetery, then along the sunken road running south east from the cemetery. But 1/7th Black Watch reported:

> '. . . owing to serious opposition at the EAST end of MAING, and the fact that the forward companies had suffered heavy casualties both in officers and men, the advance was held up here. . . in the afternoon orders were issued for a relief by 1/6 A.& S.H. . . . our casualties were 6 Officers and 82 Other ranks. Our captures were 2 officers, 167 O.R.s, 3 Light *Minenwerfers*, and 22 machine guns.' [23]

On the 25th the plan was to take the high ground beyond the railway east of Maing, Famars and Mont Huoy, 88 metres high, north of Famars, which overlooked the southern approaches to Valenciennes.

The attack was carried out, from right to left, by 6/7th Gordons, 1/6th

Seaforths and 1/6th Argylls. It began at 7 a.m. behind a barrage and by 11 a.m. 6/7th Gordons had crossed the railway and were at Caumont Farm and Grand Mont. 1/6th Seaforths had a harder time crossing the railway and took Rouge Mont, but were stopped by the Germans dug in west of Famars. 1/6th Argylls' right made progress but on their left the enemy opposite La Fontenelle and Trith-St. Leger kept them from their objective until noon.

As the 51st consolidated they were shelled with a mixture of gas and conventional shells and at 4 p.m. the Germans fired a hurricane barrage, followed by a counter-attack which suffered heavily from the British artillery, but pushed 6/7th Gordons and 1/6th Seaforths back to the railway line. The German attack was held by 1/6th Argylls, established on the railway line since the morning. At 6 p.m. the Germans launched their second counter-attack against 1/6th Argylls, and instead of firing at them from cover they charged the oncoming enemy, drove them downhill, and established a new line in trenches 500 yards ahead of their previous position.

The only officer left in C Company, a 25 years old subaltern, won the V.C:

'Lt. William Davidson Bissett 1/6th Batt. Arg. & Suth'd Highrs. (T.F.)
'For most conspicuous bravery and leadership East of Maing
on the 25th October 1918, when in command of a platoon,

Lt. William Bissett

which he led to its objective with great dash.

Later, owing to casualties, he took command of the company and handled it with great skill after a determined enemy counter-attack had turned his left flank. Realising his danger, he withdrew to the railway, thus temporarily saving the situation. The enemy, however, continued to advance in force after his men had exhausted their ammunition. Thereupon, under heavy fire, he mounted the railway embankment, and, calling upon his men to charge with the bayonet, drove back the enemy with heavy loss, and later, again charging forward, established his line.

'By his splendid example and fine leadership Lt. Bissett was the means of saving a critical situation.' [24] [Bissett became a Major in World War II and served in the R.A.O.C. and the Royal Pioneer Corps. He died at Wrexham on 12th May 1971.]

'The charges were brilliantly carried out, and thirty-two men mustered on the bluff facing Famars. Bissett aggressively waved an empty revolver, and the party made a feint of having enough ammunition to repel any attack. . . only annihilation was expected.' [25]

A less dramatic summary is in the diary of Lt. J. McPhie 1/6th Argylls:

'25th October. Doctor forbade Latta to take Coy over the top, so I had to take command. Jumped off from Maing at 7.15. Went for about 500 yards before we met any real resistance. Got about 200 prisoners, 6 M.G.s & 2 Anti-Tank Guns. Casualties fairly low. Gained about 100 yds more than final objective laid down. Boche easily handled also counter-attack easily repulsed.' [26]

1/6th Argylls registered the spoils as 74 unwounded prisoners, 10 machine-guns, one trench mortar and 2 anti-tank guns. 'Fairly low' casualties were one officer and five other ranks killed, four died of wounds, three officers wounded, one gassed, 48 other ranks wounded, 50 other ranks gassed and one missing. [27]

On the 26th· objectives were Famars and Mont Houy. From right to left 6/7th Gordons, 1/4th Gordons (both 152nd Brigade) and 1/6th Black Watch (153rd Brigade) were deployed. At 10 a.m., following a creeping barrage, 6/7th Gordons took Caumont and Bettraeve Farm, then, in co-operation with some 1/4th Gordons took Rouge Mont, and reached their objective, facing the Rhonelle river, south of Famars village. The 1/4th Gordons took Famars by 11.30 a.m.

By 11.30 a.m 1/6th Black Watch had fought their way through artillery and machine-gun fire and neared Mont Houy. Its right company attacked the hill, and the left company moved towards Le Poirier station. It was held up by machine-gun fire from houses on the other side of the Canal d'Escaut, and stuck 200 yards from the station. The right company, despite casualties, took the summit of Mont Houy and held it for most of the afternoon, until the Germans outflanked them on both sides and drove them back to a line between Famars and La Fontenelle. Bewsher's description of the engagement emphasises the lack of accurate information available, and states:

> '. . . when the situation became clear, orders were issued that at dusk the 6/7th Gordon Highlanders, with artillery support, should advance and secure a bridgehead over the Rhonelle river at Aulnoy, while the 6th Black Watch, with a company of the 6th Argyll and Sutherland Highlanders, were ordered to push forward beyond Mont Houy.' [28]

As they prepared to move they were shelled by high explosive and gas, which heralded a German counter-attack, which drove the forward companies of 1/4th and 6/7th Gordons battalions to the south end of Famars but the Gordons 'showed the dour mettle of their race'[29] and fought their way back into Famars. Aulnoy was too strongly held for 6/7th Gordons to take, and on the left 1/6th Black Watch and a 1/6th Argylls' company were held up by machine-gun fire.

Over the night of 26th to 27th October 1/4th Seaforths took over from 1/6th Black Watch. 1/7th Argylls moved to the railway and put one company in the line north of Famars. 1/4th and 6/7th Gordons remained in the line. At 10.30 a.m. the Germans shelled Famars and obtained a foothold in the village. The inevitable counter-attack was delivered two hours later and despite strong German resistance 1/4th Gordons took back their original positions east of the village.

The Germans' domination of Mont Houy gave them a clear view of the British and Canadian advance on Valenciennes, and made its capture essential. 1/4th Seaforths were to attack, their objective being a line from cross roads west of Aulnoy to 400 yards north of Le Poirier Station. 1/7th Argylls were to maintain the line between the right of 1/4th Seaforths and 1/5th and 1/6th Seaforths who had relieved 1/4th and 6/7th Gordons on the right.

At 5.15 a.m. on 28th of October, following a barrage by four field and one heavy artillery brigades, and a machine-gun barrage, all 1/4th Seaforths' companies attacked. The right company fought its way into Mont Houy Wood and set up a line in it. The twelve survivors of the centre company took a quarry in the north west of Mont Huoy then advanced to their objective, a trench beyond Chemin Vert. Half of the support company succeeded in reinforcing them and its other two platoons reached the crossroads west of Aulnoy and were killed, wounded or captured: this was the furthest penetration by the 51st. 1/4th Seaforths' left company was halted 400 yards north of Le Poirier station by machine-gun fire from La Targette. The battalion had suffered heavy casualties and the German counter-attack drove it back to the southern edge of Mont Houy Wood, where 1/7th Argylls reinforced it and the two battalions stopped the German attack. It is fair to reflect that 1/4th Seaforths 'received relatively little support from the rest of the Highland Division' [30] but Bewsher justified the lack of reinforcements and maintained that:

> '. . . the situation, however, remained obscure, and as the
> runners from the most advanced troops had to traverse areas
> swept by machine-gun bullets few of them survived to deliver
> their messages. It was therefore not known in what serious
> straits the 4th Seaforth Highlanders were.' [31]

This smacks a little of retrospective justification for a failure to ensure that the attack was reinforced by more than just one battalion. It has rightly been concluded that the 51st 'had fairly relatively modest artillery support' and that 'it must have been obvious that it was very tired.' [32]

It was decided that the Canadians would attack Mont Huoy from the south in co-operation with the 49th Division which relieved 1/5th and 1/6th Seaforths, but the situation around Mont Houy was too fluid to carry out a divisional relief. 1/4th Seaforths were replaced on the night of 28/29th October by 1/6th Argylls, who, with 1/7th Argylls north of Famars held the 51st's front. On the 29th the Germans attacked the Argylls twice, at 6.30 a.m. and at 4 p.m., but the line held. At 9 p.m. on the 29th of October 1/6th and 1/7th Argylls were relieved by 44th (Manitoba) and 47th (British Columbia) Battalions, 10th Canadian Infantry Brigade, 4th Canadian Division. The division's artillery remained in position until 2nd November, then returned on the 6th under the orders of the 56th (1st London) Division.

On November 1st, supported by eight field and six heavy artillery brigades which fired:

> 'one of the fiercest bombardments of the War. . . the ground, much of it a swamp, between Chateau de Pres and Valenciennes was a horrible litter of German dead. Our barrage had been laid down with the utmost precision, and through [Trith] S.Leger, Poirier and Aulnoy its area of destruction was so accurate it might have been set with a rule.' [33]

Had such overwhelming support been organised by XXII Corps for the 51st, it might have taken and held Mont Huoy. The Canadian 10th Infantry Brigade took Mont Huoy.

In the nineteen days preceding its relief the 51st had suffered 112 officer and 2723 other rank casualties, of which 21 officers and 292 men were killed and 6 officers and 184 men were missing. Bewsher thought this 'not so proportionately high as had been the case in some of the previous battles.' [34]

The 51st moved back to the environs of Cambrai. At St. Roch, a northern suburb of Cambrai 1/7th Argylls noted:

> 1st and 2nd November. Companies engaged cleaning equipment and billets.
> 3rd. Church parade. Corps Commander present.
> 5th-9th. Companies on training and practising attack formations.
> 10th. Church parade and two named officers posted. [35]

While the October battles were taking place newly liberated villages were fed by the British Army. In a letter of thanks from Clemenceau to Haig on 30th December 1918 the 51st and 66th divisions were singled out. 'The 51st Division alone thus provided food, free of charge, for 3,500 persons a day. An admirable ingenuity was displayed in the supply of ingredients for the making of these free soups. . . ' [36]

Rorie and his RAMC personnel and other units were responsible:

'On entering a half-smashed village, the first hunt was for a
'boiler' or 'copper', the kind of thing found in a washing house
for boiling clothes or in a farmyard for making hens' meat or
cattle food – of sufficient capacity for the job. This when found
was thoroughly cleaned out, filled with water, and a fire lit
beneath. Into the water went the contents of several tins of
'bully', a bag of biscuits, some Bovril, or a piece of meat cut
from some convenient and recently shell-killed horse. The
neighbouring remains of gardens were searched for possible
turnips, carrots, cabbages or any green things of the vegetable
order; and (after due washing and chopping) in they went too. . .

The news – and the fragrant odour – of what we were
manufacturing soon got abroad, and the starving inhabitants
commenced to gather. . . ' [37]

This continued until the French civilian authorities were able to take
over responsibility in mid-November.

As the 51st prepared for the next battle the German fighting retreat
continued, but rumours of an armistice were rife until, on the 9th, Private
Wrench, 1/4th Seaforths wrote: 'I hear tonight that Mons has fallen.
Mons! Well, and that is just about where the war started too.' And on the
10th:

'It is official about Mons and that the Canadians have
advanced far beyond. . . I dodged church parade again. . . it
was so cold and frosty too that who should want to stand out
in a frosty field for that? And now it is night . . . it is officially
announced that an armistice has been signed to take effect
at eleven o'clock tomorrow, when the hostilities will cease.
Firing has already ceased on certain parts of the front to
allow the German plenipotentiaries to come through the
lines. And so what a racket. The Argylls band are out in force
and even here we can hear them play. These drums are being
beat as they never were beat before. I never dreamed the
skins could stand so much 'walloping' nor the pipes sound
so wild and great. What a great and glorious feeling it is. The
war is over and we have won. Out in the yard there is a crazy

bonfire of boxes of German rockets and star shells and they are spurting and fizzling dangerously in every direction and just like us, 'bursting' with enthusiasm at the glorious news. And the noise is almost deafening.' [38]

1/7th Argylls' history described the atmosphere:

'At 11.30 p.m.on 10th November 1918 the door of our Battalion Headquarters mess was rather suddenly and by no means gently forced open by a member of the Brigade Staff, who disturbed a peaceful evening by announcing that the 'Bosche' had given in.'

'The officers roused the N.C.O.s to the tune of the best slogan they had ever heard, 'The War's finished!' The N.C.O.s pulled the men out of their beds and the men routed out the pipers. The whole cheering mob 'paraded' en masse in front of the battered house that labelled 'H.Q. 7th A.&S.H.' and raised their voices in a chorus of demands for their Colonel. He appeared and was forthwith hoisted on the shoulders of a group of sturdy Highlanders from which point of vantage he assured the assembled and motley throng that the glorious news was indeed true.

'The Sergeants raided the Quartermaster's stores, while that dignitary looked on unmoved. They took therefrom all the Very Lights, gas gongs, rattles, flares, S.O.S. signals, biscuit tins and anything else that could make a noise or otherwise add to the evening's fun.

'Somewhere after midnight adjournments were made to a local brewery that had been used for all as a concert hall, and there each officer in turn was firmly requested to 'sing, dance, or tell a story' on pain of being instantly ejected from the window and debarred from taking any further part in the celebrations.' [39]

November 11th, Private Wrench, 1/4th Seaforths:

'It is really quite hopeless to try to describe what today means to us all. The actual, official news of the armistice was issued at 8 o'clock this morning. It read 'Hostilities cease at 11.00 hours today. Today will be observed as a holiday.' '

Wrench was sent on horseback with this message to units and officers in the Cambrai area and as he moved through the streets he passed the good news to civilians:

'. . . although for a brief moment some of them seemed to doubt me. Then I dismounted and told them over again that the war is finished and when they at last came to realize it was so and that I was telling the truth and the war was really to end at eleven o'clock, they would start and shout out of pure joy and I had a hard time taking myself away then to escape their embraces.'

At noon on the 11th Private Wrench was in a reflective mood:

'An hour ago it was war, and now it is peace yet the transition is too subtle for us to comprehend at the moment since we are not actually in action. . . I have come through it after all and I pray and hope to God there will be no more of such political misunderstanding and madness that will start off another war. Surely this is the last war that will ever be between any civilized nations. And after this, what is to become of us now? Are we to be better off or worse and shall we say to Germany, 'Let us forget and forever henceforth be at peace'? Then 'Man to man the World o'er will brothers be for a' that'.' [But in the evening:] 'It is pandemonium and I think we must all be mad. . . the bon fire is blazing again out in the courtyard and boxes of German star shells and signal flares are being piled on it to feed it. . . while we are letting ourselves get loose it is certain that each one of us has time to give a thought of regret for our late pals who have 'gone West' and have not been spared to become mad with us as well. . . ' [40]

1/6th Argylls' Lieutenant McPhie:

'Armistice signed, all hostilities stopped at 11 a.m. No Parades. B played C at 11.30. Officers played Sgts. at 2.30. Bonfire and concert at 6 p.m. Batt.officers dinner at 8 p.m. [41]

Two battalions exemplify the price paid by the 51st's infantry. A peacetime battalion numbered just over 1000 men. In 1/4th Seaforths

273 officers and 3783 men served in the battalion – the equivalent of four battalions, of whom 60 officers and 1110 men died, or 28.8% of those who served. [42] 1/7th Argylls lost 53 officers and 898 men. [43]

From 11th November all were consumed with the priorities of demobilisation, but the process was slow and the army had to keep the men occupied.

Typical of the 51st's battalions, 1/7th Argylls were preoccupied with education classes and battlefield salvage from 6th to 10th January 1919, then moved from St. Roch to comfortable billets at La Louvrière, 20 kms east of Mons. The routine of church parades, education, salvage and sport continued, then on 27th January there is a note of 'odd men proceeding for demobilization', thereafter batches of 50 to 70 officers and men left the battalion every few days until 'the cadre of the Battalion arrived at Stirling on 21st May 1919, and handed over its colours.' [44]

Private Wrench, 1/4th Seaforths, caught the frustration of seemingly endless delays in demobilisation:

'Monday 17th February 1919. There wasn't one of us but who looked with envy and longing at the big draft leaving today on the way home. But I am lucky to be in the first platoon for the next Georgetown draft so I have visions of dinner at home tomorrow yet if we leave tonight. . .
    'Tuesday 18th: at 12.15 we sailed . . . at 6.40 the engines stopped and we were in the Solent but there was no word of moving further. Everyone is growing so impatient at the delay.
    'Wednesday 19. Well, it appears I won't possibly be having my dinner at home today yet. It was 7.o'clock this morning when the engines started again and my heart thumped harder than the boat when it gave its first bump against the quay at Southampton. I was third man off the ship and not by the gangway either but over the side. . . we left at 12.15 [from Southampton] and it was a direct run right into the station at Georgetown [Bishopton, Renfrewshire] where we arrived at 3 a.m. [on the 20th].'

    'Thursday 20. Had dinner in the canteen at Georgetown on arrival then hung around for ages waiting for the staff to arrive on duty. They got a start at 6 a.m. when we went from one

table to another answering questions and dumping our
equipment etc. Then we each received two pounds sterling
and at last were sent struggling over the snow covered yard to
the railway station again. The train left at 8 a.m. and I got off
at Pollokshields [Glasgow] at 8.30. Now here I am finally home
and when I get rid of this uniform I will have washed my
hands of the army forever and so may the Good Lord be
praised. LA GUERRE EST FINIS. VIVE L'ECOSSE.' [45]

. . .

The 51st had a varied war. In 1914 it provided battalions piecemeal to
reinforce the Regular Army in France and Flanders and when it arrived
in France it had an unfamiliar Lancashire brigade, two newly arrived
Highland battalions, and little training appropriate to modern trench
warfare. The 51st was put into the trenches, then into battle, without
the familiarisation normally accorded to new divisions. Unsurprisingly
its inexperience showed at Festubert, although the men were brave in
the face of insurmountable odds.

After Festubert it learned the skills of trench warfare, and many of
its Territorial Force C.O.s were replaced by regulars, with a subsequent
raising of standards. The establishment of divisional training
programmes and the exigencies of modern war, gave it similar
experience to other divisions. The appointment in September 1915 of
Harper, unafraid of his superiors, an innovator in training and tactics,
with experience of civilian Volunteers, and a flair for leadership and
publicity, began to build the 51st's unique reputation.

So great was its reputation perceived to be by some that an unnamed
commentator told Haldane, author of the *History of the* 4th *Battalion,
Seaforth Highlanders* that 'the two most terrible engines of destruction
ever made by man were the 51st and 15th Divisions, both Scottish. . .' [46]
Such an accolade would be contested by many with a partiality for other
divisions.

In the foreword to 1/6th Gordons' history Harper wrote:

'What was the secret of their excellence? They were imbued

> with the highest regimental *esprit de corps*; they were proud of
> their Division; they considered themselves the best Battalion
> in the best Division, and they endeavoured to act up to that
> standard.' [47]

Under a good C.O. every battalion of the 51st would have nurtured such
self-belief, and the net effect was a good division.

The 51st had four unique ingredients. It was Scottish, despite one
author encapsulating 'Scottish' in inverted commas, and implying that
it was so leavened by other nationalities of the British Isles, as not to be
Scottish. [48] This could be interpreted as an attempt to diminish
Scotland's contribution to the war. Haig invariably referred to English,
Scottish or Irish troops in his dispatches, despite any dilution of divisions
with 'outsiders'. Analyses of the birthplaces listed in *Soldiers Died in the
Great War* confirms the predominantly Scottish nationality of the
battalions: the rural 1/8th Argylls, whose recruitment area was so thinly
populated that they recruited Mancunians, had 85% Scottish born. 1/
7th Black Watch, semi-rural, encompassing the farming and fishing
villages and the industrial towns of Fife: 93%. 1/4th Gordons, from the
City of Aberdeen: 90.1%. 1/8th Royal Scots, from the Lothians, to which
some medically downgraded soldiers were sent: 80.7% [49] 51% would
define a division as being barely Scottish: these figures fully justify the
51st being described as Scottish.

Although Scots had emigrated in large numbers, most of those who
had stayed at home had not travelled far: long working weeks and poverty
kept them in their own localities. They knew where they came from, they
spoke their own dialects, they had unique rivalries, just like men from
any part of the British Isles, but in addition they had a fierce sense of
national identity, exaggerated by being a minority. Nicolson observed
that 'Scotland for Ever' was then still a valid battle cry, unlike 'St. George
for Merrie England' – if it had ever existed. [50]

Secondly, like the Canadians and the ANZACS, Scotland had a more
widely accessible educational system, divided less by class than
England's. England's more entrenched class system tended to keep
soldiers in their subordinate place, [51] whereas Scotland's egalitarianism,

whilst sometimes manifesting itself in negativism born of envy, gave individuals who were oblivious to the niceties of real or perceived status the freedom to exercise initiative on the battlefield.

Thirdly, in a society in which snobbery, real or contrived, exaggerated distinctions amongst regular, territorial and new army divisions, the 51st, as the only Highland division was in a minority of one. Being a Territorial Force division, Scottish, and drawn from one readily identifiable area gave it an easily defined corporate identity, giving it an advantage over New Army divisions drawn from throughout the United Kingdom. [52]

Fourthly, all the 51st's infantrymen were kilted, which made it a unique institution on the Western Front. That this gave the off-duty soldiers an edge is clear from the early reports of the young Lancashire billeting officer on the Somme in 1915, who was welcomed, but overshadowed by the kilts of the 51st. One wonders if that presaged an apparent willingness by some to criticise or disparage the 51st. Nicholson stated that there was nothing comparable to the massed pipes and drums of the 51st: others may have resented this.

An English regular, Sergeant David Layton M.M., discussing the relative merits of the nationalities involved in the war described the Scots as 'dour and determined – the only troops who loved using the bayonet. The best fighting troops in the world and the most feared at close quarters.' [53] Is this reported propensity for close quarter battle a variant of peacetime brawls or of romantically recalled clan warfare?

Sergeant Major Robert Goddard, 1/5th Seaforths, convalescing at his father's home in Denton, Kent wrote to his late officer's sister: 'though I am English I think there are none like the Highlanders both for their fighting ability and character.' [54] He does not expand on these characteristics, but they were recognisable to him. The Mancunians who marched behind the 2/4th Seaforths' band singing about 'hills and 'eather' were trying to become adoptive Scotsmen. Perhaps they too had been beguiled by the myth of the invincible Highland charge.

Many of the men came from the harshest parts of the United Kingdom, where climatic conditions were not as benign as they are in

Southern England, and those who came from the industrial slums of the 51st's recruitment area were accustomed to hardship.

The battalions maintained strong local links and thought of themselves as the Fife Battalion, the Black Watch, or the Argyllshire Battalion, The Argyll and Sutherland Highlanders. The 51st's training battalions were often led by officers and N.C.O.s imbued with fierce regimental and divisional pride, who instilled it in the recruits, and demanded high standards.

Historian Paddy Griffiths categorised the 51st as an élite division, albeit referring to Harper as erratic. [55] He reinforced this by commenting on the high command's inclination to choose 'trustworthy formations for the dirtiest jobs' [56] and citing the composition of V Corps at Beaumont Hamel, which included the 2nd, 3rd, 51st and 63rd (Naval) divisions. In a review of the professional origins of the B.E.F.'s Corps Commanders he concluded that corps commanders from non-regular divisions had usually commanded élite divisions, as had Harper before he was appointed to IV Corps. [57] Richard Holmes described the 51st 'as one of the best divisions in the war'. [58] Private Bill Partridge 1/7th Middlesex thought the 51st special: 'We used to say, 'If there's any shit to be shoveled, give it to the 51st Highland Division' and they always did!' [59]

The judgement of the Germans on 1st January 1918 dispenses with any historian's partiality, and is an objective assessment founded on the best intelligence available to their staff. The Germans put the 51st in the top 15 excellent assault divisions. But where did it stand in that assessment? The three divisions appearing in the alleged German list of the autumn of 1917 appear in the 1st January 1918 list: the 51st, 29th and Guards.

Contemporary opinion, as expressd by Army and Corps Commanders to the 51st as it departed from their commands was contained in formal notes of appreciation, which sometimes recorded specific thanks for a distinguished action. On 30th August 1918, as the 51st left the Canadian Corps, Lieut. General Sir A.W. Currie, sent a congratulatory letter to the 51st, which noted previous occasions on which the Canadians and the 51st had fought side by side and recognised:

'That your Division was able after the continuous fighting in which it has been engaged this year to take and keep the strong position of Greenland Hill, testifies in the strongest possible manner to the fact that the fighting qualities of the 51st are second to none in all the Allied armies.' [60]

This is a stunning endorsement by a general who reputation is universally respected.

Amongst such parting shots is another ranking. General Ivor Maxse, famous trainer of the 18th (Eastern) Division, which was successful on the Somme, and latterly Inspector General of Training, and critical of the 51st when he first came across it in its tentative introduction to war at Givenchy, wrote on the 51st's departure from his XVIII Corps in September 1917:

'What has struck me most is the thoroughness of the organisation within the Division, and the fact that all usual war problems have been thought out beforehand, discussed in detail, and are embodied in simple doctrines well known to all ranks. The result is the Division always fights with gallantry, and can be depended upon to carry out any reasonable task which may be allotted to it in any battle. For this reason I venture to place it amongst the three best fighting divisions I have met in France during the past three years.' [61]

Maxse's wife often hosted generals who were home on leave and on 23rd September 1917 Maxse asked her to make a point of trying to see Harper on his return to the UK, as Harper's division was 'one of the two or three best divisions in France.' [62] This was a private letter to his wife, not for publication, or to congratulate a division. At worst it leaves the 51st in the top three in Maxse's estimation: if it was 'one of two', Maxse, as a Guards' officer would never concede that the Guards would be anything but the best, which could put the 51st second to the Guards in his estimation.

Second Lieutenant Wilfrid Bion, Tank Corps, commented:

'the 51st Division, Highland Territorials, had won a reputation second only to the Guards. In their own opinion, and many could be found to share it – even amongst the enemy – they ranked even higher. For steadiness and reliability the Guards could not be matched. But the virtue that was their strength also led to the defect of rigidity in some situations where the flexibility of the 51st would have been more valuable.' [63]

This from a tank officer who served alongside the 51st at Cambrai – but who was recommended for the V.C. by the 51st. [64]

The fairest conclusion derives from Arthur Behrend R.G.A., who observed the 51st in the March retreat and rated it 'equally redoubtable' [65] to the New Zealand Division which he ranked 'high amongst the highest'. [66] With the 51st's conceit of itself, its fighting record, the *Furchbarkeit* list, the January 1918 German list, the opinions of Currie, Maxse, Bion and Behrens, there is no doubt that the 51st (Highland) Division was 'high amongst the highest'.

NOTES
1. Lt.Gen.Arthur Currie, Canadian Corps to 51st 30.8.1918
2. I & R Sheldon-Williams *The Canadian Front in France and Flanders* (Black) 1920 pp.118-119.
3. Neillands *The Great War Generals on the Western Front* Neillands Page 493
4. Sutherland p.178.
5. 1/6th Black Watch narrative of battle. TNA.
6. 1/6th Black Watch narrative of battle. TNA.
7. Lieutenant-General Arthur Currie 30.8.1918.
8. Bewsher p.369.
9. Bewsher p.371.
10. War diary 1/6th Argylls 6.10.1918.
11. MacKenzie p.180.
12. Morrison pp.49-50.
13. Sutherland pp.177-178.
14. Mackenzie p.18.1
15. Bewsher p.379.
16. Farrell Plate 8.
17. War Diary 1/7th Argylls 13.10.1918.
18. Lt.J.McPhie diary 20.10.1918 A&SH Museum.
19. War diary 1/7th Black Watch 19-20.10.1918
20. War diary 1/7th Black Watch 19-20.10.1918.

Fred A. Farrell

Lieu St. Amand

21. Bewsher pp.390-391 and Farrell Plate 3.
22. Queen of the Battlefield, Chris McCarthy, Command and Control on the Western Front ed.Sheffield and Todham Spellmount 2004 p.190
23. 1/7th Black Watch narrative 24.10.1918.
24. London Gazette 6.1.1919.
25. Farrell Plate 9.
26. Diary of Lt. J.McPhie 1/6th Argylls A&SH Museum.
27. War diary 1/6th A&SH, 25.10.1918.
28. Bewsher p.398.
29. Mackenzie p.183.
30. J.P.Harris *Amiens to the Armistice* (Brassey) 1998 p.267.
31. Bewsher pp.401-402
32. Harris p.267
33. Sheldon p.165.
34. Bewsher p.404.
35. War diary 1/7th Argylls 1-10.11.1918.
36. Rorie quotes Clemenceau to Haig p.257.
37. Rorie p.259.
38. Wrench 10.11.1918.
39. Morrison pp.52-53
40. Wrench 11.11.1918.
41. McPhie diary 11.11.1918.
42. Haldane Table at end of history.
43. Morrison p.56.

44. Morrison p.53

45. Wrench 17-20.2.1919

46. Haldane p.305

47. Mackenzie foreword

48. Hammond Myth of the First Great Tank Battle p.60.

49. Count based on places of birth, the only indisputable criterion of nationality, and a random sample, selected by enemy action. Place of enlistment or family names would add to the percentages of Scots but are not foolproof: e.g. men came from England to enlist in Scotland.

50. Nicholson p.149.

51. McKee p.254.

52. Nicholson p.149.

53. McKee pp.254-255.

54. Letter to Muriel Mackintosh, sister of Lt.E.Alan Mackintosh 1/5th Seaforths kia 21.11.17

55. Griffiths (Battle Tactics on the Western Front) p.80

56. Griffiths p.82

57. Griffiths p.217

58. Richard Holmes *The British Army and the Western Front* Caledonian Research Foundation/Royal Society of Edinburgh Prize Lecture, May 2003.

59. Nicholls p.170.

60. Bewsher p.369.

61. Bewsher p.231.

62. Baynes p.179.

63. Wilfrid R. Bion The Long Week-End, 1897-1919: Part of a Life (Abington, Oxfordshire:Fleetwood Press 1982) by permission of the Marsh Agency on behalf of the Estate of W.R. Bion, quoted Hammond Page 81. It could be argued that the VC recommendation coloured Bion's view of the 51st. On the other hand, he was a noted psychoanalyst when he wrote the book, capable of informed and objective judgement.

64. Bion Pages 172-173

65. Behrend p.13.

66. Behrend p.118.

POSTSCRIPT

The 51st ceased to exist in March 1919, but 1/4th Seaforths, 1/4th Gordons and 1/6th Black Watch had left in February to serve in Germany with the Army of Occupation. Apart from the novelty of serving in Germany there was a special excursion for the 1/6th Black Watch:

> 'July 12th 1919, remains a red letter day in the history of the 6th Battalion, for on that day a small detachment took part in the peace rejoicings in Paris and received the rare honour of having the French *Croix de Guerre* pinned on the Regimental Colours. . . a tumult of cheering greeted the appearance of the detachment of Highlanders as they passed through the Arc de Triomphe on their way to the ceremony, when the Military Governor of Paris, General Berdoulet, presented the decoration in the presence of the French and Colonial troops assembled for the Victory March. . . drawn up on three sides of a square, with The Black Watch colour party in the centre and the massed bands of the Welsh and Irish Guards in rear, the troops presented arms as the French General approached. . . he paid high tribute to the valour of Scottish troops during the war. . . pinning the *Croix de Guerre* to the Regimental Colour of the 6th Battalion, and kissing the Colour, the General shook hands with Colonel Green. . . All officers and men of the Battalion now wear the ribbon of the *Croix de Guerre* on the sleeve of the jacket.' [1]

As regular battalions replaced the New Army and Territorials in the Army of Occupation the last of the 51st came home: on 20th October 1/6th Black Watch:

> '. . . reduced to Cadre strength, entrained for Perth, arriving the following morning. The same day the officers and men were given a public reception and dinner in the City Hall, where they were joined by about a thousand members of the Battalion who had come together from all parts of Scotland

... two days later the Cadre was finally demobilized.' [2]

The Territorial Forces were reconstituted on 7th April 1920, and the 51st (Highland) Division was reformed in the same month. On 1st October 1920 the Territorial Forces were renamed the Territorial Army.

Individual battalion memorials had been erected during and after the war, and towns and villages raised their own memorials. At an unveiling in 1919 the C.O. of a recently returned cadre advised his listeners that the best thing that young men could do was 'join a Territorial Unit at once, and spend any other leisure time that they had at a miniature rifle range. . . for the Germans had no idea that they were beaten.' [3]

At the 51st's officers' First Reunion Dinner in Edinburgh, on Friday 20th November 1920, an appeal was launched to raise £10,000 for a divisional memorial. The Maire of Beaumont-Hamel offered a site on the Beaucourt Road, which overlooked the village, but it was was undermined by ancient workings that the Germans had not discovered when they were building dugouts. An alternative site was offered in the Newfoundland Memorial Park and Bannatine-Allason and Lt. Colonel Robertson, the honorary secretary of the memorial organisation, chose the top of 'Y' Ravine.

£8,300 was raised by donations and flag days, which was, as a result of fluctuations in exchange rates, sufficient for the project.

On Sunday 28th October 1924, before the unveiling of the divisional memorial, Major-General Bannatine-Allason, the only surviving 51st divisional commander, handed over a flagpole to the Maire of Beaumont-Hamel. Situated at 'Windy Corner' on the road to Auchonvillers: it was 45 feet high and bore a plaque stating:

'Presented to the Inhabitants of Beaumont-Hamel (Somme)
by the Officers, Non-Commissioned Officers and Men of the
51st (Highland) Division, in commemoration of the recapture
of the village by the Division on 13th November 1916.' [4]

The Honorary Secretary of the Memorial Committee, Colin MacLeod

Robertson, described a meeting on the unveiling day:

> 'There is many a son lying here on the Somme. One who
> fought in the 51st Division will have the soil of his grave
> turned up a little today. His aged parents – simple folks from
> the North of Scotland, to whom Continental travel is by no
> means a holiday – have brought over the best gifts they can
> give him. The mother carries a sapling from Scotland, with the
> earth still about its roots, and the father has a biscuit box filled
> with soil from the little garden at home. 'I want the boy to
> have a bit of the home ground about him,' he says. When the
> ceremony is over, he will set out, with 'Mother', for the
> cemetery at Mailly-Maillet, a mile and a half away, with the
> sapling, a box of home earth and a simple sprig of heather.
> That is what the Beaumont-Hamel Memorial means to many
> a Scottish heart.' [5]

Immediately after the flag ceremony at Beaumont-Hamel, in
Newfoundland Park, Marshal Foch unveiled the divisional memorial,
and speeches were made, in the presence of military and local
dignitaries: a guard of honour was provided by the 51st Regiment of the
French Army and by men from all the infantry battalions of the 51st, or
their successor amalgamations, and men from the 51st's R.F.A.,
Divisional Ammunition Column, Trench Mortars, R.A.M.C. and Machine
Gun Corps, amongst whom was B.S.M. Gosling v.c. After the formalities
lunch was provided for five hundred pilgrims in a marquee near the
Newfoundland Log Cabin.

The memorial plinth is surmounted by a Highlander, staring out over
Y Ravine. In French and English there are plaques:

Scotland
By this monument
In the lands of her ancient ally
And comrades in arms
Commemorates those officers and men of the 51st (Highland)
Division
Who fell in the Great War
1914-1918

And in Gaelic:

La a'Blair s'math n Cairdean.
Friends are good in the day of battle.

estate of Thomas Lindsay

NOTES

1. History of 6th Black Watch pp. 202-203 The ribbon was worn by Black Watch elements of 51st Highland Regiment, until it became 51st Highland, 7th Battalion, The Royal Regiment of Scotland, when, despite requests to continue to wear it, its use was ended. A sample of the ribbon is in the 1914-1918 rooms in the Black Watch Museum, Balhousie Castle, Perth.

2. History of the 6th Black Watch p.203

3. The History of the 51st (Highland) Division, Salmond, Blackwood, 1953, Page 4

4. The flagpole was renewed at a ceremony on 13th November 2006, on the initiative of Derek Bird of the Scotland [North} Branch, Western Front Association

5. 51st (Highland) Division War Memorial Brochure, 1924, Lt.Col. Robertson, Page 14

APPENDIX I

Battalion and divisional numbering

Between the skill levels of the Territorial Forces and the Regular Army was the Special Reserve, composed of men who signed on for 6 years, of which the first six months were full time, followed by a liability to serve for a month per year, with a liability for call up into the Regular Army at mobilisation. These battalions were the 3rd and sometimes 4th (Special Reserve or Militia) battalions of their respective regiments, which provided reinforcements for a regiment's two regular battalions. There were other reserve and special reserve categories of officers and men.

As volunteers answered the call, pre-war Territorial Force battalions formed duplicate battalions, thus the 9th Royal Scots became the 1/9th Royal Scots and 2/9th Royal Scots, and 3/9th Royal Scots were the second and third line battalions which sent trained drafts to their first line battalions and carried out garrison duties. The second line battalions were in second line divisions, and the 64th (2nd Highland) Division was initially the 51st's main source of replacements. Some English second line battalions and second line divisions, served in France.

Severely depleted battalions were sometimes amalgamated with others of their own regiment e.g the 7/9th Argyll and Sutherland Highlanders were amalgamated for a few months in 1915 before being separately reconstituted.

Where the county to which a Territorial Force battalion belongs was in its official title, this will be mentioned once, for example 1/6[h] (Renfrewshire) Battalion Argyll and Sutherland Highlanders, thereafter the battalion will be referred to as 1/6th Argylls. When the county is not incorporated in the official title of a battalion first reference to it will have its county after the name, in parentheses e.g.1/7th Battalion Argyll and Sutherland Highlanders (Stirling and Clackmannan).

Divisions were based on their regular, territorial or new army (Kitchener's volunteers) origins. Territorial Force formations are identified in orders of battle by the initials T.F. All others are regular or new army formations. New Army battalions were defined as 'S' Service battalions, thus when any division is first mentioned, or when its origins are pertinent to the text, its origin as a Regular, Territorial Force or New Army (S) division will be shown. Regular divisions were numbered 1-8, 27 – 29, New Army divisions 9 – 41 and Territorial divisions 42 – 75. The 63rd was the Royal Naval Division, largely composed of Royal Marine Light Infantry and surplus naval resevists and volunteers, who, instead of going to sea, became infantrymen.

APPENDIX II

Died while serving with the Highland Division 1914-19

Addison, Lt.Noel Goodricke MC 1st King Edward's Horse kia 9.4.18. Loos Memorial Panel 2 Natal, South Africa

Brooks, Private Charles, 1/6th Seaforths, S/17666, Formerly 158599 R.F.A. 32 d.o.w. 31//3/18. Etaples Military Cemetery Grave XXXIII. B.8 North Thoresby, Lincolnshire.

Burnett, Private James, 275360 1/8th Royal Scots, 20, k.i.a. 9.4.1918, Mont Bernanchon Churchyard B.6. Edinburgh/Innerleithen

Calthrop, Lt.Col. Everard Ferguson, 38th Brigade, R.F.A., 39, k.i.a. 19.12.1915. Ypres Reservoir I.B.11, Attaché Tokyo 1914-1915. Stourport, Worcestershire

Christie, Sergeant J, DCM, 406136, R.E., 51st Division Signal Company, k.i.a. 24.5.1917. Level Crossing Cemetery, Fampoux. I.C.6

Clark, Captain Donald Gordon, D.S.O., M.C. 1/6th Gordons, 25, d.o.w. 13.04.1918 Etaples Military Cemetery XVIII H.5. Echt and Alford, Aberdeenshire.

Collins, Private Vincent Lionel John, 2491, 1/8th A&SH, 18, died of wounds, 4.10.15, Authuille Military Cemetery B.41, of Crowborough, Sussex

Dow, Lt. David Edward, 1/6th Seaforths, 24, d.o.w. 17.5.17 Aubigny Communal Cemetery Extension VI.G.9. Elgin, Moray.

Drummond, Second Lieutenant Alexander Gilmour, M.C. 1/6th Black Watch. d.o.w. 5.4.1918 Cologne Southern Cemetery XVII.A.1 Glasgow

Edwards, Sergeant Alexander, V.C. 265473, 1/6th Seaforths, 32, k.i.a., 24.3.1918, Arras Memorial, Bay 8.Drainie and Lossiemouth, Moray.

Edwards, Captain George Eric D.S.O., 1/6th Seaforths, aged 29, k.i.a. 20/11/1917, Grave I.B.8 Orival Wood Cemetery, Flesquieres, Lossiemouth.

Gemmill, Lt.Col. William D.S.O., 1/8th Royal Scots, 40, k.i.a., 25.3.18, Arras Memorial, Bay 1 and 2

Grant, Second Lieutenant D., 1/6th Seaforths, k.i.a. 20.11.1917,

Orival Wood Cemetery, Flesquieres. Grave I.C.13

Gray, Corporal David, 406298, R.E., 51st Division Signal Company, k.i.a. 24.5.1917, Level Crossing Cemetery, Fampoux.I.C.7 Aberdeen.

Greer, L.Cpl. John T., 21165 1/6th A&SH, aged 24, k.i.a. 30.10.17, 12 Williamsburgh, Paisley. Bedford House Cemetery Enclosure No.2 III B I. 12 Williamsburgh, Paisley (gassed, former Babcock and Wilcox employee: Paisley's Fallen in the War p and p Lochead, Express Buildings, 1920 Page 18)

Hewat, Capt. James Govan Argyll, 1/6th Black Watch, 20 k.i.a. 16.4.18, Lapugnoy Military Cemetery VIII D 6, Edinburgh

Lauder, Captain John, 1/8th Argylls, k.i.a. 28.12.1916 Ovillers Military Cemetery I.A.6. Dunoon

Lawrie, William, Serjeant (Piper), Pipe-Major, 1/8th Argylls, died of pleurisy, London, 28.11.1916 Ballachulish (St.John) Episcopalian Churchyard. Ballachuilish, Argyll.

Leith, Lieutenant Douglas Meldrum Watson M.C., 1/4th Gordons, 26, k.i.a. 21.3.1918, Lebucquiere Communal Cemetery Extension, IV.A 16. Old Meldrum, Aberdeenshire.

McCallum, Sergeant Alex , 729, 1/8th A&SH, 21, born and enlisted in Campbeltown, k.i.a.15.6.15 Le Touret Memorial to the Missing, Panel 43.Campbeltown, Argyll.

MacDonald, Sergeant Alexander, 711, 1/5th Seaforths, 32, Mailly Wood Cemetery, Mailly-Maillet, I.G.12, Kirkmichael, Perthshire

McKay, Sergeant George, 240427 1/5th Seaforths k.i.s. 9.4.1917 Highland Cemetery, Roclincourt II.A.47 Hallkirk, Caithness.(Comemorated in 'Farewell', E.A Mackintosh, War the Liberator p.23/Campbell and Green p.189)

Mackintosh, Lieutenant Ewart Alan, M.C, 1/4th Seaforths, k.i.a. 21.11.17 Orival Wood Cemetery I.A.26. Brighton, Sussex.

McKellar, Lt.John Thomson, A Coy 1/8th A&SH, 25, kia 13.11.16 Mailly Wood Cemetery, Mailly-Maillett, I.D.29. Dunoon, Argyll.

MacTaggart, Captain Archibald Murdoch, 1/8th A&SH, 22, k.i.a. 16.5.1917, Arras Memorial Bay 9. Bowmore, Islay Argyll.

Meikle, Sergeant John, V.C.,M.M., 200854, 1/4th Seaforths ,19. k.i.a. 20.7.1918, Marfaux British Cemetery, VIII.C.1. Nitshill, Renfrewshire (now Glasgow from 1926)

Moffat, Private Harry, 1/7th A&SH, 275783, k.i.a. 24.5.1917. Level Crossing Cemetery, Fampoux I.C.8. Bonnybridge, Stirlingshire.

Munro, Lt.Hugh A., 1/8th A&SH, 22, k.i.a. 22.9.15, Millencourt Communal Cemetery Extension Grave F.71. Helensburgh, Dumbartonshire.

Pinckney, Lieutenant John William, 1st King Edward's Horse k.i.a. 11.4.18 II. K.2 Bailleul Road East Cemetery, St.Laurent Blagny, II. K.2. Waikaia, Southland, New Zealand

Ross, Lt. James Andrew, 1/4th Seaforths, 34, k.i.a. 26.7.1916, Thiepval Memorial 15 C. Bearsden, Dunbartonshire.

Scougall, Private George M.M, 351130 2nd Royal Scots att. 1/9th Royal Scots died (Spanish influenza) 5/11/18. Abbeville Communal Cemetery Extension V.B.4. Peebles/Edinburgh

Sinclair, Private Duncan, 2794/300929, 1/8th Argylls, 19, k.i.a. 13.11.16, Thiepval Memorial, Pier and Face 15A and 16C. Campbeltown, Argyll.

Stalker, Lt. Robert MacAllan, 1/5th Seaforth Highlanders, 25, k.i.a. 8.8.1916 1/5th Seaforths attached 22 Squadron RFC, Arras Flying Services Memorial, Wick, Caithness.

Thomson, Private Duncan, 952 1/5th Seaforths , d.o.w. 20.1.1916 Villers-Bocage Communal Cemetery Extension C.4

BIOGRAPHY AND SOURCES

Anderson, Private, Personal account. Imperial War Museum.

Andrews, William Linton, Haunting Years, *The Commentaries of a War Territorial*, Hutchison: London. No date of publication but author has copy dated 25.4.1930 under Andrews' signature.

Ashworth, Tony, *Trench warfare 1914 – 1918: The Live and Let Live System*, Pan-Macmillan 2000 London.

Baker-Carr, Brigadier C.d'A., *From Chauffeur to Brigadier*, Ernest Benn London 1930.

Baynes, John, *Far From A Donkey* , Brassey's: London 1995.

Behrend, Arthur, *As From Kemmel Hill*, Eyre and Spottiswoode: London 1963.

Bewsher, F.W., *The History of the Fifty First (Highland) Division 1914-1918* N&M reprint.

Bion, Wilfred R., *The Long Week-end 1897-1919, Part of a Life*, Fleetwood Press 1982, Free Association Books 1986.

Brown, Malcolm, *1918 Year of Victory*, Imperial War Museum, Sidgwick & Jackson: London 1998.

Buchan and Stewart, *The Fifteenth (Scottish) Division 1914-1919*, Blackwood: Edinburgh and Glasgow 1926

Burnett, Pte. James, letters.

Cairnie, Lt. James Bruce, Diaries ww1/memoir/cairnie1915

Campbell, C. and Green R., *Can't Shoot a Man With a Cold*, Glendaruel: Argyll Publishing 2004.

Cheyne, G.W., *Last Great Battle of the Somme Beaumont Hamel*, Edinburgh: John Donald 1988.

Collins, Norman, Ed. Richard van Emden, *Last Man Standing*, Norman Pen & Sword: Barnsley 2002.

Croft, W.D., *Three Years with the 9th (Scottish) Division*, John Murray: London 1919.

Cooper, Bryan, *The Ironclads of Cambrai*, Macmillan: London 1970.

Commonwealth War Graves Commission website.

Crozier, Brigadier-General F.P., *A Brass Hat in No Man's Land*, Jonathan Cape: London 1930.

Dandie, Lieutenant James Naughton, Correspondence, diaries, notebooks 1914 – 1919, National Library of Scotland.

Duffy, Christopher, *Through German Eyes: the British and the Somme 1916*, Orion Books, Weidenfield and Nicolson: London 2006.

Dunn, Captain J.C., *The War the Infantry Knew*, King Ltd, 1938, this ref. Cardinal/SphereBooks London: Sphere Books 1989.

Edmonds, Brigadier-General James and Miles, Captain W., *History of the Great War, Military Operations, France and Flanders*, various volumes MacMillan and Co: London.

Ewing, John, *The History of the 9th (Scottish) Division*, John Murray: London 1921.
Royal Scots 1914-1919 (Territorial battalions), Oliver and Boyd: London 1925.

Falls, Cyril, *History of the Gordon Highlanders 1914-1919*, Aberdeen University Press 1958.

Farrell, Fred A., *The 51st Division War Sketches*, Jack: Edinburgh 1920.

Ferguson, Niall, *The Pity of War*, Penguin: London 1998.

Fuller, Major-General J.F.C. *Memoirs of an Unconventional Soldier*, Nicholson and Watson: London 1936.

Furse, Major, *Cavalry Memories of the Great War*, publisher unknown.

Gliddon, Gerald, *V.C.s Handbook 1914-1918*, Sutton Publishing: Stroud 2005.

Gough, General Sir Hubert, *The Fifth Army*, Hodder and Stoughton: London 1931.

Graves, Robert, *Goodbye To All That*, Cape: London 1929; Penguin London 1960.

Grierson ,Maj.Gen. J.M., *Records of the Scottish Volunteer Force 1859-1908*, Blackwood and Sons: Edinburgh and London 1909.

Griffith, Paddy, *Battlefield Tactics of the Western Front The British Army's Art of Attack 1916-1918*, Yale University Press: Newhaven and London 1994.

Griffith, Paddy, Editor, *British Fighting Methods in the Great War*, Frank Cass: London 1996.

Haig, Field Marshall Sir Douglas, Diaries, National Library of Scotland.

Haldane, M.M., *History of the 4th Seaforth Highlanders* , Witherby 1927.

Hammond, Bryn, *Cambrai 1917 The Myth of the First Great Tank Battle,* Weidenfeld and Nicolson London 2008.
General Harper and the Failure of the 51st (Highland) Division at Cambrai 20th November 1917, *Imperial War Museum Review* (10) 1995.

Harper, Major-General G.M., *Notes on Infantry Tactics and Training,* Sifton Praed: London 1919.

Harris, J.P., *Amiens to the Armistice. The B.E.F. in the Hundred Days Campaign, 8 August–11 November 1918,* Brassey: London 1998.

Hay, Ian, *The First Hundred Thousand*, Blackwood : Edinburgh and London 1915.

Holmes, Richard *Tommy – The British Soldier on the Western Front,* Harper Collins: London 2004.
The British Army and the Western Front, Richard Holmes, CRF Prize Lecture, May 2003.

House of Commons Research Paper 99/111 A Century of Change, Trends in UK Statistics.

Hussey, John, 'Uncle' Harper at Cambrai, a Reconstruction, *British Army Review*, No 117 Dec.1997.

Keegan. John, *The First World War,* Hutchison: London 1998.

Lauder, Harr, *A Minstrel In France*, Andrew Melrose: London 1918.

Liddell-Hart, Capt. Basil, *The Real War 1914-1918* Faber and Faber: London 1998.

McCarthy, Chris, *The Somme, The Day to Day Account*, Brockhampton: London 1998.

McKee, Alexander, *Vimy Ridge,* Souvenir Press: London 1966.

Mackenzie, Capt. D., *The Sixth Gordons in France and Flanders*, Rosemount Press : Aberdeen 1922.

Mackintosh,Lieutenant Ewart Alan, *A Highland Regiment*, Bodley Head: London 1917.
War, The Liberator, Bodley Head: London 1918.

Macksey, Kenneth, *The Shadow of Vimy Ridge,* William Kimber: London 1965.

Malcolm, George, *Argyllshire Highlanders 1860-1960*, Halberd Press: Glasgow 1961.

Maxse Papers, IWM and West Sussex Records Office, Chichester.

Maze, Paul, *A Frenchman in Khaki,* Printed and bound by Antony Rowe Ltd, Eastbourne.

Middlebrook, Martin, *The Kaiser's Battle,* Allen Lane: London 1978.

Middlebrook, Martin, *Your Country Needs You,* Pen and Sword: Barnsley 2000.

Moore, William, *A Wood Called Bourlon* Leo Cooper: Barnsley 1988.

Morrison, A.D., *The Great War – 7th Battalion Argyll and Sutherland Highlanders* , Cunningham and Son: Alva no date.

Neillands, Robin, *The Great War Generals on the Western Front 1914-1918*, Robinson: London 1999.

Nicholls, Jonathonn, *Cheerful Sacrifice – The Battle of Arras 1917,* Leo Cooper: London 1999.

Nicholson, G.W.L., *Official History of the Canadian Army in the First World War: Canadian Expeditionary Force 1914-1919*, Roger Duhamel Queen's Printer: Ottowa 1962.

Nicholson, Col. W.N,. *Behind the Lines,* Jonathan Cape: London 1939. Reprint Tom Donovan Publishing Ltd : Stevenage 1990.

Norman, Terry, *The Hell They Called High Wood – The Somme 1916,* William Kimber: London 1984.

Oliver, Second Lieutenant John W., letters, April-July 1918. (per Jack Alexander)

Peel and MacDonald, *Sixth Seaforth Highlanders: Campaign Reminiscences* , Elgin 1923 .

Pitt, Barrie, *1918 The Last Act,* Reprint Society: London 1964.

Prior, Robin and Wilson, Trevor, *Command on the Western Front – The Military Career of Sir Henry Rawlinson 1914-1918* Pen and Sword: Barnsley 2004.
The Somme, Yale University Press: New Haven, CT. 2005.

Robertson, Colonel, *51st (Highland) Division War Memorial Brochure,* 1924.

Ross, Captain Robert B., *The Fifty-First In France,* Hodder and Stoughton: London 1918.

Rorie, C olonel David, *A Medico's Luck in the Great War,* Milne and Hutchison: Aberdeen 1929.

Salmond, J.B, *The History of the 51st (Highland) Division 1939-1945,* Blackwood: Edinburgh and London 1963.

Sheffield, Gary and Bourne, John, *Douglas Haig, War Diaries and Letters 1914 -1918,* Weidenfeld & Nicolson: London 2005.

Sheffield, Gary and Todman, Da,. Editors. *Command and Control on the Western Front. The British Army's Experience 1914 – 1918,* Pen and Sword: Barnsley 2004.

Sheldon-Williams, I and R, *The Canadian Front in France and Flanders* Black: London 1920.

Sixsmith, Major-General E.K.G., *British Generalship in the Twentieth Century,* Arms and Armou: London 1962.

Stewart and Buchan, *The Fifteenth (Scottish) Division 1914-1919,* Blackwood: Edinburgh and London1926.

Simpson, Andy, *Directing Operations, British Corps Command on the Western Front 1914-1918,* Spellmount: Tonbridge 2006.

Stirling, Major J., *The Territorial Divisions 1914-1918* J.M.Dent and Sons Ltd: London 1922.

Sutherland,Captain David, *War Diary of the Fifth Seaforth Highlanders* John Lane: London 1920.

Tattersfield, David, *Discipline in the BEF An Analysis of Executions in British Divisions 1914-1918;*
Stand To! (Aug/Sept.2008) Western Front Association.

Terraine, John, *General Jack's Diary 1914-1918,* Eyre and Spottiswoode: London 1964.
The Road to Passchendaele Leo Cooper: London 1977.

The Long, Long Trail website.

Tolland, John, *No Man's Land,* Eyre Methuen: London 1980.

Travers, Tim, *The Killing Ground – The British Army, The Western Front & the Emergence of Modern War 1900-1918* Pen and Sword: Barnsley 2003, Allen & Unwin: London 1987.

Wadham, Lt.Col. and Crossley, Capt., *The Fourth Battalion The King's Own (Royal Lancaster Regiment) and the Great War,* Privately published 1920.

War Office. *Soldiers Died in the Great War Royal Scots, Black Watch, Gordon Highlanders, Seaforth Highlanders, Argyll and Sutherland Highlanders,* H.M.S.O.; reprint J.B.Hayward and Son: Suffolk 1980s.

Wauchope, Major-General A.G., *A History of the Black Watch in the Great War 1914-1918* Vol. 2 Territorial Forces, Medici Society: London 1925.

Westlake, Ray, *The Territorial Force, 1914,* Ray Westlake-Military Books: Gwent 1988.

Woolcombe, Robert, *The First Tank Battle,* Arthur Baker: London 1967.

Wrench, Private Arthur, Personal Account, IWM.

Wyrall, Everett, *History of the 19th Division,* Arnold: London 1932.
History of the 62nd (W.R.) Division, John Lane: London1924.

ACKNOWLEDGEMENTS

The following have been of invaluable assistance, from answering e-mails or letters, obtaining books, lending books, advising, giving me the privilege of using hitherto unpublished family treasures.

Peter Donnelly Curator, King's Own Museum Preston

David Sutherland, War, Diary of the 5th Seaforth Highlanders and photos, London

Lorn MacIntyre, St. Andrews re John Lauder

David Murphy, Curator Royal Scots Museum and his staff, Edinburgh

Eileen Morris, Royal Scots Home Headquarters

Jack Alexander, Edinburgh, author of McCrae's Battalion encouragement and advice

Maeve Dixon, Glasgow, Pte. Thomas Lindsay letters and paintings

Peter Dixon, Scottish Borders, Pte. Thomas Lindsay letters and paintings

The Estate of Thomas Lindsay, paintings and letters.

Alan Cairnie, Lyn, Ontario. ,Lt.James Bruce Cairnie, Cairnie diary 1915 and 1916

The late Sam Rennie, Elgin and Marge Rudy, Saskatoon, Rennie recollections

Thomas Smyth, archivist, Black Watch Museum Perth

The Black Watch Regimental Association.

Brynn Hammond, Imperial War Museum-exchange of notes on E.A.Mackintosh's death location.

John Lee – encouragement.

Stephen Lowe, Macclesfield, Manchester men in Scottish battalions

Jack Sheldon, France, comment and contact with: Dr.Alex Fasse, Germany per Jack Sheldon.

Rod MacKenzie Argyll and Sutherland Highlanders RHQ Stirling

Ian Donn and Christine Hood, Renfrewshire Council Mobile Library (Kilbarchan, Wednesdays)

Christine MacLeod, Kilbarchan – compiler of Burnett letters.

Margaret MacLeod, Howwood, owner of Burnett letters.

Dorothy R Mein Pte. Herbert Steele's account

The National Archive Kew, battalion, brigade, divisional records and maps.

National Library of Scotland – Haig and Dandie diaries

Kenny Mclennan, Currie, Midlothian, details of EA Mackintosh's death

Ian Trushell, Kilbarchan access to his library

Imperial War Museum, London Pte.Anderson diary, Pte Arthur Wrench diary.

Staff of Q.O.H. (Seaforth and Cameron) Museum. Now the Highlanders Museum, Fort George

Staff and volunteers at the Gordon Highlanders Museum, Aberdeen

Douglas Gillespie, Kilbarchan, badge expert

Museum nan Eilean, Stornoway, Pte. Thompson letter

Colin Gray, Kilbarchan, translations from German.

Mitchell Library, Glasgow

The Marsh Agency Ltd on behalf of the Estate of W.R.Bion

David Bowman, Kilmacolm, L.Cpl.Fraser's account

Gregor Campbell, Bridgeof Weir, for the maps

Ailidh Campbell, Kilbarchan, for research

McCrae's Battalion Trust, photographs, images and information.

Every reasonable effort has been made to contact copyright holders.

INDEX